THE
GOSPEL ACCORDING TO
LUKE

THE
GOSPEL ACCORDING TO
LUKE

STEVE LUKATHER

Constable • London

CONSTABLE

First published in Great Britain in 2018 by Constable

3 5 7 9 10 8 6 4

A CIP catalogue record for this book
is available from the British Library.

ISBN: 978-1-47212-642-9 (hardback)
ISBN: 978-1-47212-641-2 (trade paperback)

Typeset in Bembo by Hewer Text UK Ltd, Edinburgh
Printed and bound in Great Britain by Clays Ltd, Elcograf S.p.A.

Papers used by Constable are from well-managed forests and other responsible sources.

Constable
An imprint of
Little, Brown Book Group
Carmelite House
50 Victoria Embankment
London EC4Y 0DZ

An Hachette UK Company
www.hachette.co.uk

www.littlebrown.co.uk

To Tina, Trev, Lily and Bodhi – the true loves of my life
(forgive your old man for his crazy antics)

BEFORE YOU START . . .

I was shocked to get asked to do a book. I mean who the fuck am I? I am not a superstar, poseur, pretty-boy musician. A few years back, the Grammy Museum asked me to do a Q&A about my career. I had 300 people stuffed into the place, pissing themselves in the aisles, laughing at my stories. My agent said, 'You MUST write a book.' My publishers sought me out: I never searched for a deal.

I said no at first, remembering some of the wild, insane things I have said and done. I thought this was a bad idea. Then I thought, 'No, wait . . . I don't have to get ugly.' I can tell my story in my words. And yes, I left some stuff out. I am terribly sorry I can't 'name-check' every person I have ever worked with, or done crazy stuff with, and some of it I just don't remember.

Oh yeah, I swear a lot too. If you are offended by that, stop reading now. See, I wanted this book to sound like I am telling it, so I didn't edit the way I speak. I come from a long line of angry men who shout and swear. There was my grandfather, Lee, my dad's dad, and my dad, an ex-marine. Dad went into showbiz behind the camera just like Grandfather Lee, an assistant director/

production manager. They yelled at people all day and my dad was never at a loss for words when pissed off at me or my sister. I believe my oldest son Trev has thankfully broken the chain. He is calm, cool, collected and quiet and does not outwardly let shit and/or haters bother him. I mean, people who hate me will go after him on the internet, but he takes it real cool. He says, 'Fuck it, Dad, those people are losers and would do anything for your job.' He has a point. I am proud of him, as I am of all four of my kids. They are the real, true, pure loves in my life.

First off, it was hard enough to make all of this fit into a 300-plus-page book – sixty years of life – and a crazy life at that. Many people have also asked me, 'How did you make this record?' and, 'Who came up with what parts?', so it's not a book about where I put my dick or what I put up my nose: such a tired old cliché anyway. Yeah, yeah, everyone did it . . . Next! In other words, this is not a manual on excess, nor is it OK that I did some of the insane things that *are* in the book.

Life is more interesting anyway. I DO throw myself under the bus a few times and got permission from the guilty attendees at some of my less-than-fine moments. And kids, trust me when I tell you: do NOT try ANY of this. Or else!

I tell my story not to brag, not to glamorise the OVER-use of booze or drugs. I stopped all that nonsense many, many years ago. I tell the stories in the book that are just TOO good not to. People won't believe some of it, but I swear it's all true. There may be a nice girl who is married now with four kids with a husband who knows nothing about a one-night stand a hundred years ago, and I shall let you live in peace. Other people I do name. I called and read them what I wrote and said to them: 'Is it cool for me to use this, 'cause if it's not I won't put it in the book.' They said, 'You gotta tell THAT story', and here we are.

See, I want to have friends at the end of all this and I could write a really salacious book, name names and fuck people over, but that's just a mean thing to do. People have written things about me and I was like, 'WTF, man . . . That was private', or whatever. But we live in a world now where privacy does not exist. I thought I might as well tell MY side of the story, try to be as honest as I can and show who *I* am.

Some things I allude to. Use your imagination. That's why books are better than movies, because YOU can see or dream up a scenario that may be better than what I experienced. A lot of stuff just didn't fit. I had to edit. Writing this book did dig up a LOT of old memories and I cried a lot – as well as laughed my ass off. Doing this book made me miss a LOT of people, some of who died while I was writing it. Some of my best friends . . .

I turned sixty writing this book. I've spent forty-one years of my life making real records and touring. Corporate rock? WTF does that mean? Anyone who ever signed a record deal is corporate rock, and those 'indie' labels are still labels. If you sold ONE record, YOU sold out. Sorry. The idea was to be a successful musician and pay for your life by doing so. I did that and I'm an asshole because of it? Yet I still got hired to play on a lot of hit records. I don't get it.

In Toto, we sold a lot of records, and made hits, and played well. We were first-call studio players and played tight, in the pocket and in tune, and studied our instruments and came up with parts on the spot in no time. Somehow this got to be considered a deficit. I have to put up with a lot of shit: like the internet haters who actually waste hours of their lives setting up accounts just to tell you that you suck, you're ugly, or I'm wearing a wig, or I'm drunk or high on drugs when I'm none of these things. Or tell me I'm a cunt when they have never even met me. Say it to my face, asshole, and see what happens. But I prefer, 'Hello, how are ya?' I am a decent guy if you actually *know* me. Sure, we all have a few people in our lives who we have imagined killing slowly and with great detail spent on pain and torture, but then I end up wasting the time on them and in the exact same way I've just bitched about. As I age, I realise you can't make people like you and you can't please everyone, so there is no point in trying. You always get disappointed.

I have trusted people who have fucked me and my family over, lied about me . . . all the horrible shit. At some point, you have to let it go or it will eat you alive and THEY win. I let them go. I am free from the haters because I took their power away. I stopped reading about myself because so many fake-named people were trying to click-bait me into a shit-throwing contest. I fell for it a few times. I so dearly wish I had not.

It's taken a LOT of work for me to get here. I am a highly sensitive person, despite the reputation as a wild man. Yeah, I was 'that guy' many times, but not as much as everyone says. Not so as I remember anyway, and like I have said many times: they tell me I had a great time. I admit to being less than wonderful on occasion. I am weak and I will tell people to fuck off when pushed and poked at.

I have no fear of death any more. I've finally realised that we chose everything we experience in this life before we got here. I know . . . 'There he goes on some wacko rant'. I will spare you. And laugh as you may, I really don't know and none of us do, but I believe that we choose even the most painful things to experience in flesh and body. People talk of hell. This life is hell. Think about it. If you didn't know extreme love, pleasure and happiness, how could you know what the opposite of all that is? We live a heaven-hell life. No one gets away without heartbreak, loss, physical pain, relationship pain, etc. But in order to know what both things are, you have to experience both. Think about it: this earth is the hell we read about. Look around. Read stuff, and *lots* of it, not just jaded versions of the truth. Try and find the actual truth.

So the devil with a hot poker up your ass for all eternity theory is BS. I have already had that experience. I believe it's called a lawsuit! And then another, and another . . . There is no red guy waiting for you because you rubbed one out in the shower, or didn't wear your hat. My opinion . . . God is in the heart and I never have to look for Him. He is always with me, even when I have been awful (and I have). I am of no particular religion. There is much good in religion and also much bullshit. Those televangelists should rot in hell. Seven hundred and fifty bucks a seat to talk to God – tax-free! REALLY? And people believe that shit?

And come the end, God, or whatever you wish to call him, will sit with you and go over your life with you while YOU judge yourself. That's what I believe. That is the hard part. I know what's coming! I pray he has a fucking *great* sense of humour and is the great, all-forgiving God I believe in. Otherwise, uh oh!

Anyway, I may not have gotten it all right. My memory lapses and there is some of my life I simply don't remember. I have had a great time and now things are better than ever. I am a junkyard dog in every way, but I do have a sweet and gentle side that the people I love know. There are so many untrue rumours about me. I can't address them all. For example, all the lies about how much blow we all did in the late seventies and eighties. Look how many records we did. If we were that high how could we have worked with the greats that we did and all the time – sometimes up to twenty-five sessions a week, day and night, five, six days a week – and keep on getting called back for more? If we sucked and were all messed up, would I be here now? Sure, we partied. Everyone did. Fuck, a pool man once asked me if I wanted 'a bump' back in the late seventies. The shit was everywhere. And yes, I overdid it many more times than I wish to admit to, but it was the thing to do. Dropping by someone's pad at 4 a.m. was *not* weird back then.

I wish I could take back some of the awful things I said and did while blazing on day two of a coke-booze bender, but that was another lifetime ago. I am sorry to anyone I hurt, or was an asshole to during that time. I stayed at the party too long, losing myself, my playing and my marriages. I hate myself for it. I did it until it was no longer fun or funny, or anything else good. I fucked myself up bad and it cost me in ways I can't fix. I can only say I'm sorry – and I am. Many times my humour was not funny to others, and trust me when I tell you that every stupid, 'holy shit I fucked up' thing I ever did while I was drunk and high, I wish I could go back in time and re-live and fix what I did to hurt people, but I can't.

Forty years later, it seems the hard work has now turned things positive towards our band. Boy, I have some wear and tear inside from all the touring and particularly once records stopped paying and selling. It was the road that fed my family and paid the divorce cheques and allowed us to send money to Jeff Porcaro's wife and kids. Even still, we have quietly sold twenty million plus records since Jeff's death and that is due to the road and hard work.

I watched my older kids grow up on a plastic telephone, cried myself to sleep many a night missing them. I still do. Thank God they now have iPhone, FaceTime, Skype. I can see and talk to them. Shit, now is like out of an old Bond movie, or *Star Trek*. I never imagined one day I would carry a computer with me every-where. On one hand, it's great. On the other, we have lost our humanity.

People think being famous is nothing but great fun. Truth is, even at my level it is scary and mean, and strangers attack me and write shit they would *never* say to my face – although some of them do even show up at my house. Right now I am finishing building my fortress. It is an angry world that we live in. I miss the old days. I know . . . what an old-guy thing to say, but I guess every generation says the same thing for a reason. Things don't seem to be getting better right now in the world. I pray that they do for my kids.

I hope you all enjoy this little tome. There are a few who won't, but they are assholes anyway so . . . *fuck off* again. Forty years in, I have earned the right to say that now. I took my ass-kickings and so many that I can't count. There is a price to success. Sometimes it's a huge price. I don't recommend this life to many, but I am most blessed. I'm one of the very few people in life who got to write on their tax returns 'Musician' under 'Occupation', and since 1975, the year that I graduated high school at Grant High in Van Nuys.

I got to be what I dreamed about being – and that was a lofty dream. I pulled it off with a lot of help from my friends! I tell my kids now, 'When you grow up, be happy and be kind and pick a job that you look forward to doing . . . No matter what it is and don't take shit from anyone. Fight for what's right!'

OK . . . on with the show . . .

PROLOGUE

My story is like a gigantic artichoke buried in the dirt. Once you dig it up and start peeling away at it, there are all kinds of different aspects and layers. Very probably, you don't know even the half of it. You see, our band Toto truly is the redheaded stepchild of rock-and-roll and for forty years now critics have hated and eviscerated us. There was a time when I would cut out and keep some of my favourite bad notices. During the global oil shortage of 1978, one guy wrote that it should be made illegal to press our albums and waste the oil. Another wished in print that each of our parents had been sterilised so that we could never have been born to make music. That was a particularly memorable example of a scathing review, but here's the thing: we have brought way more to the party than any of these critics have ever realised.

On the wall of his office, a former manager of ours once put together a display that showed off every artist that members of Toto past and present had played with and every recording we had played on. Starting with three of the four Beatles, that chart was like looking at the history of rock-and-roll. Put it this way: how many bands collectively can say that they've played on around

5,000 albums, and that they have something like 225 Grammy nominations and combined sales of something like half a billion? Well, we can. We were sort of the house band on the biggest album in history – *Thriller* by Michael Jackson. In fact, between us we played on just about every record that came out of our home-town of Los Angeles between 1975 and 1995.

There was a point when I looked at the top one hundred records in *Billboard* and was amazed at how many I was on. My new friend, the movie director J. J. Abrams, called me Zelig when we met because he said I'm on so many records that he grew up listening to. I've worked with Paul McCartney, George Harrison and someone who has become a very dear friend, Ringo Starr. Elton John, Joni Mitchell and Miles Davis asked me to be in their bands. I don't think there's anybody on Planet Earth who was hipper than Miles Davis. We were good enough for Miles, but not for *Rolling Stone*'s publisher Jann Wenner and his cast of like-minded morons? Give me a fucking break, man.

Right off the bat, some context might be helpful. I knew precisely what I wanted to do with my life as a very young boy. Growing up in the 1960s in North Hollywood, music was my best friend because I sucked at sports. There were, though, very few musi-cians. It was only later in life, when I met my brother Steve Porcaro and got to know his family, that I discovered what a studio musician was all about. That raised the bar for me from being a rock-and-roll kid to wanting to be a very serious musician.

I found out that I wanted to be like the guys who are now known as the Wrecking Crew and the musicians who followed them. The Wrecking Crew were cats such as Tommy Tedesco and Glen Campbell on guitar, Don Randi and Mike Melvoin on keys, Joe Osborn and Carol Kaye on bass and Hal Blaine on drums. Together, they played on most of Phil Spector's hits. They *were* Spector's Wall of Sound and also the band that Brian Wilson used on *Pet Sounds*. Just about every record back then enlisted at least one or two of these guys, because the young rock musicians didn't have their studio skills just yet. I found it fascinating.

Following right on from the Wrecking Crew, the next generation of first-call, A-list session musicians to come out of LA were the guys who made up the Crusaders, the LA Express, the Section and guitarist Lee Ritenour's band. In the Crusaders you had Larry Carlton on guitar, Joe Sample on keys and drummer John Guerin, and then Robben Ford on guitar and saxophonist Tom Scott among those in the LA Express. The Section, meanwhile, was made up of bassist Leland Sklar, guitarist Danny Kortchmar, drummer Russ Kunkel, keyboardist Craig Doerge and sometimes a second great guitar player, Waddy Wachtel. Those guys were all virtuosos, and altogether defined the classic LA sound of the early seventies and played on records by Joni Mitchell, James Taylor, Linda Ronstadt and Jackson Browne. For all of us budding guitar players in LA, what Carlton did on Steely Dan's 1976 album *The Royal Scam* was seminal. It was rock-and-roll being played with alternative jazzier notes and that was a watershed moment for me. I looked up to all the other great guitar players of the era such as my friends Jay Graydon, Lee Ritenour, Dean Parks, Ray Parker Jr. et cetera.

Then through Steve Porcaro, Jeff Porcaro and David Paich took me under their wing and we all became Toto. We were sort of the rock-and-roll upstarts. Many of the guys immediately before us were pretty much jazz players who could rock, whereas we came at it from being rock-and-roll guys who could play everything else. We comingled with all of those other genius players and then went on and became the last generation of the great LA session-musician era. Let me tell you now, it was a magical time. At the height of it, every page of my date book was filled up weeks and months in advance. I spent at least twelve hours a day in a recording studio, six days a week and for years at a time. I had headphones on my head more than I didn't, but what a life it was. Being with your friends, creating music all day long and with some of the most legendary artists, musicians, producers and engineers that there have ever been. It was beyond a dream come true.

On any given day you didn't know who or what you were going to be working with. You just had to be ready for anything from 10 a.m. to 2 a.m. That was the only problem – we never slept. What we got paid to do, as studio musicians who made records, was fill in the blanks. We came up with all the hooky little parts and rearranged things in the blink of an eye. If it was a shitty song, we used to call it 'polishing a turd'. We would rewrite those songs from scratch: change the chords, put together a different way to get to the bridge. What we would end up cutting would be nothing like what we had originally been handed and had been written on just an acoustic guitar or acoustic piano. Essentially, we were intrinsically involved in the production and arrangement of each of the basic tracks that we played on, whether the artists, managers or producers wanted to give us the credit for that or not. There was no law that said they had to and it was the same for all of us. Rarely, if ever, did the Wrecking Crew guys get any credit for the records that they helped to make. Even today, people generally don't know that Hal Blaine was the drummer for damn near every major American rock band of the sixties. Hal played with the Byrds, Jefferson Airplane, countless others. The man is a beast and that much should be common knowledge.

I came in as a young session musician and followed Larry Carlton, Lee Ritenour and Jay Graydon when they were pursuing the next level of their careers as producers, arrangers and/or artists themselves. This is how it worked for me and so I was told: if you got to have a solo on a hit record, soon enough everybody would go, 'I want *that* guy.' Things really took off for me after I played on Boz Scaggs's *Down Two Then Left* record in 1977. There was a song on that record called 'A Clue', and the solo I did on that broke me out. After that came out, and with the endorsements and recommendations from all my new friends, my phone started to ring off the hook. Also, a nod from Jeff Porcaro and David Paich meant everything in this town and soon I got called in to play with everybody from Elton, Joni, Stevie Nicks and Don Henley to Quincy Jones, Michael Jackson and Aretha Franklin. I was fortunate to be geographically well placed, because right then Los Angeles was the epicentre of the music business. In that respect, I was very lucky to get my foot in the door of the session scene in LA at a very early age and I owe that to Steve Porcaro and his family. When I met Steve, my life changed. It's not luck, though, that keeps you in the game for forty years. You had to be able to bring it every time or else you would have got fired, game over.

The guys from Toto got hired because people knew that we would get the job done. We were very creative and also versatile. Not only did we play on a scary number of records, but they were in every style of popular music. We also didn't sound like anyone else. Like the Crusaders, the LA Express, the Section guys and Steely Dan before us, we too fashioned a signature sound that defined a place and time. It was rock-and-roll with an undercurrent of R & B and funk, with adult chords thrown in, and you had multi-part harmonies and hooks. All of the records that came out of LA from the late seventies onwards had that sound, and most especially our own.

See, here's the other thing. We were unique in the sense that we also became hugely successful in our own right. Our band is the biggest part of my story. Toto has sold forty million records, and has over half a billion Spotify plays. Somebody does a version of our most famous record, 'Africa', what seems like every other year. It has now become a legit standard in popular music. And we totally get the joke. There was a great one that Jimmy Fallon did with Justin Timberlake on his late-night show back in 2013. That alone has had seven million views on YouTube. I have twice been a character on *South Park*. We've become a part of pop culture and this totally cracks me up. We're honoured that guys like that would make fun of us and we'd like to think it's done with affection. There's even such a thing as a Toto bidet and I just had to have one in my house. Nothing cleans my prune like one of those guys. Press the right button and I'll sit there all day.

No doubt about it, mine has been an extraordinary life. Yes, there have been hard times and tragedies along the way, and I've had to take some really low blows too, but it's also been the most amazing journey and I wouldn't change a bit of it for the world. I don't want to sound weird here, it's humbling really, but I happen to believe it's important that those of us who lived through those incredible, heady times should also share our recollections of them.

That golden period of music really needs to be documented and preserved, because it's gone now, never to be repeated. At this point, there are only a handful of guys still doing sessions on records. Most of them do it from their own home studios. These guys engineer themselves. They're great, but they themselves admit that they miss the day-to-day things that I got to do, which is showing up not knowing who you were going to play with, or what you were going to do. These days, budgets are gone for studio musicians, or they've been cut in half at least. The producer's maybe on Skype and between them guys share things on files. To me, that's such a cold, clinical way to make music. All of the craft and spontaneity has gone.

The Wrecking Crew guys would do a take on Friday and it would be on the radio on Monday. That was the record. People just don't have the chops, desire or the money to do that any more. You have a whole group of young musicians who can't play a take from top to bottom. Technology is king now. The general rule is, 'Just Tool [put it on Pro Tools and fix] it.' That is, instant gratification with no studio chops required. And once a computer can figure out how to write its own music, guys like me will be extinct and perhaps looked back upon with favour historically. The jury is out.

Back when I came up, you had to be thinking on your feet the whole time. Jeff, Steve Porcaro, Paich, David Hungate and I became renowned for being able to get things done in one or two takes. The first couple of times you're going to get the best stuff anyway, because it's then that you're playing by instinct and not over-analysing everything. That is a metaphor for my life. I guess what I'm trying to say is that you can't think too much about any of this shit. Oftentimes the best thing to do is just sit back and enjoy the ride.

Jay Graydon: A baseball player who hits .300 is doing real well. To be a top session player back in the day you needed to bat a thousand. That was the job. And Luke was an absolutely outstanding musician. He had got down what you strive for as a session guy, which is to say good feel, and good time and pitch. And he's a pretty good singer, too. The guy had the gift and honed it very well.

CHAPTER ONE

I can tell you the exact date upon which I decided precisely what I wanted to do with my life. It was the evening of 9 February 1964. At the time I was just six years old and that was when I saw the Beatles perform on *The Ed Sullivan Show*. For me, that experience as a whole was like the point in *The Wizard of Oz* when everything turns from black-and-white into colour. Seventy-three million Americans watched that show, but there's no one who could have been more transfixed by it than me. There was just something about it that got down deep under my skin.

By today's standards, their look seems rather tame. After all, it was just four young men in suits singing incredible songs, but it was a sound that I had never heard before in my life. They had energy for sure and their harmonies were beautiful, but it's impossible now to overstate the cultural impact of that moment on those of us who were then growing up in America. Put simply, we had absolutely nothing to compare it to. Until that point, we had never seen guys with electric guitars who played that kind of music. My world stopped around that television set and I can't even begin to describe the sense of euphoria that I felt sitting there in our living room, bug-eyed. It was as though aliens had landed in the back yard and handed me the secrets of life.

Afterwards, my parents bought me the first Beatles album. Every song on that record was pure magic, but it was 'I Saw Her Standing There' that did it for me and, more specifically, George Harrison's guitar solo. Hearing that, it was as if something otherworldly was being injected into my very soul. The way that George bent the notes, the sound of what I now know as reverb on the guitar and how the whole thing was recorded blew my mind. It hit me harder than anything in my life to that point. On *Ed Sullivan*, it was the way that George had his guitar slung over his shoulder. The way each of them looked and moved. Right then, I thought to myself: 'I have to do *that*, I want to be George.' But then, I loved all of the Beatles equally and always thought of them as a group.

Funnily enough, when my mom, Kathy, was nineteen and pregnant with me, she was visited by a psychic friend of my grand-mother, Mia. This woman put her hand on my mom's belly and told her: 'Well, Mrs Lukather, you're going to have a baby boy and when he's six years old something is going to happen to him. He will hear music and someday people will know who he is.' Mom was really bummed out because she was hoping for a doctor or lawyer. This *was* the late fifties.

The only other passion I had as a small kid was Tonka trucks. They were made out of real steel back then and I used to collect them. I loved to see the garbage men come up our street because of the huge truck that they'd be riding. For much the same reason, I was also enamoured with our gardener's lawnmower, which he would let me push. At seven years old, I thought that was the coolest thing in the world. I would tell both of my parents, 'If I can't be a musician, I want to be a garbage man.' To which they would reply, 'Well, perhaps you should work at this music thing, son.'

Once my parents realised how enraptured I was with the Beatles, they thought it was cute and encouraged me in my earliest musical endeavours. They bought me my first guitar, a cheap Kay Acoustic from the Thrifty drugstore down the street. Getting that guitar totally changed my life. Mom and Dad knew that was the case, too, and had it made into a lamp for my twenty-first birthday. I still have it now in the guest room of my house.

On my parents' record player, I wore that *Meet the Beatles* album out playing 'I Saw Her Standing There' over and over again. I would keep lifting the needle up and putting it back to the start of the song. I didn't know how to play a note, but I would mime along to the record. Dad would shout out to me, 'Do you *have* to keep playing the same fucking song?' (Dad had been a Marine at sixteen years old.) I heard that mantra a lot growing up. Mom used to tell me, 'That's your father's work talk,' and if I ever swore, she'd make me eat from a bar of soap that she used to clean the garage floor. Man, it tasted like shit, or puke almost, but parenting was different when I was a kid.

This is really crazy and even I still find it hard to believe, but one day I was sat out on the porch of our house on Elmer Avenue, North Hollywood, struggling to play my Kay guitar. My hands just fell into the first position chords, like I knew how to play them, even though no one had shown me. It was so weird, I even surprised myself. I was like, 'How the fuck am I doing this?' I may not have said those exact words, but in an instant I had gone from having this thing hurt my fingers and not being able to play a single note on it to somehow knowing the first folk guitar chords – E, A, G, C and D. I was excited and scared all at the same time, and I've not told anyone that story until now. I know how nuts it sounds, but it was as if somebody had turned an 'on' switch inside of me.

It still feels to me now as if I was really born in the moment of that one *Ed Sullivan Show*. In reality, I came into the world on 21 October 1957. Though of course I didn't realise as much back then, I was a showbiz kid all along. Both my dad, Bill, and paternal grandfather, Lee, were in TV and film. Lee Lukather worked as an assistant director and production manager. Mom told me he was on many of John Wayne's movies and I also heard the legend that he was the Duke's drinking buddy. He was a macho man of the old school. My dad joined the Marine Corps to get away from a very unhappy home life. By the time I came along, Dad was working as an assistant director as well, on a well-loved TV sitcom, *The Adventures of Ozzie and Harriet*. Later, he worked on *I Dream of Jeannie, Bewitched* and *Happy Days* and also movies such as *The Deer Hunter*. You still see his name on late-night TV all the time. There are only a few true Lukathers in the world. Anyone born with that name, they're a relative of mine.

Dad had a brother, Paul, a good man with a kind heart until politics kicked in, and a half-sister, Jane, who got married young to a guy named Ernie. Jane and Ernie lived with us at my parents' house for a time. They seemed so cool to me because, even though my mom was young, they were even closer to my age and liked the same kind of music. Both of them were good to me, too. When I was fourteen, they took me water-skiing and I remember sneaking off and getting drunk. I used to spend a lot of time with them and their daughters. Sadly, we had a difference in opinion about politics and lost touch, which makes me sad to this day. I will always remember the many good times that we had. They were also so supportive of my dream to be a real guitar player and make a living at it.

Once, Dad took me with him to the set of *I Dream of Jeannie*. Seeing Jeannie herself in colour was awesome and she was very nice to me. The thing was, though, the crew would spend ages setting up the lights and then have to do take after take. I found it to be the most boring thing imaginable. Dad hadn't even gone into showbiz on account of any deep-rooted passion; it was just a job to him and one that he was able to get through Lee. Also, it suited him, having been a Marine, because he got to yell at folks all day long. I inherited my short-fused temper from my dad and perhaps also from my grandfather, who was just the same. Sometimes this was good, sometimes bad. I got to see some famous actors and my dad would tell me: 'I work with these people. Some of them are nice, but some of them are assholes.' Dad wasn't impressed by fame. He got to see the dark side of it in his job.

The other drawback was that Dad was away from home a lot. Regularly he would be gone for up to six months at a time to work on a film somewhere far-flung like New Guinea or Guam. If we did get a phone call from him, it was so prohibitively expensive that I would only be allowed to speak with him for a couple of seconds. The sum total of our conversation would be Dad going, 'Are you doing good at school? Are you being nice to your mom? OK, I love you and I'll call you next month.'

I adored my parents and my younger sister by three years, Lora. Looking back, I can't believe how young my folks were at the time. Mom was still a teenager when she had me and Dad was seven years older. Mom was a beautiful woman and doted on me and my sister. Her mom, Mia, was also an incredible human being and ended up being my spiritual advisor in life until she passed. My Aunt Jean was always there for me, too.

My dad's mom, Phyllis, was the classic loving, overbearing grandmother. The running joke in the family was that she had worked her way through seven husbands. When I was young, she had a house in the city on Valley Vista Boulevard. Later on, she moved out to a place in Palm Springs where we used to go and see her. She would always greet me by squeezing my cheeks between her thumb and forefinger. Grandma Phyllis was very permissive and adored me. She would let me do all of the things that my parents wouldn't. She took me to see *A Hard Day's Night* what seemed to me like a hundred times and bought me my first pair of Beatles boots. My mom had forbidden me from getting them. She made up some bullshit story that I had flat feet. Both Mom and Dad hit the roof when I came home wearing them. Mom thought my feet would turn into hooves, but I *loved* those boots!

When Lora was around two years old, she got horribly burned. She somehow pulled a pan of boiling water off the stove and all over herself. Lora scalded most of the skin off one side of her body and damn near died. I don't have any actual recollection of the incident, just what I have since been told. I might even have witnessed it, but it messed me up so bad that I have erased it from my memory.

Lora miraculously recovered from her burns, but she had a really rough childhood. Later on, she had to be in leg braces. She also had these horrendous allergies. When she was a teenager she would suffer extreme bronchial attacks, worse than asthma, and have to go into hospital to get adrenalin shot into her heart. That would happen on a weekly basis and scared the shit out me. Ironically, the attacks stopped just as soon as she took up smoking at fourteen. Explain that one to me!

The two of us were pretty close when we were young, but when I got to be a teenager, I drifted a bit. I think Lora believed I was the favourite child and that Mom liked me best, though I never saw it that way. Like any other bratty little kid sister, Lora would also rat me out to Mom and Dad, but now I can honestly tell you that I couldn't function without her support. If ever something goes wrong for me, I call Lora and we talk. She's a very wise, spiritual woman and she's like Grandma Mia on steroids. Lora's my rock and I love her so much.

Lora Lukather: When I was in single digits, my brother would call me into his bedroom and force me to be in his fake band. My parents would come in with their cigarettes and coffee and sit down to watch us play along to my brother's Beatles records. I had no musical talent at all, so my brother would set me up behind makeshift drums and have me play the simplest, most repetitive stuff.

My brother was very small and shy and got picked on at school. I would go and stand up for him. One time at kindergarten, this kid was bullying him in the playground. I saw it, and went over and kicked this kid in the shin with my metal corrective shoes. I broke his leg. Mom did everything she could not to laugh when the principal called her about the incident. My brother is still now an insecure person, but he's just able to hide it. He puts up this protective wall so that people can't see how sensitive he really is.

As a young kid, I had problems enough of my own. I was very shy, small for my age, horribly insecure and terrible at all sports. The bigger kids didn't need any more reasons to pick on me and I was never able to stand up for myself. I tried to over-compensate. Lora, God bless her, eventually beat up one of the bullies for me, but it didn't help my situation that I'd had to depend upon my little sister – quite the opposite in fact. There was this one asshole who lay in wait for me on the school bus. He was relentless, humiliating me on a daily basis so that the other kids would laugh at me. I used to beg Mom not to make me get the bus. In school, there was one time that the teacher wouldn't let me go to the bathroom and I pissed my pants. Kids don't forget stuff like that and I got tortured about it, but I had to tough it out. For me, bullying was just a part of growing up.

It's a cliché, I know, but it truly was music that saved me. By the mid-sixties, every kid in the neighbourhood wanted to be like the Beatles. The older kids could get away with having long hair because they were rebelling, but not us little guys at Rio Vista Elementary School. A bunch of older kids up the street from my parents' house had a band called the Hedges. They used to rehearse at night in one of their parents' garages and I would go along and listen. They were teenagers and I was just eight, but they would let me hold their electric guitars. One guy had a Rickenbacker just like George Harrison's. This guy, Steve, showed me how to play a bit. One of the first songs I learned was 'Dirty Water' by the Standells. It was a simple little riff from the time, but it set me going along with everything else I was taking in on a daily basis on guitar.

By then, my parents had got me a shitty mini-electric guitar, which had an amplifier that was about the size of a large walkie-talkie. A childhood friend, Jon Brewer, who lived round the corner from me, had just gotten a drum set. I would take my guitar and amp over to Jon's house. I could manage a couple of chords and we thought we were the greatest thing in the world. Together with another neighbourhood kid, Dave Gibbs, we even gave ourselves a name, the Nails. Soon, I could play stuff like 'Gloria' by Van Morrison's Them and 'The House of the Rising Sun' by the Animals. I was like a sponge. I would listen to the older guys up the street doing all of these songs and learn them right away. Slowly, I was also able to pick things out by ear from off the radio. I would fumble around on my guitar until I could find the right chords. Mind you, the music back then wasn't so hard.

By the time I was nine, I wanted nothing more than to be in a proper band of my own. The trouble was that I was two foot tall, weighed twenty pounds wet and nobody my own age was interested. In this regard, my dad inadvertently helped me out. He very much wanted me to be good at baseball, so signed me up for a local Little League team. You can't make this up, but we were called the Beavers. I got given a team suit with 'Beavers' written right across the front of it. I still have a photo. I was so bad I couldn't manage to throw the ball over the plate. Even my own teammates would make fun of me. The plus point was that our coach's son, a kid named Jimmy Nestor who was a couple of years older than me, played a little bit of guitar too. Jimmy had a friend, Doug, with a real drum kit. Jimmy's brother, Jon-Ren, was a really cool guy.

Jimmy's and Jon's folks lived just a couple of blocks from my parents. Every chance that I got, I would ride my bike round to their place with my guitar. We would jam together in their apartment. It was a pretty basic set-up. Jimmy had a bass guitar that he would plug in through his parents' giant record player and TV set in the living room. He also had a small VOX amp, which was *the* coolest thing I had ever seen. The Beatles had VOX amps. We would do 'The House of the Rising Sun', 'Gloria' and the couple of Beatles songs that I knew. I managed to work out the solo in 'Gloria', which I later found out was played by a young Jimmy Page. Later we became a Grand Funk Railroad tribute band. I did my first gig ever with those guys when I was nine years old. We played at a girl's birthday party in Jimmy's apartment building. All the girls screamed and I made one dollar. I was hooked.

My school also had an orchestra that I wanted to get into, but the music teacher didn't consider the guitar to be a proper instrument. That is unless it was classical guitar, which I could not have cared less about. He ended up giving me a violin and some written music to learn, which I could not figure out at all. The violin felt alien in my hands. My parents, on the other hand, were very excited by the appearance of this violin, at least at first. They just assumed I would grow out of the guitar and become a 'real' musician. Anyway, I was hopeless at the violin. If you have ever had the misfortune to hear anybody trying to play violin who doesn't know how to, you will know that it sounds like two rabid cats fucking. The music teacher called my parents up and told them, 'Your son has no talent for music whatsoever and you should really discourage him from ever playing an instrument.'

To show you what that guy knew, later on when I was in fifth grade, we got a piano. My mom used to love game shows and got on *Hollywood Squares*, which was a big deal at the time. Mom won and her prize was a Spinet piano. It was delivered to our house and to begin with Mom tried to get Lora to take lessons, but my sister hated doing them. My grandmother, Mia, used to have a Hammond organ at her house and would let me mess around on it. Just like with the guitar, I found that I could pick things out. I started to fumble around on the Spinet as well, working out simple chords, until I was able to make a nice noise. Since Mom wanted someone to play this piano, she eventually had it moved into my room. These days, it's in bubble wrap in my garage.

The thing that I most wanted, though, was a *real* electric guitar. I had outgrown the mini and I literally begged my parents to get me a good one. It wasn't until the Christmas that I was fourteen that they finally relented. Even then, it was another shitty little thing called an Astrotone that once again they picked out from the local Thrifty drugstore, probably for about five to ten dollars. This thing had four pick-ups and was really hard to play, but today the vintage guitar guys collect these pieces of shit and are able to sell them for big dollars. Why, I have no idea.

In the meantime, I made do with borrowing good guitars off other guys. My other friends had Gibsons and Fenders. On one occasion, I got hold of a really fine Gibson SG from this kid who lived on the same block as Jimmy Nestor and couldn't play at all. Years later, I found out from Jimmy that the guitar owner was Leif Garrett, who went on to become a huge teen idol in the seventies. I haven't seen him since those early years in the neighbourhood.

Throughout my childhood, there was another familiar refrain in our house. My dad would ask me, 'So kid, what is it that you're going to do with your life? What do you want to be when you grow up?' I would guess that most kids of my age in the late sixties would have said an astronaut and to follow Neil Armstrong to the Moon, but a musician was all that I ever wanted to be. When I told Dad as much, he patted me on the head and said, 'Kid, you've got a billion-to-one chance of making it.' To which I would reply right away, even at nine, ten and eleven, 'Yeah, but I'm going to be that one guy.'

From the start, I had tunnel vision. Music was the only thing that I truly cared about. Dad wasn't about to break my dream for me, but he expected me to snap out of it. Both of my parents thought that I had lost my mind. In those days, if you said you were going to be a musician, it was tantamount to admitting that you intended to be a drunk, womanising bum. All I can tell you is that I never was a bum.

CHAPTER TWO

One of the first real best friends I can remember was a kid named Bobby Brown who I met in fifth grade at grammar school. I was ten or eleven at the time and Bobby lived just a few blocks from me. There were a couple of other kids in class who were interested in playing music, too. One was a great guitarist, Steve Caton, whose dad, Roy, I later found out, was the contractor horn player and arranger with the Wrecking Crew. The other was a kid named Scott Sublette on drums. Steve was a little more advanced than me and showed me a bunch of stuff. He also taught me 'Blackbird' by the Beatles, which I really loved, but mostly I spent my time at Bobby's house.

Bobby's mom had a swimming pool, so it was *the* place to hang out in the neighbourhood. She was also a friend of my mom and would let us have full run of the house, so I may as well have moved in with the Browns. It got so that I would spend the weekends there. I would ride over on Friday after school and on Sunday my mom would call up Audrey and say to her: 'Would you send my son home? We would like to have dinner with him.'

Bobby and I got up to so much no good together. Audrey would leave money out for us for food. We would order a single pizza and, when the delivery guy turned up, I would distract him at the door while Bobby stole more pizzas from the back of his van. We would do horrible, unthinkable things to these pizzas and then redeliver them to random houses in the neighbourhood. I want to say sorry now to anyone who was one of our victims. We would steal from off the ice-cream man's van, too. Again, one of us would distract, while the other climbed on the moving van and stole as much ice-cream as possible. We would also set off pipe bombs, and climb up onto the roof and throw lemons or apples at the mailman or the ice-cream man. They were fun, ridiculous times.

There were two other big advantages for me in having Bobby as a best friend. Number one, he was a real tough kid and so became my protector. It turned out at grammar school that I got picked on for sucking at sports and being able to play guitar. One or other of the school bullies would tell me, 'You think you're so fucking cool, Lukather. Be at the flagpole at three o'clock and I'm gonna kick your ass.' I would even show up, but then Bobby would accompany me and stare my tormentors down.

Secondly, Bobby could play the bass guitar and guitar. He and his elder brother, Doug, had a Fender Duo-Sonic guitar and some amplifiers set up at their house. (It turned out that Bobby's older sister was friends with Jeff Porcaro through her boyfriend Kelly Shanahan.) A guy much older than us, Mark Hollingsworth, would also come over and show us how to play songs, and also taught me my first blues scale. That was a big moment. Mark had a Fender Jaguar guitar, a Fender Twin reverb amp and the first fuzz tone I ever saw, the Fender Boss-tone, which plugged into the guitar, not on the floor. He was my first real guitar teacher.

Eventually, we all hooked up with another local kid, Rudy Battaglia, Tony Rizzo, who played drums, and in fifth grade we formed a band that we called Blueberry Waterfall. No doubt it was a stupid name, but nonetheless we had it written up in bold right across Tony's bass drum. We also wore these little uniforms that our parents made up for us, pinstriped pants and shirts with a tie. Bobby's mom would find us places and parties to play at and drive us to and from these weekend gigs. We would get paid five bucks each a pop. I could make ten, twenty bucks over a weekend, which for an eleven-year-old was a small fortune. It was more than enough at least to keep me in candy and strings.

Blueberry Waterfall lasted for around a year and a half. We worked up about forty minutes of music and I sang. It was Beatles and Rolling Stones, and some top-forty tunes, but the first Jimi Hendrix album had also just come out and I was able to play 'Foxy Lady'. That one had the famous 'magic raised nine chord', also known as the Hendrix E chord. The song was actually in F# on the record, but I digress . . .

Wherever it was that we showed up, people would always go on to us about how they couldn't believe a bunch of kids were able to play this stuff. One of our most memorable shows was at a talent contest called the Teenage Fair, which was staged at the Hollywood Palladium. It wasn't just that we got an honourable award for being the youngest act of the day, but there was also a wall of amplifiers for us to plug into. That was the first time that I got to play really loud. And I had the shit zapped out of me. The microphone wasn't grounded right and when I stepped up to sing, I got an electric shock from it right into my lips. I saw God, Jesus, the aliens, all at the same time, and it burned my lip like someone had punched me in the face. Not fun, but we won a special prize because we were so young and so it was worth the pain.

Our most memorable performance was at our school, Rio Vista, in the packed auditorium; and when we played all the girls screamed. I never looked back. There was a second memorable talent show that I played at that same year. That was at summer camp in Mount Shasta and the results for me were much less pain-ful. I did a solo spot and right afterwards the prettiest girl on the camp came up and gave me my first kiss. I think it was just then that I went from being a little kid to a fully fledged adolescent. I started to want to be cool and to do what the older kids were doing, and in the view of my parents it was all downhill for me from there. Bobby and I would throw pool parties at his house. We would have girls come over and admire their bikini bodies in the pool. The change had begun . . .

It wasn't too long, though, before my folks worked out the best way to keep me in line. Once I got too big to be hit with a belt and could fend off Mom's hands, they would instead deprive me of my music. Whenever it was that I transgressed, they would remove the guitar and stereo from my room. That would hurt me much worse than a beating.

The hippy movement was also happening in LA just then and the next thing I heard after the Beatles that blew my mind was Eric Clapton and Cream. As I remember, Mark Hollingsworth taught me how to play 'Sunshine of Your Love', and that was another significant step up for me. I would spend days in my room listening to Cream and Hendrix's *Are You Experienced*. That was a further bone of contention between Dad and me. He would rush into the room whenever 'Third Stone from the Sun' came on, with all the feedback, and shout, 'Goddamn it, will you turn that noise down!' One time he snatched the album cover off my bed, looked at that great fish-eye-lens photo of Hendrix and just stared back, open-mouthed, at me. Then he threw it back on the bed, shook his head and said, 'I have no words.'

At the end of the sixties, the first Led Zeppelin record hit and that was yet another game-changer. That was actually my first make-out record. For something like two weeks round about that time, I had this very cute girlfriend, Diane. We would go over to Bobby's house together and make out in the upstairs room above the garage. When Diane broke up with me, I was a total mess. Many years later, I ran into Robert Plant at some rock festival. We got a bit of a juice buzz going and I told him, over and over again, that *Led Zeppelin I* was my first make-out record. Robert was very patient with me. All that he said was, 'Yeah, I get that a lot.' I think I owe him a slight apology for being up in his face, filled with liquid courage and trying to make conversation.

Bobby and I were thought to be such bad influences on each other that in 1970, when it came time for us to go on to junior high, both sets of parents decided it would be for the best to separate us. Bobby went off to the public school, Walter Reed. My mom sent me to a private school, Laurel Hall. It was a Lutheran school and I guess Mom thought I needed some religion in me. In reality, Laurel Hall was a pretty liberal establishment and also not like the public schools I had been at in the sense that I had a fresh start. I thought perhaps this school would be different for me. The sad thing was that Bobby and I ended up drifting apart. He had been like a very dear brother to me and I loved him. Tragically, he died young from liver failure. Far too many times now I have had to endure the pain of losing my dearest friends all too soon.

The other kids at Laurel Hall had grown up together from kindergarten, so I came into the seventh grade as the new kid. Anyone who's been the 'new kid', especially at that age, knows what a traumatic experience it can be. I was also a bit of a troublemaker, as well as something of a smart ass. I was over-compensating for my insecurities. It might sound like a cliché, but my guitar became my closest friend.

I made a couple of friends at Laurel Hall who could also play. One was Ronny Sarian. His parents were very strict. They wanted Ronny to be a lawyer, but had got him a guitar and a bass. His little brother Donny played drums, so he might have played once in a while with us too. When Ronny and I got caught smoking cigarettes by the principal, I think I took the fall.

The other kid was Kevin McCormack. Kevin played drums on a very small kit and it turned out his father was a recording engineer. The three of us would get together at one of our houses and mess around playing Grand Funk Railroad and Creedence Clearwater Revival songs. One afternoon, Kevin's dad happened to hear us and offered to take us into a recording studio to cut a couple of tracks.

For the occasion, we decided we should write two songs of our own. Ronny, who was a really good guitar player, came up with one I called 'Grass', a feeble attempt at writing a 'weed song' at twelve years old. I wrote the other, which I titled 'Leave It'. It was quite raw and basic, nothing earth-shattering, and I made the words up on the spot, 100 per cent live and one take, but as I remember it was a pretty good effort for 1970 or early '71. We also hit upon the next in what was to become a sea of dumbass band names that I've had to wallow in – English Muffin (of course that could now mean anything). The big day arrived and it proved to be an amazing experience. My first time in a studio and straight-away it seemed to me an amazing place. It tripped me out just seeing the big mic-stands and the sound board. The control room appeared like a spaceship to me. The studio even smelled good. I wanted to move right in and live in a place like that.

I remember Kevin's dad had put headphones on us and we set up and played live. In those days I would get uptight about my voice as it hadn't broken, but I was able to carry a tune and Mr McCormack put a little reverb on it so that it sounded like a professional record-ing. At the end of the session, he made us up an acetate disc of our two songs and on the Monday morning we took it into school and played it to the class. In my mind, I had a fantasy of fame and fortune, but in reality I was only twelve or just thirteen.

I simply devoured music. Records were relatively cheap back then and when my parents asked me what I wanted for Christmas or my birthday, I would just hand them a list of albums. I wanted to grow my hair long and wear psychedelic clothes and beads like Hendrix, but that wasn't going to happen for a twelve-year-old at Laurel Hall. If my hair got down close to my eyes, a teacher would assuredly call up Mom and tell her not to send me to school until I got it cut. Out of school it was a different story and right around that time was when the wonders of black-light rooms, booze and weed came into the picture for me.

Even taking into account the fact that English Muffin hadn't made me an instant star, here I was twelve years old and already playing in bands and making money. I didn't go anywhere without my guitar. I found it to be the best way to root out people who were as obsessed with music as me. During the next year or two, I got to meet a lot of like-minded kids. Many of these guys have gone on to have real careers in music and remain great friends to this day.

One such guy was John Pierce, who truly was my first friend ever. Our mothers were pregnant at the same time in the same neighbourhood. John now plays bass with Huey Lewis and the News and has done hundreds of recording sessions as well. There was David Levey, the son of the great jazz drummer Stan Levey, who later became a doctor. Another was now-legendary guitarist Mike Landau, who has gone on and played with everyone from James Taylor, Joni Mitchell and Pink Floyd to Miles Davis. I thought I was pretty good, but Mike was *really* good, one of the best players I have ever heard. He was even smaller and younger than me, this teeny little kid, but had a natural gift for the guitar. I became a better player just from hanging out with Mike and seeing what he could do.

John Pierce: The two of us lived three blocks from each other and so I have no recollection of life before Lukather. One memory does stand out. There's a knock on our back door. It's Luke and he says to me, 'I know the chords to "Hey Jude". He picks up my nylon-string classical guitar and, sure enough, he knows the chords. But this is not the typical eleven-, twelve-year-old kid fidgeting his fingers to accommodate each chord, but a seamless, perfectly in time, 'correct' rendition of the song.

Luke got really good, real fast. I've never seen a guy improve at the pace that he did in that period. I would go over to his house just to watch him play. I'm sure I was pretty jealous of him, but that didn't stop me from being totally blown away. It was amazing to see raw talent take flight like that, and in his bedroom no less. Talk about a front-row seat.

Mike Landau: I can remember very vividly the first time that I met Luke. I was twelve years old and one of my buddies told me about his friend who also played the guitar. He went to a different junior high, but lived in the same neighbourhood. One day after school, I walked over to a house nearby where these kids would have a jam in a room out back. As I turned the corner of the street that the house was on, I spotted in the distance this crazy-looking kid on a bicycle and with a big bush of hair. It was trash-collection day in the neighbourhood and this kid was entertaining himself by riding his bike into the trashcans that were neatly lined up all down the street. He knocked every one of them over, made a huge mess, but was laughing his ass off. He also had a T-shirt on that read, 'Born to Raise Hell'. Needless to say, it was for me love at first sight.

Luke always seemed to me to have complete self-confidence, even at that age. He was quick-witted and charming, so could get away with pretty much anything around the grown-ups at my house. My mother would have guests over and Steve would entertain them for hours by telling these completely foul-mouthed, filthy jokes. He would say things around my mother that I would never dream of, but she would be delighted and yell, 'Oh, Steven!' He just had a personality that was infectious and endearing.

Basically everyone I hung out with could play and jammed with everybody else. And we all wanted to outdo each other. It was healthy competition and we splintered off into a couple of rival bands. In one, there was Mike, John Pierce, drummer Jon Brewer, bass player Chris Cibelli and a great cat named Mark Thornberry. Mark was a really good guitar player and the first of us guitar-heads to really take it seriously in terms of study. His parents were very tolerant people, because we would be round their place all the time. The other was my band, which was made up of Mark's brother Jerry, who played drums, a real good bass player, Tom Hunt, who could sing too, and me. Later on, we also met a guy named Bob Selvin who had a Hammond organ, and so our band was able to play anything by the Doors, Deep Purple and 'In-A-Gadda-Da-Vida' by Iron Butterfly. Their band was called Atlantis, ours Prophecy. When one band had a gig, the other would go along to watch and we would all share and borrow each other's gear and support each other. I played with a lot of people in the neighbourhood, especially Matt Dancy, Phil Young and Eric Wallengren and some of his buddies at Walter Reed Junior High.

All of us would hang at two places on the corner of Moorpark Street and Tujunga Avenue. There was Henry's Tacos, or else a burger joint called Barnaby's right across the street. In the back, Barnaby's had a jukebox, and I figured a way to make that thing work without having to put in any money. There was also a nice girl named Kathleen, who'd give me free food because I was broke most of the time. I would sit in there for hours at a time listening to the Free song, 'All Right Now'. Those days, all you had to do was hop on your bike, ride down Moorpark and you'd find some-one to get up to no good with. What's so weird to me about kids today is that they're all stuck in front of their game boxes. Home was the last place we wanted to be.

My friend Tom Hunt's parents had six kids and he was the youngest, so he had full run of the house. By the time they'd had their sixth child his folks could give a shit what was going on. Tom's dad had a carpentry workshop out back. The two of them would make incredible stuff together, such as a huge bass cabinet for Chris Cibelli, nicknamed 'The Log'. Tom also had an entire room in which we could rehearse and leave our gear set up. It was like a fortress in there; you had to squeeze through a crawl space and Tom had turned it into a black-light room. He had hung up all these tie-dyed sheets and posters, and it would be lit by candles. I'd never seen anything like it.

The first time I ever got high, I smoked a lot of joints with Tom, the Thornberry brothers and a bunch of people in that room. Tom also had a killer stereo set up in there and at the time we were listening to *James Gang Rides Again*. There's a part on the song 'Bomber' where Joe Walsh plays this insane slide solo. When he slowly slid up the neck of the guitar on that solo . . . it was at that exact moment that I got my first weed rush. Not an hour later, I had to go home to dinner with my parents. My eyes were purple-red and I was totally paranoid. I was too high. I told Mom and Dad I had flu and that my eyes were red from swimming, some more BS, and excused myself. I went up to my room, curled into a ball, listened to Hendrix's *The Cry of Love* and didn't smoke pot again until I was like twenty-one. That was when Jeff Porcaro showed me the proper way and not to overdo it.

Instead, I started to drink booze at the weekends with Mike Landau and a bunch of our friends. Everybody else was a reefer-head, but for Mike and me it was beer and Boone's Farm Strawberry Wine. The latter was this cheap, sweet wine that you could buy a bottle of for eighty-five cents. Mike, myself or one of the crew we hung out with would get hold of it because we were underage. The bunch of us wore these big pea coats and would go into the liquor store as if to buy candy. While one of us was paying the owner for sweets, the other would be shoving a couple of bottles of Boone's Farm's finest inside his coat. We would just get shit-faced. And when you threw up Boone's Farm, it would look like blood.

LSD was also making its way into the neighbourhood, but I didn't want to be any part of that scene. From what I saw, it was way too intense. The way kids were on acid freaked me out and no one more so than Jerry Thornberry. At junior high, kids would throw house parties on a Friday or Saturday night. There would be drinking and we could also go along to play as a band and hopefully meet girls. One Saturday, Tom Hunt got us a gig at one of the Walter Reed parties. Tom, Jerry and I showed up as a power trio. There we were, ripping it up, when right in the middle of a song, Jerry lurched up from behind his drum kit and ran out of the house. Turned out somebody had given him a hit of Purple Haze acid and he was tripping out of his mind.

Jerry told us later that he was convinced there was a grizzly bear in the room, trying to get at him. He ran all the way home, which is where things got truly fucked up for him. By dreadful coincidence, as he was running up his street, his mom was apparently having a heart attack out on their front lawn. An ambulance and police car were parked up out front, lights flashing, and the medics were trying to revive Mrs Thornberry. God bless her, she pulled through, but by this point, Jerry told me later, all he could see were lots of Porky Pigs spinning around her head saying, 'Errr – that's all folks!' As this life-or-death scene with his mom was being played out, he was running around the place freaking out, yet trying to maintain a straight face and not get caught. Fortunately, everything turned out OK.

Later that year, Dad got me a Gibson Les Paul Deluxe, like the one Pete Townshend used to play. Rather than have him take me to the toy store when he was home, I would plead to go to Guitar Center in Hollywood. *That* was my toy store. The guys in there got so used to seeing me they'd be like, 'Oh, *that* kid's back!' I could play pretty good for my age, so they would let me grab all these guitars from off the walls and try them out. There was a little back room that I'd go into, with an amplifier. On that particular day, I had taken down this really cool Les Paul Deluxe (which now resides at The Musicians' Hall of Fame in Nashville) and plugged it in to an Ampeg VT-22 amplifier. I finished up playing as usual and was ready to leave and Dad said to me, 'OK, let's get this stuff in the car.' I didn't know what he meant, but he said: 'I want you to have them – that guitar and the amp.'

Even thinking about that now, it brings tears to my eyes. It was the greatest gift my dad ever gave me and it changed my life. All of a sudden, I had pro gear and that was a defining moment. Dad had also been talking about buying for himself a new car, a Firebird or something flash like that. Ever after, Mom would remind me:

'Your father gave up a car for you to have that guitar, so you better be nice to him.'

There was another time at Guitar Center that has also stuck fast in my mind. Once again, I was playing in the back room, and one of the guys who worked there came in to listen. When I was done, he said to me: 'You know there's another kid comes in here just like you. He's from out in Pasadena and real good too – you should meet him.' In fact, the two of us wouldn't get to meet for a few more years yet, but it turned out that other kid was Eddie Van Halen.

CHAPTER THREE

For me as a young teenager, there weren't a lot of wild sexual escapades, though I had a few girlfriends for brief periods in high school. Doubtless it would be true to say that this was partly on account of the crippling shyness that I was afflicted with around most girls. Yet also it was because, in those formative years, music was just about all that I thought and talked about and did. No sooner had I gone to Grant High School than I heard about this kid of my age, Steve Porcaro, who had the most bad-ass band.

Steve's elder brother, Jeff, was already by then some kind of local legend. The first two Steely Dan albums were out and Jeff Porcaro was their drummer. A group of us went to see Steely play at Santa Monica Civic and that was the greatest band and Jeff the most amazing drummer that I had ever seen in my life. The third Porcaro brother, Mike, was in twelfth grade and a killer bass player. Those guys had been raised around music. Their father, Joe, was a highly respected studio percussionist and jazz drummer who had recorded with Sinatra, Stan Getz and Sarah Vaughan.

When Jeff Porcaro had been at Grant High, he'd had a band, Rural Still Life, with his best friend, David Paich. Steve had now inherited the mantle, but had adapted the name to just Still Life. The first time that I got to see them play was at the tenth-grade dance and they were incredible. They were doing Sly and the Family Stone and Edgar Winter-style stuff, this very slick rock and blues, and my immediate reaction was: 'I want to play with *that* guy.' On drums they had Carlos Vega, who would go on to be a session drummer and play with James Taylor, and Guy Shiffman. Carlos was a sweet, funny cat and Guy and I worked on a lot of projects after we graduated. The band also had a horn section, fronted by Andy Leeds, and a great guitarist, a sweetheart named Danny Costello.

Steve and I got to know each other through the school's music teacher, a Mr Neal, who kind of took it upon himself to hook us up. It was my good fortune that Steve had decided to change things up in Still Life and wanted to bring in another guitar player for Danny. Steve asked his friend Andy Leeds to become our manager. He asked me to audition over at his parents' house and learn Edgar Winter's 'Free Ride', some Steely and a couple of other things. In turn, I hit upon the idea of bringing Landau along with me. I had the notion that if we played well together, Steve might want both of us. Between us, Mike and I had that double-guitar, Steely thing right down. At the time, Mike was more like Denny Dias, Steely's jazzier guy, while I was the Skunk Baxter, rock-and-roll dude who would be jumping off the amplifiers and being the class clown as per usual.

We got together in Steve's dad's garage studio, which was a very professional kind of set-up. It was fully sound-proofed with a drum kit and Joe had all his percussion stuff laid out. Steve called up 'Free Ride', Mike and I nailed the double harmony solo and that was it, we were both in Still Life. In time, we also got John Pierce in the band. From then on, we would get together every day after school at the Porcaros' house to rehearse. Steve was a great band leader, very serious and strict, a bit of a taskmaster but in a positive way. He'd had a proper work ethic passed down to him from his dad and his two elder brothers. Joe was a famous, first-call studio musician, but would come home and practise every day even after work and Steve wanted it real bad too. It was seeing how hard Joe worked that instilled into all of us the fact that being merely good wasn't enough, you had to be great.

I spent more time at the Porcaro household than I did my own. There would always be great Italian cooking going on from their mom, Eileen, and they were altogether a magical, beautiful family. I even had a little schoolboy crush on their kid sister, Joleen, but that was very much off limits. Jeff had moved out by then, but would drop by all the time and sit in with us. He had this distinct aura about him. He would walk into the room with his glasses and a vest on and the whole place would light up. He was a rock star *before* he was a rock star.

In Still Life, we thought that both Jeff and Paich were unbelievably cool. They were everything that we wanted to be. At the time, they were just twenty-, twenty-one years old, but superconfident and already becoming successful musicians. And, man, the way that those cats played time and grooved together. Something chemical happened between them. You can't learn that shit; it was as if they had come into this world as kindred souls. In actual fact, it was their fathers who had brought them together. David's dad, Marty, was this genius cat – a pianist, conductor and arranger who had produced Sinatra, Sammy Davis Jr and the great country sessions for Ray Charles. From 1969 to 1972, Marty was also the musical director of *The Glen Campbell Show*, for which Joe Porcaro was percussionist. Jeff and Paich were tight from their early teens. They grew up together and straight out of school were both playing in Sonny and Cher's band.

Funnily enough, I had also met Sonny and Cher when I was twelve. My dad was assistant director on an ill-fated movie, *Chastity*, which Cher was starring in and Sonny had written and was producing. The movie was shot in Arizona and Dad flew Mom and me down to the set. Both Sonny and Cher were incredibly nice to me. In the flesh, Cher was a stunningly beautiful woman and I followed her around like a little puppy dog.

Every bit of the work that we put in with Still Life paid off. We became *the* shit-hot band in the entire Valley area. All of the local bands would audition to get prom gigs because they were big events and we would rent proper PA systems – they paid around 500 dollars. We would rehearse for a month solid just to kick ass at these high-school dances. Basically, we were a Steely tribute band. We learned everything from their records, from the vocal harmonies on down. By 1974, Jeff was making Steely's fourth album, *Katy Lied*. He played us the tapes of the basic tracks, so we were able to jam those songs months before the record was even out. Jeff and Paich would also come and play the odd prom date with us. Jeff would claim later that he had even brought Donald Fagen and Walter Becker down to see us play. According to Jeff, the pair of them snuck in back for a little bit, then snuck out again. Jeff told me that they said something to him like: 'Shit, we should just hire these guys to do our stuff.'

Through John Pierce, another musical guy I met in high school was Mark Williams. Mark's dad was John Williams, the famous film composer. He also had a little brother, Joseph, who was fucking nuts and who twelve years later would become the singer in Toto. He was, and still is, one of the funniest humans I know. John, Mark, Mike Landau and I got together in another little side band. We would hang at Mark's house and while we were upstairs making a bunch of noise, Mark's dad would be downstairs composing. John Williams was already a top-call, go-to film-score composer, and around then he got the gig to write the score for *Jaws*.

It was through being exposed to that kind of world, and with the inspiration of Jeff and Paich, that the ideal of becoming a professional musician began to seem more attainable to me. It was also then that I first got to know about all of these other great studio guys who were playing around town – cats like Carlton,

Ritenour, Graydon and Robben Ford. There were a couple of Hollywood jazz clubs where you could go along to see these guys play, the Baked Potato and Donte's. Both of these clubs had a two-drink-minimum rule and food, and you could get in underage.

A lot of the studio players like Ritenour would have standing jam bands. Don Randi of the Wrecking Crew and Shelly Slussman owned the Baked Potato. I would go down there to see Ritenour and Harvey Mason, and a killer, ever-changing band of A-listers. It's a teeny little hole-in-the-wall place down in Studio City and still open to this day. You can stuff just about a hundred people inside and folks used to wait outside from 4 p.m. for the 10 p.m. show. Donte's was just down the street from the Baked Potato in North Hollywood. That club would have Carlton and Ford, Pops Popwell on bass and Greg Mathieson on keys, and Jeff Porcaro would sit in with those guys. When I started going to the clubs and meeting the real studio guys, it became apparent that they were all insanely great players and these were the guys I wanted to be. I would get myself a couple of Coca-Colas and watch them playing this extraordinary kind of jazz fusion. Through Jeff, I got on the night's guest-list and I would find a good table to be able to see this shit going down up close. It was inspiring, plain and simple.

I would also go into the local record store and hunt through the bins to find even the most obscure records that these guys had played on. I would buy them and study them to try to work out all of the parts that they had come up with. For me, one of the key cult records to come out during that time in school was Jay Gruska's *Gruska on Gruska*. Jay's now a successful composer for film and TV, but back then was trying to break through as a singer-songwriter. His album was produced by Michael Omartian, who has since worked with everyone from the Jacksons to Christopher Cross on his Grammy-winning first album. Michael is a genius keyboardist and at the time was playing on Steely Dan records, so Jeff and Paich played live with Gruska. Steve Porcaro played

Gruska's album for us in Still Life and we fell in love with it immediately. Even though it was never anything like a hit, we would do Jay's songs at our high-school gigs. Now, I do know for a fact that Jeff brought Jay down to see us because he introduced him to us. As far as I was concerned, I had got to meet a real rock star.

The one thing you had to be able to do to be a successful studio musician was sight-read music. We had a next-door neighbour, a guy named Mike Berkowitz, who was doing sessions and also played drums on the road with Helen Reddy. Dad would say to me, 'Look, this guy's not famous, but he's making a living.' That in itself was a big realisation for Dad, that you could actually have a career out of playing music. It was Mike who told Dad that if I was serious about music, I ought to have a guitar teacher and take formal lessons. Dad then went and spoke to his friend, Carl Fortina, who was head of the music department at Paramount Studios. I think Mike and Carl recommended to Dad the same guy, Jimmy Wyble.

Jimmy was a soft-spoken, gentle giant of a man and one of the great swing guitarists to come out of Texas in the 1940s. The so-called King of Western Swing Bob Wills had picked Jimmy out for his band the Texas Playboys and he went on to play with Sinatra and Benny Goodman among others. Jimmy was also endlessly patient, which made him the ideal tutor for me. He had to teach me from scratch to read music and I had a really hard time of it, like a lot of guitar players do. There is a good reason for that, which is that the guitar is one of the few instruments on which you can play the same note in several different places. On, say, a piano or horn, middle C is just, ping, right there. On guitar, middle C is on several strings all the way up the neck. It's all the same note and, because of the way the strings are set up, it's in fourths and then, Jesus God, just the one time, in a third.

It took me a while to get even competent with written music and theory, but I was determined and would practise a lot. I was also a pretty fast learner and Jimmy was great with me. He passed a few years back now, but fortunately I was able to tell him just how much he and his teaching had meant to me. Not too long before he died, I took him out to dinner at the Hotel Bel-Air. The funny thing was Jimmy was more into talking about how to date an Asian woman than music. It was hysterical. He passed soon after, but he changed my life and turned me into a 'real musician' in my parents' eyes.

I would also take every music class that was on offer at Grant High, and as I progressed with my studies I considered applying to the prestigious Berkeley School of Music. However, a more affordable option presented itself to my parents, which was the Dick Grove Music School. Dick Grove was a real hipster jazz guy and his was the first jazz improvisation school to open up in Los Angeles. Steve Porcaro, John Pierce, Carlos Vega, Mike Landau, Bruce Gowdy, most of our high-school band and I were all in Dick's inaugural class. Dick's wasn't just a great place to learn music: you could also meet people there and get work from them. Guys would often come into class and go: 'Hey, I know a cat who's looking for a guitar player' for this or that gig.

Soon enough, I started to pick up casual work. I could play rock-and-roll and also now a little bit of jazz and funk. Often as not, I would have to wear a suit and sing the goofiest songs of the era, but hey, I got paid to do it. You would also get asked to go into studios and play behind wannabe singer-songwriters on their demo tapes. Those gigs would pay twenty-five dollars a song. It was kind of like being in the minor leagues and that was where I did my training. Doing all these different kinds of sessions was how I got to be able to develop confidence and my own style, and find my voice as a musician.

One of the other real landmark things to happen to me in high school was that I got given my first car. Just as soon as I had got my licence at sixteen, Dad had me go with him over to my grand-mother's house. Parked out front there was this turquoise 1963

VW with a bow tied onto the roof. What that meant most of all for me was sweet freedom. I could come and go now as I pleased, and what's more I had somewhere to put all of my gear. I ripped out the back seat of the car to make room for my Ampeg VT-22 amp, just like Keith Richards played through on *Exile on Main Street*, a heavy bastard, and I still have it. I also got in there my Les Paul, a Gibson 335 that I by now had, plus the first generation of MXR foot pedals. The sole drawback to this was that, in order to be able to pay for gas, guitar strings and picks, I had to take on a couple of really shitty weekend jobs.

The first of these was cleaning toxic solvents out of a dry cleaner's for minimum wage, which at the time was a dollar sixty-five an hour. They didn't even equip me with a pair of gloves, and this corrosive shit would burn my fingers. The second was a gig bussing tables and washing dishes at a Japanese restaurant. At the very least, both of these were motivating. I mean to say, if I didn't make it with music, I was going to have to do *this* for a living. Are you fucking kidding me?

In the end, one of my close friends, Scott Carlson, got all of us budding-musician guys a better gig parking cars at an exclusive Hollywood restaurant, Chasen's. It was through doing that job that I was first able to get behind the wheel of a Ferrari, a Porsche and a Mercedes. We parked cars for everyone from Sammy Davis Jr to Joe Walsh, which was a big deal as we were fans. We would do crazy shit like tear off down the street at 150 miles an hour in rich people's cars. Landau one time roared into the lot in a Cadillac and smashed into three Rolls-Royces that were parked up. He bent the Caddy's fender all ways up and then had to drive it back out front.

Our boss was this guy named Joe Arnold who'd had his eyebrows burned off in a fire. This prick wouldn't even let us keep the tips. We figured out a scam. Some of the rich folks would come out after dinner, half-hammered on booze and ask for their car. Sometimes we would get a ten- or even twenty-dollar tip. We would keep a bunch of one-dollar bills in our back pockets. We'd grab a few of these bucks to show Joe and palm the ten or twenty. One night after we had graduated, a bunch of us drove up in front of Chasen's. I had a rubber monkey face mask on and a fire extinguisher. When Joe came over to move our beat-up car along, I emptied the fire extinguisher on him and buried the asshole head to toe, along with everyone else waiting for their cars. Mission accomplished.

As I was making money and Dad was away so much, I started to implore Mom to let me drop out of school. That, though, was never going to be allowed to happen. Mom told me in no uncertain terms that I would finish my high-school education no matter what, so I took her at her word. I figured that I would do the bare minimum to graduate and nothing more. To determine the class you were placed into, they would give you what's called an Iowa Test. I failed it on purpose, so I could be put into the 'scholastically challenged' classes. I would pretend to go to school but cut class through the week, and instead study music and rehearse with people who were paying me to play. At the end of the week, I would then ace the test, which was the only requirement for my parents to be happy. My teacher was on to me, but looked the other way. I also paid Lora twenty dollars a throw to do my homework and term papers for me. Lora was happy enough to take the dough, but Mom would keep on at me: 'You need something to fall back on.' My answer to that was: 'Like what – a knife?'

It was while we were still in school that Steve Porcaro got a call from this guy Gary Wright, who had been the singer in Spooky Tooth. Gary was just then about to have a huge solo hit with a song called 'Dream Weaver', and wanted Steve to audition for his band. Steve went along and got the gig, which was to play keyboards on a proper rock-and-roll tour. They were going to be doing stadium shows with Yes and Peter Frampton. At seventeen, Steve got to leave Grant High and to go out on the road. He was the first of our crew to hit the big time and, in the minds of the rest of us, that now meant that the same could happen for any of us. We might all be studio musicians. Being an actual rock star, on the other hand, still seemed as viable as finding a needle in a haystack.

CHAPTER FOUR

Ask me and I'll tell you that there are two ways to consider how it was that I came to be a session player. On the one hand, you can apply straight logic. That is to recognise that in Los Angeles in the mid-seventies there was a community of top-class musicians and that all of those guys were friends. Once you got a thumbs-up from certain people, such as Jeff Porcaro and David Paich, then you might be able to make your way around the whole scene.

The other perspective is altogether different. See, so many serendipitous things happened for me in such a short space of time that now I feel as if I were blessed. With hindsight, I have come to think that there might just be something bigger going on. That perhaps there are aspects of life that are pre-ordained before we even come into this world and that we end up doing just what we're supposed to. And then again, you could say that I think about this shit too much.

One thing is for sure and that is that I got my first legit job in music straight out of Grant High. An arranger, a wonderful guy named Gary Stockdale, hired a couple of us from Dick Grove's school to be in his pit-band for a run of performances of

Shakespeare's *Two Gentlemen of Verona* at LA City College. I got paid 250 dollars a week for the gig. Being able to show my parents I was getting a weekly pay cheque from a real job was a proud moment. It was also my first step towards a lifelong career.

It happened that Gary knew Frank Wolf. Frank went on to become a venerable engineer and recorded artists such as Barbra Streisand, Smokey Robinson, Randy Newman and Asia. Back then, he had a little four-track place out in La Cienega called Little Night Studio. With Steve Porcaro off with Gary Wright, I had thought of trying to get a record deal as a solo artist. I had written three or four songs that I wanted to demo up, and for such purposes Little Night was perfect. My parents offered to give me the money to cover the cost of a session, so I went in there with Mike Landau on second guitar, Carlos Vega on drums, Dean Cortez on bass. I played the basic track on keyboards and overdubbed the guitar and vocals.

Believe it or not, we got a kind of rock-ish Stevie Wonder vibe going on with those tracks, and I received a pretty positive response to them. It wasn't enough to land me my dream deal, but certainly that Little Night session paved the way ahead for me. Gary was well-connected and tight too with Jay Gruska, who he also got to come down and sing background vocals on my stuff. Turned out Jay dug what I was doing. Straight after the session, he invited me to play some gigs with him at this club where he had just got a regular Wednesday night spot. The Bla Bla Café was on the Valley side of the Hollywood Hills. It was a little dive bar and you could squeeze maybe a hundred people in there, but Al Jarreau had not long been discovered at the Bla Bla and it was a jumping place. There was just room on the stage for a piano and a four-piece band, so Jay had Mike Porcaro, Carlos and me to back him up. These were great times and we started to gel as a little band. A lot of the studio guys and friends, such as Jeff and Paich, would come to see us every week.

Jay was very much my conduit into a bigger, wider world, all the elements of which were inter-linked. He was living at the time with a great session guitarist, Dan Ferguson, who had also played with Jeff and Paich in Sonny and Cher's band. Dan's then girlfriend was a girl named Dee Dee Andros, who wanted to be a singer and whose father was wealthy enough to fund her ambition. Dee Dee's dad paid for her to put together and rehearse with an incredible session band. Intermittently, Steve Porcaro became part of Dee Dee's set-up. Another of the guys was Jai Winding, who was a huge talent. Jai was already by then well on his way to becoming a first-call keyboard player and would go on to work with Michael Jackson, Don Henley and many more stellar artists. He would also become a close friend of mine.

Dan Ferguson was a busy guy, and so was on the lookout for another guitar player to help out with Dee Dee. As I remember Gruska put him on to me and I was only too happy to jump into that scene. For three to four hours every weekday, we would get together to rehearse with Dee Dee out at a place called Alley Studios in the Valley, which was being used as well by Jackson Browne and Lowell George of Little Feat. Thanks to Dee Dee's dad, I got paid another 250 bucks a week for my time. Right then, you could rent an apartment in downtown LA for 300 dollars a month, so I was properly able to call myself a working musician.

Yet another great cat who played in Dee Dee's band was the talented session drummer Willie Ornelas. He became a close friend and got me an invite to the weekly poker game that the top session guys held on Friday or Saturday nights at each other's pads. Getting a nod into that was a big thing, a kind of mark of acceptance. Carlton and Graydon were regulars at the game, and so also was a fast-rising guy from Canada, a keyboardist and songwriter named David Foster. Paich had got Foster his first pit-band gig in LA, doing *The Rocky Horror Show* at the Roxy on Sunset, and in general in those days, it would be true to say that where Paich led, Foster followed.

For their part, Paich and Jeff would kind of float into the games, bluff some, take everybody's money and then split. Man, those guys were magical characters. Everybody respected the pair of them, and such was his elevated status that Jeff especially could have been forgiven for being arrogant, but he wasn't. It was a mark of the man that he pulled his whole deal off with a knowing nod and wink. It was also Jeff's place that was *the* cool bachelor-party pad. He had a great sound system, the finest weed, and the most beautiful girls were always around.

Altogether, all of those guys appeared to me then like the hippest cats on Planet Earth. There I was among them, a zit-faced teenager still living with his mom and dad. When it came to my turn to host the game, Dad even sat in and played with us. I begged of him beforehand, 'Please God, don't tell childhood stories that will embarrass me.' Nevertheless, all of these guys that I so looked up to also took a shine to me. I guess it was my sense of humour that helped me to break the ice. I truly admired those guys.

Graydon would give me advice on the best gear to get for pro sessions, such as a Fender Princeton amp or a Deluxe and a new stereo device called a Boss Chorus, which I would follow to the letter. Jay's been one of the constants in my life ever since and has helped out so much. He's my brother and my son Trev's godfather and a constant bro in my life. Carlton invited me up to hang at his house and I ended up playing Hammond on one of his demos, 'Nite Crawler'. Foster and I were becoming fast friends as well. Long before he got to work with everyone from Chicago and Alice Cooper to Whitney Houston and Madonna, the two of us would have breakfast together almost every day at a joint down the road from my folks' house called Charlie's Rest. There, we would chain-smoke Marlboros and talk about our dreams of making it big. Back then, I loved the guy and he was also very instrumental in helping me with my early career.

As well as his music buddies, Jay Gruska also ran with some of the young Hollywood crowd, and it was that which got me into another circle. Among them were David Jolliffe (star of 1970s show *Room 222*); Bill Mumy, who had been the child star in the TV series *Lost in Space* and *The Twilight Zone*; Ben Weiss, who became an assistant director and director on *Friends*; a couple of the Cassidy brothers, Shaun and Patrick; and Debbie Reynolds's and Eddie Fisher's son, Todd. I also got an initial meeting with Miguel Ferrer, who would later become one of my best friends. To this day I still am great friends with all of those guys.

It was on account of getting to know Shaun Cassidy through Jay Gruska that I got to make my television debut. Just as his elder brother David had done with *The Partridge Family*, Shaun wanted to make his name as an actor-singer. By then, he was already doing a TV show of his own, *The Hardy Boys*. The first time that he ever got to sing on the show was doing a version of 'Da Doo Ron Ron', which Phil Spector had originally produced for the Crystals back in 1963. Jay, Mike, Carlos and Scott Page (of Pink Floyd, Supertramp and Toto) and I appeared in that very episode as Shaun's backing band. Later on, it turned Shaun into an overnight sensation and teen idol.

Meanwhile, Todd Fisher had got the first mobile recording truck in LA and Gruska started to use it to work on new material. Recording in that truck was a surreal experience because Todd would have it parked up in the driveway of his mom's house. We never did get to see hide nor hair of Debbie Reynolds. Todd was a really good guy, too. He is someone I have not seen in forty-odd years now, but Jesus, have I felt for him. That was a hell of a beating he took in 2016 losing his mom and sister within just a day of each other.

At the same time that I was playing with Dee Dee and at the Bla Bla with Jay, I began to get calls to do other sessions. One I did was for a guy called Phil O'Kelsey; we rehearsed for a while and then ended up at United Western Studios, where the Beach Boys had cut *Pet Sounds*. I got union wages, so it was a real recording session. For a musician at that time, LA was boomtown. Once you broke on to the circuit, there was a natural cycle to how things would happen. Guys would every few years jump off the train and move on to become an artist, arranger, songwriter or producer. That left a void for younger players such as me to come in and fill. Graydon and Carlton were just then getting ready to make that jump, and Graydon started recommending me for the sessions he couldn't do and the ones he was producing.

Some of the first pro dates I did were alongside Graydon, and also Foster and Willie. There was another early one for the debut album by an aspirant singer-songwriter, Michael Clark, which was significant for me at least. Clark's record didn't do squat for him, but on the date I got to work with Lee Ritenour, Leland Sklar, Greg Leisz and Mike Baird. I hit it off with those guys and they also began to pitch me for gigs. That's when the snowball really started to roll.

Leland Sklar: That session was at Conway Studios and Luke couldn't have been more than nineteen years old. He was a real punk, but I loved him instantly. Soon as he started to play, he blew me away. He had the soul of an old man in his young body. After that date, any time that anyone asked me to recommend a guitarist I would tell them, 'Call Luke!' He has gone on and kept getting better over the years, too, matured like a fine wine. Any time that I would go into the studio and see a road case with either of Luke's or Jeff's names on it, I would know it was going to be a fun day. The other thing about Luke was that no matter who it was that we were playing for and whatever the quality of music, he would always bring his A-game to the date, never the B.

Not that I didn't have setbacks. Back then, they would hold open auditions for gigs and I got to hear about one for Frank Zappa's band. Frank was looking for a rhythm player and all the usual suspects were vying for the slot. I rolled up to the open audition at

SIR, a Hollywood sound stage, and there were a hundred other players stood around the place. Frank's band at the time was incredible and they knew each lick and nuance of every piece of music that he had ever recorded. Frank hadn't arrived when I got there, but the band, which included Terry Bozzio on drums, Eddie Jobson on keyboards and violin and Patrick O'Hearn on bass, were already set up and playing this insane, intense stuff.

It was dazzling. Watching them, I started to think that this was one deal that was slightly above my pay grade at that point in time. I decided to hide in the shadows and just watch how things unfolded. Frank walked in the room. He was every bit as charismatic and imposing as you would have expected him to be. He grabbed the mic and glared around. I was trying my best to make myself invisible, but he looked straight at me and went: 'You!' Instantly, every eye was on me. I couldn't breathe. It was as though I had sucked my cock up through my lungs and time had stopped dead.

The first thing I did was plug into a Marshall and play a little bit, just to prove that I could. What Frank did was to rip open a chart and thrust it at me. This thing looked like someone had randomly wiped their ass with black ink in a twenty-one/eight time signature; it had strange groups of eighth notes and more alien time signatures. I could feel Frank's stare burning into me, but all I could manage was to mumble something about how I would need to learn this stuff first. He said: 'It's OK, I believe you,' and threw the chart to one side. 'Let's see how your comprehension is,' he continued. 'I'm going to play you a phrase and I want you to play it back for me.'

In my entire life, I don't think I have ever been as terrified as I was just then. If you would have shoved a piece of coal up my ass, a diamond would have surely come back down. Frank proceeded to play this weird, oddly coupled phrase. All I could fathom was that it was in the key of A. I managed to get the first few notes, but then fumbled. Frank said, 'It's all right, I'll do it for you again.'

Then he played something that was completely different and longer. It was sixteen bars and all but impossible for anyone to take in on one listen. I was horrified and once more fumbled. This time, Frank sneered at me: 'You have terrible comprehension. Next!'

I put my guitar back in its case and had to do the walk of shame out of there, trying my damnedest not to cry. Frank Zappa had just told me that I sucked in front of what seemed to me like every guitar player in LA. I felt as if my life was over. Years later, I would become close friends with Steve Vai and he was in Frank's band after this period. I told Steve the story of my humiliation and he just laughed. He said Frank wouldn't have wanted to audition a hundred players, so he made me, as the youngest and most unqual-ified-looking candidate, the sacrificial lamb in order to empty the room. Apparently, almost everyone did end up following me right out of there. Cats were thinking, 'I'm going to have to do *that*? Fuck this.' Driving home that day in my little VW, I had tears pouring down my cheeks. But then, I had a moment of clarity. I thought to myself, 'I'm going to prove that motherfucker wrong.' I resolved to study harder, and deeper, and that I wasn't going to be kicked in the ass and walk away. (Years later, I got to know the Zappa family; I told them the story and they laughed.)

Once more, fortune favoured me. Paich and Jeff, who were inseparable in most every respect, were both by then riding a hot streak. Paich especially was on fire. Jeff had got him in to play on Steely's *Katy Lied* record and together they had also made an album with one-time Allman Brothers Band guitarist Les Dudek. Les had gone on to join Boz Scaggs's band, and Boz in turn produced Les's solo record for him. Which was how it came to pass that Jeff got to play on and Paich got to co-write one of the most successful and influential records to explode out of LA in all of the 1970s. When it emerged in March 1976, Boz's *Silk Degrees* all at once laid down the template for the LA-derived, blue-eyed, rock/R & B sound that was to reign supreme for the next five, six, seven years, and it went on to sell more than five million copies. It was a game-changer of a record.

The immediate result of this was that Paich and Jeff struck a deal with Columbia Records to put their own thing together. By the start of 1977, they were getting free time to work weekends on their own demos at Davlen Sound, the state-of-the-art studio in North Hollywood where *Silk Degrees* had been made. Two of the other slots in their nascent band already appeared to have been filled. Steve Porcaro had gone out with his brother and Paich in Boz's band on the *Silk Degrees* tour, as had a friend of theirs from the Sonny and Cher days, David Hungate, a brilliant bass player. However, a big rave was going on around town over who the guitar player would be. *That* chair was still open and, more than anything in the world, I wanted to be the guy to fill it.

It wasn't as if Jeff and Paich hadn't been following my progress. The pair of them would often come along to the Bla Bla to see Mikey and me play with Gruska. My cause was also helped by the fact I was so close to Steve. On 9 January 1977, Jeff called to invite me down to Davlen Sound to play on a track that Paich had just written. It was obvious that they wanted to check me out up close and so badly did I want to impress them that I was shaking with nerves by the time I got there. That was such a great studio. The room was big and loud, and it had in it a beautiful Bösendorfer piano. The track they teed up for me was titled 'All Us Boys', a version of which would eventually appear on our second album in 1979. Paich's original was a bit rockier, and I plugged in and ripped into it. What I played was good enough for the two of them to ask me to come back the next weekend.

That I had been invited to try out at all was seen as a huge deal. There were a whole bunch of other guys who thought they were in line for the gig, so the vibe on the scene was very much, 'Who the hell is this punk-ass kid jumping the queue?' Neither were Jeff or Paich about to make things easy for me. In fact, it would be fair to say that for the next several months, the two of them delighted in fucking with me. They kept on having me come down to Davlen Sound, but never once let on whether or not I was actually going to be in their band.

One time, I turned up with the girl I was then seeing. Her name was Christy, and she was beautiful, blonde, six years older than me and a divorcee. Short-lived though it was, my mom was appalled by our relationship.

That day, Paich and Jeff had me wait outside in the corridor with Christy and my guitar, just to fuck with me some more. Finally, Paich came out of the studio. He looked at me, looked at Christy, and then made his move. He swept her up . . . and stuck his tongue right down her throat. What's more, she went for it! My face was on the floor and I was a bit shocked but that was over soon enough.

CHAPTER FIVE

Doors were opening up for me. On the one hand, there were my ongoing weekend visits to Davlen Sound. The way these would go down was that Jeff and Paich would cut tracks live to tape. Paich would also add Moog bass and, man, he was so good at it. I would overdub onto the tracks. Together, Jeff and Paich were an intimidating but also magnetic force. They were tearing it up right in front of me. On any given day, I would watch magic go down between them and with a shit-eating grin on my face. I was so happy just to be there in that room that I could have burst into flames.

Added to that, once word got out that I was working with those guys my credibility shot up and I was thrust into the orbit of other incredible musicians and producers such as Richard Perry and the whole Studio 55 scene. One in particular was James Newton Howard. Nowadays, James is best known as the Academy Award-winning composer and conductor of film scores for such block-busters as *The Dark Knight* and the *Hunger Games* movies. Back in the day, he had made his name as a keyboard player, synthesiser wizard and arranger for Elton John's band. I met James through

Paich and Jeff and Steve Porcaro. They were doing a lot of sessions together at the time and also introduced me to Robin Reinhardt, who was Richard Perry's assistant and booker for sessions. James and I hit it off straight away. He liked my playing and we shared a very wrong, sick and demented sense of humour. Robin was really cool, as well. She started booking me for Richard's sessions and hiring me for other stuff, too. I owe her a lot.

Like Carlton, Graydon and Ritenour, James was in the process of breaking out from session work and, in his case, into producing. He had just then landed a gig producing a record, *Wild Child*, for a singer-songwriter named Valerie Carter, and brought me along to play on it. I had dug Valerie back in high school, since her first solo album, which Lowell George of Little Feat fame produced. *Wild Child* turned out to be a wonderful record to make. The songs were great. It was done at one of my favourite studios, Sunset Sound, and that was when I started to feel as if I had been welcomed into the A-list of guys. James had me write a tune with him for the record, too, called 'Lady in the Dark'. Other than me, he also called in Jeff on drums, David Hungate on bass and an unbelievable jazz pianist and percussionist, Victor Feldman, who was twenty years older than the rest of us and was another to have worked on Steely's stuff.

James had an enigmatic assistant on the record, this little black dude from Minnesota who was supposed to be the new wunder-kind. This guy was meant to be there in a co-producer capacity, but didn't actually speak. I would be doing a guitar overdub and his head would just appear over the top of the console. He would stare at me for a few seconds and slowly disappear from view again. It was really fucking weird. He didn't once even acknowledge me, never mind introduce himself. I only found out later that this cat was Prince.

Four years later, the two of us would both be back at Sunset Sound. I was doing a session for Greg Mathieson and Prince was working in an adjoining room with his band. I would see him outside the complex at ten in the morning, sat astride a purple motorbike and wearing a silver lamé suit. I would smile and nod my head to him, but the most that I ever got out of him in return was a raised eyebrow. He was one very strange, talented cat.

That summer, Boz Scaggs planned to go back out on the road again and was getting his band together. On this occasion, he was looking to add to the ranks a rhythm guitar player to supplement Les Dudek. Besides Les, he had Jeff, Steve and Stevie Wonder's bass player Scott Edwards, and he had also brought Jai Winding into the line-up. Jai and I had become close friends. He had got me on my first session for a record by Terence Boylan. Also on that album were Donald Fagen and Dean Parks. When it came out, all of sudden I saw my name written in the same sentence as my studio-guy heroes. (Thanks, Boona!) Anyway, Jeff and I guess all of those guys put in a good word for me, because I got the call from Boz's then road manager, Craig Fruin. Craig asked me how much money I wanted to do the gig, and I damn near shit my pants. Fuck, I hadn't a clue what to say. I had only just started doing the better sessions in town, so plucked a figure out of the air – 1,000 dollars a week. Craig went, 'OK' and hung up the phone. I was so stricken with panic that I got straight on to Jeff to make sure that I hadn't blown it by pricing myself too high. It was 1977. That was like asking for 4,000 dollars a week now.

And, man, did I ever prepare for that gig. Before rehearsals had even started, I made sure to learn all of Boz's shit, every last note. Opening day of rehearsals, I was the first one there. Second day, something went down between Boz and Les. Boz had been working with Paich on songs like 'Lowdown', which had jazzier chord changes, and Les was a stone-cold blues man. He had only played on one track on *Silk Degrees* and it soon became apparent that he hadn't got to know the other newer songs. Boz and Les walked off the sound stage. I guess they had words because it was just Boz that came back out and he told the rest of us: 'Well, Les just quit, so I'm going to have to find another lead player.'

At that, Jeff stood up from behind his kit, pointed with his sticks at me and announced to Boz: 'You've got this guy.' Then he said to me: 'Show him what you've got, man.' Boz called up 'Jump Street' off *Silk Degrees*, the song that Les was to have burned on and a tune that one can *really* play on. Now, it was a slide-guitar piece and I didn't play much slide, so instead I risked it all and just did *me*. I stepped forward and took the solo like a man possessed. By the grace of God, I shone and at the end of the tune everyone else in the band gave me a round of applause. All that Boz said was, 'Well, I don't need to find another guy after all.'

In every sense, that for me was a massive tour. We went out for the better part of three months right across the States and around Europe. I had not seen anything of the world before then, and here I was travelling in a private plane and staying in five-star hotels. All of us in the band met up at the Porcaro house to take a limo to the airport. I had my mom drop me off. To her, it was as if I was going off to join the circus but, for my part, I was barely able to contain my excitement. As a child, I had a recurring dream that I was about to walk out on stage in front of thousands of people. Right before I got to play the first note, I would always wake up.

Opening night was 21 June 1977 at the famous Red Rocks Amphitheatre, Colorado, and in front of a sell-out crowd of nearly 10,000. Southside Johnny and the Asbury Jukes were the opening act and they were great. Watching them from the wings, it was like looking out over a sea of people. In the middle of our set that night, Boz threw me a solo on one of his older blues tunes, I tore into it and the crowd reacted in a really positive way. It was the highest high that I have ever had in my entire life.

The only thing I didn't dig on the tour was that everybody on it would refer to me as 'The Kid'. Jeff started that one up and it stuck. I hated it, but took it. It wasn't even as if I was the only nineteen-year-old in the band. Both Steve Porcaro and the percussionist, Lenny Castro, were my age. The three of us couldn't even go into a bar after a gig. Boz was proud of me, though, I think. I did stand out. Back then, there weren't a whole lot of other teen-age guitar players making a noise. As opposed to today, where there's a foetus on YouTube that plays like Stevie Ray Vaughan. Every night, Boz would introduce me on stage: 'It's the Kid! He's only nineteen years old!'

> *Lora Lukather: The first time that we all went to see my brother play was when Boz hired him. It was at the Greek Theatre in LA and the whole family was there: Mom, Dad, my grandfather and me. Seeing my brother front and centre stage, the crowd acclaiming him, was when I looked at him through completely different eyes. Sure, he was always off in his room practising, but until that moment I had not properly listened to him. And the tears from my parents' eyes! We all of us knew that he was going to go on and be somebody.*

The Greek Theatre was the big hometown gig – seven nights sold out. It was 18 August 1977. I played a solo and Mom told me afterwards that she looked over at Dad and he had a tear coming out of his eye. He turned to her and said, 'I didn't know that he was *that* good.' Boz had my parents come backstage after the show and told them how I was a good kid. He was so gracious that night. He also presented me with a Gibson L-5, a classic jazz guitar, that I still have. I believe that was his way of saying he dug me. I loved the man.

By the end of the tour, I had made around 10,000 dollars. I came home off the road determined to buy a new car. I also had money stashed from sessions and I wanted a BMW. I was still driving around town in my '63 Beetle and believed it was time for a change-up. I went right on down to the local BMW place. I walked in there wearing ripped-up jeans and flipflops, and must have looked like I was twelve years old. I said to the sales guy, 'I want to drive *that* car.' He looked me over and replied: 'Are you jerking me off, kid? You know how much that car costs?' The guy wouldn't let me near the car, let alone hand me the keys to drive it.

So, I did what any other self-respecting smart ass would do, which is to say I went back home and told my mom. She took me straight along to another BMW place on Van Nuys Boulevard and I bought a brand new, top-of-the-line BMW 550i. That car was a maroon-sparkled, bad-ass ride and I spent on it every last dime of the money that I had got from Boz. Later that day, Mom called up the sales guy from the first BMW place. She asked him, 'Do you remember the little kid that came in this morning? Well, he has just now bought that car from the dealer's down the road and paid cash. Never judge a book by its cover, asshole.' I loved my mom.

When we were just about to start touring *Silk Degrees* that summer, Boz started work on his follow-up record, which became *Down Two Then Left*. In the midst of playing dates, he would also be recording. Not unreasonably, we all thought that Paich would again be involved, but instead Boz brought in Michael Omartian to write songs with him. You would have to ask Boz why that was, but *Down Two Then Left* turned out to be an even jazzier record. He had Jeff come in again on drums, Hungate on bass, Michael Omartian and Jai Winding on piano and Graydon and Ray Parker Jr on guitars. They were overdubbing on a track called 'A Clue'. So Boz called me up late one night and asked if I would come by Hollywood Sound and have a go at a solo.

This was when guitar solos were considered cool. Carlton had been made a star in the guitar community through the solos he had played on Steely's *The Royal Scam* and many others, and in general getting to take one on a record was thought of as a big deal. If it turned out to be a hit record, that would be *really* helpful to your career. There was pressure, though, too. We didn't have the luxury of doing a lot of takes in those days because records were cut straight to tape and there weren't a whole lot of tracks available to us. I hurried down to Hollywood Sound studio that night and sat out in the hallway while they ran the track. I hit upon an idea, then went in the room and nailed the take. It was my first big-time solo. Boz got me in to do another solo on the song 'Gimme the Goods'. That was the first gold record I ever got; I was very excited and grateful.

> *Mike Landau: Luke's musical growth happened very quickly. I would say the defining moment where he officially became a complete bad-ass on guitar was when he recorded the solo on Boz Scaggs's 'A Clue' in 1977. Boz was a huge artist at that point and I believe Luke was only nineteen years old at the time. I wasn't at the session, but it sure sounds to me like one of those perfect, first-take solos that just flowed out of him. That solo is a masterpiece, a beautiful moment in time. It's got it all in my opinion and was an amazing debut of things to come. It also sounds just how Luke played the guitar — effortlessly.*

Up to that point I was an up-and-coming guy, but now my career was starting to take off and my parents' phone rang off the hook with offers of work. I started to do ten, then twenty, twenty-five sessions a week. There was a competitive element to it but in a fun way, too. Guys would sit around the studios going, 'How many sessions you got lined up next week — twenty? Well, I've got twenty-two.' It became a bit of a thing to go down to the musicians' union office to pick up your cheques and measure how high your pile stacked.

David Foster began to call me in to do the sessions he started producing. We were close friends back then. I worked on one of his first productions for an incredibly talented and beautiful Canadian singer, Lisa Dal Bello, who Jeff was dating. Lisa sang on our first demo, 'Miss Sun', which went on to become a big hit for Boz. Right after working with Boz, one of the first major things I did with Foster was Alice Cooper's *From the Inside* record. Foster was producing, but he wasn't a rock-and-roller — *at all*. He understood the concept of it and could appreciate it, but he didn't live it, whereas I was the guy who cranked up his Les Paul real loud. I was also able to double-track my parts quick. That wasn't so hard, as I made up my own parts almost all the time. Foster wanted me to help him out with Alice. I'd loved Alice since junior high, used to play *School's Out* in ninth grade, so that was a huge call for me to get.

That whole record, of course, was Alice's piss-take on being in an asylum. He had just then got out of rehab, so was totally sober and focused on the task at hand. He was super-smart, super-funny and a joy to work with. Before going into the studio with Alice, Foster and I went up to his house to do some of the writing. Foster and I had come up with riffs in advance. I have to give Foster a lot of credit. He was an incredible producer and also great at bringing ideas out of me. Foster brought me in to write two songs for the album, 'Nurse Rozetta' and 'Serious'. Bernie Taupin turned up at Alice's with pages filled with these brilliant, crazy lyrics, which Foster and Alice managed to edit down. I ended up doing a lot of the musical stuff on that record and as a piece it was a very rewarding creative experience. It also introduced me to working with legendary producer-engineer, Keith Olsen. The album's single, 'How You Gonna See Me Now', was a hit and I had a solo of mine on it. My buddy John Pierce also played on that track. I wanted to surround myself with all of my childhood friends as well and get them in the club, so to speak. John and Mike Landau were the first two besides me who were more than ready to step up.

Another album of note was the first solo record from Three Dog Night singer Cory Wells. The producer David Anderle called me through the recommendation of Foster and Graydon; the session players included Leland Sklar and Mike Baird, who was best man at my first wedding (boy were we trouble at the time). The making of that record was a great experience.

I got a call to do Peter Criss's first solo album, which was altogether different. Kiss were so huge then that each of the four guys in the band got to make their own records, including the drummer. Not that Peter played drums on his own record. I showed up for the session and they had got another session guy in to do Peter's parts. I found out later that a whole bunch of ringers got called in to play on Kiss records. Mike Porcaro, for one, played bass on a Kiss album. Once Kiss became all about the spectacle, I don't think Gene Simmons, who has always been nice to me, had a whole lot of patience in the studio.

At that time, there were also contractors who would book up musicians for sessions. A couple of those guys in particular, Frank DeCaro and Trevor Veitch, were really good to me. Disco was still happening and Trevor got me on a hell of a lot of sessions for guys such as Giorgio Moroder and Greg Mathieson, who were the producers and arrangers of that stuff. Giorgio produced a lot of these records, but wouldn't be around most of the time. Cats like Winding and Mathieson, who was Carlton's keyboardist as well, would be the arrangers of these sessions. I would show up at a studio called Rusk in Hollywood where Giorgio had a team of people that worked on his stuff. That place was like an assembly line. We would get thrown a bunch of charts, have a quick read over them and then do our parts in one, two takes. They didn't have time for any bullshit and that was fine by me. I could do a solo, an overdub and – boom! – be out of there. You wouldn't even have a clue which artist it was that was going to be on any given track. Oftentimes, I would hear a song on the radio and go, '*Hey* – I played on that!' And it would be like a Donna Summer record.

It was through Frank that I got to be on Barbra Streisand's *Wet* album in 1979. Frank's call was: 'Streisand, a week at Capitol, twelve till six, be there!' I showed up and Graydon was also on the session and Jeff too. I played acoustic guitar and Streisand stood no more than three feet from me in the vocal booth, singing live. With the reverb in the vocal booth, she had the most beautiful sound to her voice. Once we had run the tape, she came out to us and said, sweet as you like, 'Guys, it sounds great, really. I just need you to take a break while I go work on the chart a little bit more.' Then she turned to the producer, Gary Klein, and the arranger, who was Frank's brother, Nick, and gave them a piece of her mind. All of us musicians were sitting there trying not to laugh while she just laid into these two poor guys. I ended up doing her next two albums. Barbra Streisand could not have been nicer to her musicians but, man, she terrified her producers.

Jay Graydon: When I started to go into producing and songwriting full time, I would tell everybody, 'I'm done – call Lukather.' Luke always thanked me for that, but I have told him countless times that they still would have called him eventually. I just saved both him and them some time. Musically, every session I ever did with Luke was great. If one or the other of us started playing rhythm, the other guy would find a part that would complement it. There was no competition between any of us guys. We all replaced someone, and we all got replaced at some point. You start to worry about that shit and you go crazy.

We got to have a laugh, too. There was one session we did for Juice Newton, the country singer, before she'd had a hit. The band was Jeff, Foster, Hungate, Luke and me. It was getting close to 5 p.m., and I had another session to go on to at seven. We were going to go into overtime if we didn't get the last tune down quick. I had the first twelve bars to myself, a finger-picking part, and I made the mistake of telling the guys that I needed to get the fuck out of there. Of course, they decided to fuck with me. Soon as I started to play, they began to throw shit at my guitar – cigarettes, matchbook covers and the like. I would try to do a take and these things would be bouncing off my strings. OK, it was funny the first couple of times and then I had to say, 'Come on guys, give me a break over here.'

By then, I knew the part, so I wasn't looking at the sheet music. Neither was I looking at the guys, because I didn't want them to distract me. I had got my eyes fixed on the floor. I played the part and then everyone else was supposed to come in. Except, unbeknown to me, Luke had quietly put down his guitar, snuck over in my direction and took his pants off. He knew exactly when I was going to look up. When I did, his bare asshole was six inches from my nose. Close enough for me to count his bunghole hairs. I was on the floor laughing, so was everyone else. Stupid shit like that was normal.

You could never predict what an artist was going to be like, or how they would react. Hungate, Jeff and I got hired to play a session for a songwriter named Kenny Nolan. Kenny was a middle-of-the-road singer-songwriter. He had written a couple of tunes for Frankie Valli and just the year before had a hit of his own with a saccharine piano ballad, 'I Like Dreamin''. That particular session, we got to the second song of the day and it was an especially cheesy number titled 'But Love Me'. Hungate went around to everybody's charts and added an extra 't' to the title, so now it was 'Butt Love Me'. When it got to the hook, which started out, 'Do me wrong, do me right, do anything you like,' we all stood up and yelled, 'Butt love me!' Kenny almost broke down and cried. He scolded us that we had ruined his song and had us fired on the spot. Forty years later, a friend of mine happened to run into Kenny and mentioned my name to him. And he was still *sore* about 'Butt Love Me'.

The next road gig that I got offered was huge. Boz's manager, Irving Azoff, also looked after Steely and asked me if I wanted to do their next tour. They had just made the *Aja* record and were getting ready to go out behind it. For me, that was beyond being a dream job. As far as all of us were concerned, that band was the pinnacle of musical excellence. I even got as far as rehearsing with their other guitarist, the amazing Denny Dias, but then the shit went down. Right when things were about to get serious, the horn players Donald and Walter had lined up began to ask for a lot of money. So I was told. Donald and Walter just said, 'Fuck it,' and canned the whole tour.

So, I got to be in Steely Dan for five seconds. It was faster than fleeting, but that was another moment that for me changed everything. The butterfly effect of the Steely tour not happening was that Jeff and Paich were also left with nothing else to do, and decided that we should really get down to making our own first album.

CHAPTER SIX

We started to make the first Toto album in October 1977. It was only once the Steely tour collapsed that I got to know for sure that I even had the gig. The whole time we had been on tour with Boz, I had kept on going at Jeff and Paich, 'Am I in the band, guys? Am I?' Their hazing went right on, too. Jeff would look thoughtful, stroke his chin and tell me, 'I don't know, man, maybe we'll try out someone else.' It wasn't until later that he let on to me that they had known all along that I was their guy. I was fearless at the time, would do anything and was also easy to work with. Paich in particular had very specific things that he wanted to hear. He only had to tell me once and I would be able to execute any given part. He brought the best out of me. Jeff could coax me as well with just the right look or reference.

As far as Jeff and Paich were concerned, musicianship was a prerequisite of their band. They had wanted guys who could not only play, but also sing and write music. Paich would reference Fleetwood Mac and the Eagles, the kind of bands in which every member contributed. In Steve Porcaro, they had a genius keyboard player who was also a trailblazer for all of the experimental synthesiser stuff then emerging. Steve was always way ahead of the curve in that respect, whereas Paich was more of an old-school piano and Hammond organ player, but they were a wonderful, complementary team. Hungate was the most seasoned cat of us all. He was nine years older than Steve and me, but hilarious and also a first-take guy. His off-the-cuff ideas were endless.

When it was finally established that I was going to be the guitarist, Paich also decided that he wanted us to have a lead singer. At the time, he had been working with Foreigner on their second album, doing string arrangements, and got fixated upon having someone with a high tenor voice like Lou Gramm's. The first guy he and Jeff approached about the gig was Michael McDonald. Michael had been in Steely with Jeff and had also sung on a demo that Steve had made in high school. As fate would have it, Michael had just accepted an offer to join the Doobie Brothers. He told Jeff and Paich, 'If you would have asked me last week . . .' We have maintained a great friendship with Michael ever since, but how different our band could have been. And probably all of our lives, too. That's the butterfly effect for you.

The other guy Jeff and Paich were hot on was Bobby Kimball. Bobby was in a band with a friend of theirs, Joe Schermie, who had been the bassist in Three Dog Night. They went along to see Bobby rehearse with Joe. For sure, Bobby wasn't a schooled musician but he had a powerful sound to his voice, particularly back then. He was a big personality, too, and we all dug him. Like Hungate, he was older than the rest of us, and by ten years, and had come up to LA from his native Louisiana. Bobby had been working on the road for pretty much his whole life and, as we were soon to discover, he was a sweet cat.

The night of his audition, Bobby brought along with him a song that he had written, 'You Are the Flower'. On the spot, we cut a demo of it with him. Some strings were subsequently over-dubbed onto it, but essentially that's the version of the song that you hear on the first Toto album. Paich had another new song. A couple of weeks beforehand, he had invited Jeff, Steve and me up to his apartment in Westwood. On this little spinet piano, he had played for us this riff that had a kind of shuffle groove. Paich told us that he had copped the vibe from Sly Stone's 'Hot Fun in the Summertime'. He began to sing along, but all that he had at the time were three words: 'Hold the line'.

Nevertheless, the three of us were soon enough shouting out to him, 'This is fantastic, man!' I told Paich I could hear a crunchy guitar part and no one played a shuffle groove like Jeff Porcaro. From the get-go, it was obvious that this was something special. By the time Bobby came in, Paich had worked up the lyrics and we had cut a demo. He had Bobby step up and sing to the basic track, and Bobby killed it. Paich turned to the rest of us and said, 'He's our guy.'

Columbia had extended a full-blown record deal to the band by the time we had got off the road with Boz that September. Not one of the guys at the label had heard so much as a note of music. Such was Jeff and Paich's graciousness that they made the deal an equal split between the six of us. I know for a fact that people had tried to convince the two of them to treat the rest of us as hired hands, but they wanted this to be a real, genuine working band with equal splits.

However, certain decisions were still Jeff's and Paich's alone to make. One of which was over who should manage us. We met with Tommy Mottola, who was then working with Hall & Oates and had pursued us hard, but decided against him. They couldn't possibly have known that Tommy would go on to be made president of Columbia some twenty years later and of all the implications that would have for us down the line. The other guy who was interested was Irving Azoff, but since Paich and Irving had issues over the Boz thing, his name was taken off the table. Paich's dad, Marty, had a relationship with the two guys we ended up going with, Mark Hartley and Larry Fitzgerald. Both of them were very good people, but to be honest I didn't have the experience to know if that was a good idea. If I had been asked my opinion, I would have gone with Irving in a heartbeat because I knew him and I knew he was big time. If we would have done, I also think we'd have been in a very different place right now. I liked Irving; he was good to me, and like Don Henley said in his 1998 Rock and Roll Hall of Fame speech: 'He may be Satan, but he's our Satan.' You want a guy like that making sure that you're taken care of and well off later in life. (Thing is, according to Paich, Walter Yetnikoff, then president of Columbia, wanted Fitzgerald and Hartley to manage us. They had a close working relationship with Columbia, so it seemed like a great thing.)

To make the album, we based ourselves out at Studio 55 in Hollywood, which was the producer Richard Perry's place. Perry was yet another legendary cat from that time. He had made records with Ringo Starr, Fats Domino and Carly Simon, and a real scene had grown around Studio 55. All of the A-list guys would be down there day and night, and picking up work from Perry. The whole thing was very incestuous, but at the same time it was a great hang.

Among the first of the many records that I did for Perry was a Diana Ross one. At the time, it wasn't uncommon for the star artist not to be there for the tracking sessions and Diana wasn't around. Richard Perry had instead hired a Diana Ross impersonator to sing her parts. He would have us do an endless number of takes in different keys, so that they would have a choice of what to use whenever it was that Diana turned up to do her vocals.

The Section guys were very much a part of the Studio 55 crowd too, and it was then that I first got to meet both Waddy Wachtel and Danny 'Kootch' Kortchmar. Once again, Jeff and Paich had told them that they had got this kid guitar player and they came down to listen to me play during our album sessions. For their part, I may have been competition to check out. It was sphincter-tightening for me because I revered those guys, but and, for whatever reason, they liked me. I went on to work with each of them many times and loved to play with them. Kootch is a soulful cat and funky as a motherfucker, an incredible musician but also a great producer and songwriter. Waddy was more the rock-and-roll guy and I was sort of able to fit in between them. I love them both to this day. Such versatile and hip musicians . . . you know when you are hanging with greatness.

It was Waddy who taught me Keith Richards's famous G tuning (which was actually Ry Cooder's famous G tuning and maybe some old blues guy's, but who knows . . .) so that I could finally play the Stones' songs right. Whenever other people do the Stones, it always sounds wrong because they don't understand what Keith did. Waddy was Keith's buddy and here's what he passed on to me. What you do is to take the low E string off a Telecaster, Esquire or guitar of that nature. Then you tune the other five strings to G-D-G-B-D, so that when you then make a barre chord, one finger across and two fingers down, you have the third and fourth right next to each other. And then, and only then, is when you get that 'Start Me Up' thing going on and can play a host of other Stones classics properly.

It was a pleasure to go in to work every day at Studio 55. It was a beautiful big room with polished wood floors and a great custom-made console. Making that first Toto record, I got to learn on the job and was enthralled with every aspect of the process. At the same time as we were cutting, Paich was also off doing a record with the singer Cheryl Lynn of 'Got to Be Real' fame (and I watched Paich and Foster write that song). Often as not, Paich would be late along to our sessions. The rest of us would sit around and jam, but then I also started to ask our engineer, Tom Knox, to show me how the console worked. Tom would throw up the twenty-four track, let me move the faders and explain to me what each button did and what the adjustable equalisers – the EQs – were all about. It was like letting a child play with the space shuttle and began my eternal fascination for mixing records.

Otherwise, on that first album Paich and Jeff called the shots as they were the senior members. I tried to be the people pleaser. Whatever they wanted, whatever they needed, I would do, as much as anything to prove to them that they had hired the right guy. Whenever it was that Paich did show up, he would always seem to have with him yet another great song for us to cut. Songs just then seemed to flow out from him. Some we cut live as a band, like 'Georgy Porgy', which was a one- or two-take thing. Other stuff, Jeff and Paich would put down the basic track and the rest of us would overdub. Musically, the way we played rock-and-roll came from an R & B foundation because of where Paich, Jeff and Hungate felt the groove.

We were also acutely aware of and inspired by other records that came out around that same period.

Right before I cut my solo for one of the album's hardest-rocking songs, 'Girl Goodbye', Paich brought the first Van Halen record into the studio. He told me, 'You have got to hear this guy.' He played for me 'Eruption' and my jaw hit the floor. Eddie Van Halen, man, he was extraordinary. He was funky, soulful, had unbelievable time and feel, and his chops blew my mind. He was so fucking good, I knew I would have to play the shit out of 'Girl Goodbye'.

These were in the days when everybody smoked in the studio and someone had left a thick glass ashtray on top of the speakers. I had got my gold-top '58 Les Paul and went for a high harmonic note, screaming out of the big speakers, and this ashtray just went POW! It literally exploded. Now, obviously it was a freak occurrence and I had hit a frequency that could shatter thick glass, but Paich stopped the tape and went, 'Woah, what the fuck?!' to a room full of laughter.

Likewise, I remember being very apprehensive when it came time for me to cut my solo on 'Hold the Line'. There were a bunch of other cats in the control room that day, buddies of Jeff's and Paich's, and among them the legendary drummer, Jim Keltner, who was Jeff's mentor and best friend. Jeff and Paich were looking at me intently through the glass, and with their expressions clearly reading, 'You better fucking bring it, man!' What's on the record is what I played right then. Apart, that is, from the multi-tracked harmony section at the end that Paich wanted to have, because he had heard it on the first Boston album, which had not long come out, and from Queen. The rest of that solo is one take. By the end of it, they were jumping up and down in the control room.

Through the years, Keltner was always at our sessions. Jeff would call him up and invite him to come down and bless which-ever track we had just done. (He and I are still close friends to this day.) We would play him the rough mixes real loud, and nothing was ever truly done until it had got the thumbs-up from Keltner. A second tradition established on that first album was that Paich had his dad work with him on the string and horn parts, and Joe Porcaro would do percussion overdubs.

Marty was a very strict taskmaster. For one thing, like the rest of us he would also call David 'Paich', which we found hilarious. Marty did not accept average work: it had to be exceptional. He drove his son really hard, but that was what had made Dave such an outstanding musician. Marty could also command an orchestra like no one else. He was a ball-buster and I always found it highly entertaining to watch him roast the stiffs in the union string section.

The other guy who hung around us was Roger Linn. At the time, he was Leon Russell's guitar player and engineer and a very tech-minded guy, so naturally befriended Steve. One day, Roger called Steve up and told him that we all had to come over to his place. We went round to Roger's apartment, and he had set up on the living-room table this Roland box that was ripped apart with soldering irons and shit coming out from the sides of it. Roger had us sit on the couch and pressed play, and out from this box came the sounds of a snare and kick and hi-hat, playing 4/4 time. Right there, Roger had invented the prototype Linn drum machine. Now, as the drummer among us, Jeff was horrified. He leapt up off the couch, violently shaking his head, and shouted at Roger, 'This thing can never leave this room – we have to destroy it!' Funnily enough, Steve was later involved in the process of hooking a clock up to that same kind of machine so that synthesisers could be run to it, which was the birthing of synth-pop. Who knew?

We were very serious-minded as musicians, but also crazy rock-and-roll guys. There was always that yin and yang to what we did and, now and again, we would like to have a little, shall we say, fiesta? Jeff would be the great equaliser in that respect because he would never get out of control. Everything that Jeff did was straight ahead. Although, that being said, a couple of times a year he would allow himself to get absolutely shit-faced and be hysterical. On breaks making the first album, we would all go to this joint called The Mikado, which at the time was one of the only Japanese restaurants in LA. It was also one of the few places where we could drink underage, because the Japanese staff never ID-carded me.

One night at The Mikado, Jeff ordered a frozen Mai Tai and that was always the signal that he was going to tie one on. He followed it up with ten bottles of hot sake, which he made into a pyramid on the table. In short order, he proceeded to drink all the sake, and then went to pour the eleventh bottle over his head. I shit you not, just as he did who walks in the place but Marlon Brando. This was the big, beefy version of Marlon. He stopped and looked at us intently and especially at Jeff, who by then had hot sake dripping down his face and a shit-eating grin. Then he shook his head and moved on. Man, we pissed ourselves laughing at that.

That whole period of my life was almost too good to be true. At the same time as we were working on our debut album, my own session career was also taking off. I was able to move out of my parents' house and into an apartment of my own on Corteen Place, North Hollywood. I had my flash BMW parked outside, but in the apartment just a refrigerator, a bed, a little black-and-white TV, a stereo system and the gold record that Boz had so graciously given me. All that was in the fridge was beer, which I had to have Dad buy for me, and a box of Hostess Ho Hos. I also got to meet the woman who would become my first wife.

Before I could legally go into bars, after nights in the studio I would hang out at this coffee shop, Denny's, on Ventura Boulevard and Coldwater Canyon. One night, I spotted in there this beautiful, blonde eighteen-year-old girl named Marie Currie. Once I found out that she too was a regular, I was in Denny's every night. Luckily for me, I happened to know people who knew Marie, and extracted from them the information that she was just then breaking up with her boyfriend. Eventually, I got up the balls to ask her out. The two of us instantly became inseparable. Marie was the first true love of my life and I fell for her hard.

I had a little money so I had just bought my first house, but Marie didn't believe I had bought it. I was young but I paid 75,000 dollars for the pad on Radford Avenue, North Hollywood, and we moved in together. Marie was there when it all started for me and watched the whole thing happen. We had a great thing going at the time. Work was booming and Toto was wailing and the partying had not become out of control . . . yet.

My parents were also proud that I had invested in real estate. Better that than blowing all my money on a BMW.

One problem did become apparent around that time and that was with Bobby. In the first instance, there were issues with getting him to sing the higher key parts that Paich wanted him to do. From day one, Bobby struggled hard with being able to sing those in tune. He could sing his own songs great, and to this day, Bobby proves his vocal prowess by nailing Elton John's 'Burn Down the Mission'. Hearing him take that on, the rest of us would go, 'But why can't you do that on our stuff?' Every one of Bobby's vocals on every album was painstakingly put together and I have got to give Paich a whole lot of credit for that, because he really did nurse them out of Bobby. Paich is the most soft-hearted, soulful, patient man. He never screams or flies off the handle, and it took that kind of patience to work with Bobby.

In Bobby's defence, these were very difficult parts. We probably should have cut the songs a couple of keys lower, but that was the sound of rock music in the mid-to-late seventies. That whole era burned out almost every lead voice of the time, not just Bobby's.

Those guys had beautiful high tenors in their twenties, but who knew they would be singing those same songs forty years later? It's like an Olympic weightlifter can jerk 500 pounds at twenty-one, but at seventy? I don't think so. Bobby ended up singing on only about half of the record. The lower-key stuff Paich took on and I took on the middle-range songs like 'Georgy Porgy' and 'Angela'. No question Bobby had the lead on 'Hold the Line', and that was the one that broke us.

Among us, Bobby was also older and perhaps a little crazier. After hours, he would have a separate life and a very different set of friends. The rest of us were Valley kids and he came from New Orleans and ran with a rougher crowd. Some of the people he knew were very peculiar. Every once in a while, I would go and hang at his place, and sometimes we would write together. There were some very interesting goings-on at Bobby's house. One time I was there a bunch of people came out of a room, all of them butterball naked. Not pretty.

I was like, 'Ah, no, we're going to leave now.' Bobby was more than a little embarrassed.

When the album was almost finished, Jeff asked an oddball kind of guy who happened to be living in his house at the time to come up with the cover artwork. Jeff would take in any stray – and for a while Bobby lived at Jeff's too – and this cat, named Philip Garris, was an excellent artist. He had worked for the Grateful

Dead and done the iconic cover for their *Blues for Allah* album, the one of the skeleton playing a violin. With us, he fixated on a lyric in the song 'Manuela Run' about having the sword of Damocles hanging over your head. He came up with a sword motif and that has been our logo ever since. For sure, it was a cool-looking cover, but the same couldn't be said for the name we eventually hit upon for this band of ours.

Throughout the sessions, Paich and Jeff had asked the rest of us for our suggestions. Of course, all that they had got back in return were sexual innuendo and butthole terms. Then, one fateful night, Paich and Jeff got stoned together, or possibly had a couple of margaritas and then got stoned . . . I don't know . . . and they watched *The Wizard of Oz*. Afterwards, someone began to write 'Toto' on all of the boxes of tracks. I did tell the both of them that they were going to live to regret it. Right after the *Toto* album was released, Tom Scott, our friend and also legendary saxophonist and arranger, was out touring Japan and sent us a Polaroid in the mail. It was a picture of a toilet with a little 'Toto' logo written on it and Tom's shit floating in the bowl. Tom had scrawled across it: 'Nice name.'

CHAPTER SEVEN

We worked on the first Toto album for eight months on and off, mostly on, and throughout that time Paich kept up a constant mantra. Whenever it was that we were listening back to a track, he would grandly announce to the room: 'Triple platinum, baby! Triple platinum!' We all got a laugh out of that, but also we were young, silly and arrogant. Everything that Paich touched at that point turned to gold and he was proven to be right – we did indeed go on to sell three million records in the US and more worldwide. Though none of us foresaw the hate and backlash of our success.

Before we had even finished the record, we were booked to appear at the record company's annual convention in New Orleans. I think the idea was for the Columbia guys to at last be able to see what they had paid for, and the sobering thing for us was that it would be our very first live gig together as Toto. Added to that, and because we had pulled out all of the stops in the studio, it was inevitably going to be a big challenge for us to replicate the vocals live.

We had triple-tracked everything, so it was a huge-sounding, highly produced record. The other thing immediately apparent was that we needed to bring in someone to sing high over Bobby because we needed someone who had the chops to cover the harmonies above Bobby's lead vocals. We hired Tom Kelly, who had a great high voice for harmonies and was also able to play secondary guitar parts. Tom went on to became a big-time song-writer, penning 'Like a Virgin' for Madonna, 'True Colours' for Cyndi Lauper and so many others. In addition, Tom and Richard Page (soon to be lead voice of Mr. Mister) sang backgrounds on a lot of the major rock records of that period. Later, Keith Olsen and myself would co-produce a cult record for i-TEN, which featured Tom and his writing partner Billy Steinberg.

Jeff also called in Lenny Castro from the Boz tour to add percussion. Lenny's been an integral part of our family, and still is. He is a deep soul brother, and we've been through a lot of life together.

We rehearsed down at this dark, dirty, dingy place in North Hollywood, appropriately called Rats. At first, it was difficult for us to figure out how to go about rearranging the songs, the huge three-part vocal harmonies especially. However, our rhythm section was tight as a vice, we could all play great and we got up a head of steam. Unfortunately, no sooner was that the case than Paich fixated on us having no discernible image. True enough, there was no obvious star of the band back then as all we cared about was the music. I wore nothing but Pendleton's shirts, ripped jeans and beat-up Adidas tennis shoes, with my hair long and dishevelled. Paich had just been to see Yes. They had all been sporting capes onstage and that was the look that he wanted for us, and for which he tapped up a stylist who made clothes for Cher. Once Paich talked Jeff around to the idea, there was no point going back. When the cat went for his inside-leg measurement for the ninth time, I knew we had entered hell.

Paich had the stylist draw up a set of drawings of each of our intended costumes, which I can describe no better than being like silk kimonos. On paper, they actually looked pretty cool, but not so when they turned up for real, which was not until the day

before we were due to leave for New Orleans. Truly, that was one
of the great 'What the fuck?' moments in our band's history. Our
take on the Yes capes was even more horrifyingly awful and they
made us look entirely ridiculous. Mine was a lurid purple number,
didn't fit and was several miles beyond being camp. There we
were, going to walk out in front of a bunch of drunken record
executives from all around the world, and in the guise of extras
from *Madame Butterfly* on acid.

Worse still, it fell to us to open up the second night. On the first
night our heroes Weather Report had kicked off the convention
– *Heavy Weather* was wailing up the charts and was the talk of all
musicians. It was a stellar line-up of that band, too, with Jaco
Pastorius on bass, and we were mind-fucked at how good they
were. Up next was Meat Loaf, at the height of the *Bat out of Hell*
record and his own sheer Meat-ness. A big buzz about those two
performances had gone all around the place, but by the next day
fatigue had begun to set in among the delegates. We went on cold
in our kimonos and having no clue as to how to interact with each
other, much less our audience. I hit the opening chord of our first
song, 'I'll Supply the Love', and my guitar cut out. Stupidly, we
hadn't had the time to try out playing in our new costumes. What
I discovered right then was that every time I tried to hold out a
power chord my billowing, curtain-like sleeves would touch the
strings and shut off the sustain. Jeff had it even worse, since he was
so restricted that he could barely raise his arms. And just a little
cherry on top: I had strep throat.

It was beyond Spinal Tap insane – I pray to God no one will
ever see this. But still, it was just a taster for the main event and
that was to be the grand unveiling of the 'Totar'. Paich had got it
into his head that he wanted to be able to move around the stage
like a guitar player. So Steve and he developed this . . . thing.
Essentially, it was a keyboard with a guitar neck stuck on to it and
the wooden body was spray-painted red like a Strat. Paich had it
wired to a Mini-Moog, which in turn was plugged into one of

Hungate's bass cabinets. As he donned this abomination, I could see the guys in Weather Report sitting a few rows back, cracking up. By the by, though, their keyboardist Joe Zawinul got a 'key-tar' of his own and for a short while they did become all the rage.

Our misfortune was that the Totar had been a rush job and Paich hadn't got himself a long enough cable. He strode forward with the Totar slung around his neck, and proceeded to bring Hungate's cabinet and the Mini-Moog toppling over. The latter of which went bouncing across the stage and was promptly destroyed. No sound ever came out of the Totar, and the Columbia top brass were surely left thinking to themselves, 'Wait, we've just spent millions of dollars on these guys?'

The album came out in October 1978 and straight away we got our asses handed back to us by the trendy rock critics. Punk rock was the new rage and a big influence in the States, and the very antithesis of what we were all about. The press jumped on that and the hipsters would blame us for everything bad about 'corporate rock'. (Let's face it: if you sign a record deal and accept money you're 'corporate rock'.)

We had been with Boz in London just the previous year, '77, and seen all of these guys with blue Mohawks and leather jackets walking down the street. That was right before the whole punk package made its way across the Atlantic and we were like, 'What the fuck is this all about? These guys can't play. And they spit on each other?' It did nothing but confuse us. I have since met Steve Jones and he's a sweetheart of a cat, but at the time the critics started comparing us to the Sex Pistols and also the Clash. I like the Clash and I'm not going to argue with the impact that they had, but to relate us to them was totally unfair. We came from a place where our heroes were Steely Dan and were quickly made into the poster band for everything that punk was not.

Basically, we got shit on. Some of the reviews we got for the record were vicious, poisonous even, and they did hurt. There was also a misconception that began to be propagated that we had been put together in the record company's boardroom. Notwithstanding Steve and I had known each other from high school, what rankled was that the fact that we were studio players was used against us. People in general and rock critics specifically didn't, and still don't, appreciate what we session guys actually did. They envisage a bunch of guys sat around on haemorrhoid dough-nuts reading little dots and picking up a pay cheque. Now, there are people that do that, but for TV and film work. We, on the other hand, got given mere sketches of songs and were told, 'Make this great.' And very quickly we did. And lots of those records became hits. And if you do that every day, and for several years, then you get to be very good at it. Not many people understood that we co-produced and arranged and in many case rewrote the songs without as much as even hearing them beforehand.

I once went to an event honouring Jimmy Page with Eddie Van Halen and a whole bunch of guys – every famous guitar player in LA was there. We got there and when we walked in, Jimmy was there to greet us. Man, it hit me how many hours I had spent learning his parts and songs. He motioned me to come towards him, but I thought for sure he meant Eddie . . . No, he meant me. He took me aside and said, 'You have something those guys out there don't: they don't have the studio-musician thing. I was a studio player, so was John Paul Jones . . . you should be proud of that.' I hugged him and said, 'Is it OK if I tell people this?' He laughed and said yeah. The role of record session players has never been truly understood or explained to the masses – or to rock crit-ics – but here was a legend telling me that he knew what it meant. He was so kind and his music means so much to me.

The thing was that *Toto* took off organically. No matter how much derogatory stuff got written about us, the people who liked our music really liked it. I was sat at home one day when Paich called me up, very excited. The local FM rock station, K-MET, was playing 'Hold the Line'. I was at my first house with Marie and jumped up and turned on the radio just as the DJ said: 'Los

Angeles's own Toto there and a brand-new record.' That's an amazing feeling, hearing your own song on the radio, and once you have, your life is never quite the same again.

Following the debacle in New Orleans, we realised how much we needed to get our live act together prior to us being sent out on the road. With that in mind, our managers managed to get us a residency on Kauai. We were to play twice nightly for two weeks at a resort hotel. That engagement also got off to an inauspicious start. We turned up the first day to find ourselves billed as: 'Toto – Los Angeles's hottest new disco band.' Mark Hartley, though, knew Hawaii's most prominent DJ and this guy started to slam the shit out of our album, every song. Twenty-four seven, we were being played on local radio, and that got people from all over the islands to fly in to Kauai to see the band. We played to a packed house pretty much every night and got our sea legs. It was like rehearsing in front of a crowd, and we started to get good.

We also got to do our first big gig in Honolulu, opening up for Peter Frampton at Neal S. Blaisdell Arena. Frampton was on his 'Comes Alive!' tour the first time round, so was hot and the place was jumping. Thanks to our friendly DJ, the crowd also knew our songs and we had a killer set! The place went nuts and we got a huge ovation. I was a huge Peter Frampton fan and meeting him was so cool. We are still close pals – even our sons are close pals. His playing really affected me in a positive way. He played more modal stuff but he was still rocking. He is a very unique and strong player.

On our first tour, we played all over the States and basically went crazy. We were guys in our twenties, partying every night and living the life. It was a lot of fun to go through all of that stuff and I wouldn't even try to suggest otherwise. One night, we were on the bus, tearing down the freeway in the middle of the night. Jeff and I were sat in the front lounge, and I looked up and saw Lenny swaggering towards the front of the vehicle as if he were

John Wayne after a hundred beers. I suspected that Lenny must have imbibed something, because he wasn't looking too steady on his feet. He stumbled, but managed to reach out and grab the back of the driver's seat. Our driver was Dominic, a bald-headed man mountain who looked like a pirate. He had an earring and everything . . . that look was not popular in 1978. Lenny puked up all over Dominic's bald head, and the chunks of food and bile ran ringlets down his face. If the guy had let go of the wheel we would have all died. The rest of us were screaming and laughing but as much in terror as with laughter. And that was a regular night at the office. There were dares and we were just kids living the dream and doing everything naughty we could do. It was not all of us all the time at all, but usually someone got up to no good and it didn't take much for the rest of us to follow.

In February 1979, we had to fly from the road back to LA to attend that year's Grammys ceremony. Our album had picked up so much momentum that we had been nominated for the Best New Artist award alongside Elvis Costello and the Cars. If I was looking for omens, I got one that night as I climbed into the car to go to the Shrine Auditorium. The pair of white pants that I had worn for the occasion ripped right around the crotch. The whole show, I had to wear my shirt out so people couldn't see half of my nut sack hanging down. We thought Costello or the Cars would win because they were the critics' darling, but in the end it was the fifth nominated act that got the nod. That was a disco group, A Taste of Honey, who'd had a hit with a song called 'Boogie Oogie Oogie'. They were certainly barely heard of after that night. Such is life.

CHAPTER EIGHT

If your first album happens to be huge, then at some point a single thought will inevitably enter your head. It will go as follows: 'Holy fuck, what do we do next?' And here's another lesson I learned the hard way: you should never, ever read your own press, good or bad. As a direct response to all of those scathing reviews that we had reaped, by the time we returned to the studio we were resolved to do something very different. What we wanted most of all was to be taken seriously as a rock band, which was how it came to pass that we followed up our three-million-selling debut with a kind of 'prog-rock' record, which ended up not really being that at all.

We all were starting to write more about now, but Dave Paich was still our 'go-to guy' with songs back then. Paich would consistently write great, melodic songs, but we were set upon making ourselves be more like Pink Floyd or, again, Yes. With that at the front of his mind, Paich, who reads and watches a lot of fantasy stuff, came up with a rough concept. In short, it was a Dungeons & Dragons kind of story. This was at least before that became a heavy metal cliché, but we were under tremendous pressure from the record label to deliver the next 'Hold the Line' and instead conjured up a seven-and-a-half-minute song about a many-headed serpent, 'Hydra'.

The title track of the album, it was also the first band-written song. When we went into Sunset Sound Studio One, one of my favourite rooms of all time, Paich had the keyboard intro and verse. We started jamming and I came up with the song's two riffs and Hungate the alternate bass part. Paich sang the verses and Bobby the choruses. As work on the record progressed, Paich would ponder a lot conceptually, even though he had just one other related song, 'St George and the Dragon'. As things turned out, we never did get around to developing a full-blown thematic piece and, at the same time, other acts had great success with lifting the sound from the *Toto* album. Even as we were making *Hydra*, we started to get calls from people telling us how much they loved our new single. What they had actually heard on the radio was a Jefferson Airplane song, 'Jane', but based around a copy-cat of the kind of lead piano line that Paich would play. It went on to be a top-twenty hit in the States, too. Ironically, the Airplane's Mickey Thomas was one of the guys Paich and Jeff had entertained as being our lead singer before we got to Bobby.

While we were in the process of recording *Hydra*, I took a call from James Newton Howard. That was to invite me over to France for a couple of weeks and to play on Elton John's new record. In the middle of our sessions, I had to go and ask the guys for time off. Paich's response was the driest by far. He did a thoroughly convincing job of looking pissed and barked back, 'I don't know, is it cool if you leave us to go and work with my hero?' Elton was one of my all-time musical heroes too, and I went off and had a completely wonderful time.

I was flown first class over to the south of France and then driven up into the rolling hills above the commune of Berre-les-Alpes. We were to work and live in a big old house miles from the two nearest cities, Nice and Marseilles. The place was called Super Bear studio and was where Pink Floyd had just cut the basic tracks for *The Wall*. It had a tennis court and a swimming pool and, for the next couple of weeks, I got to hang out in the middle of nowhere and drink from a case filled with cognac and wine. Great times.

Elton had wanted to try out something completely different for what would turn out to be his *21 at 33* album. He avoided using his regular band and wasn't writing quite so much with Bernie Taupin. I travelled out to France with James and Elton's chosen new rhythm section, bassist Reggie McBride and drummer Alvin Taylor. Reggie and Alvin between them had played with the likes of Little Richard, Stevie Wonder, George Harrison, Funkadelic, Billy Preston and Leo Sayer. Reggie was a killer bass player and funny as hell. Alvin played great too, but the funny thing was that he couldn't tune his kit. You would think a drummer would be able to do that, but Clive Franks and I ended up sitting at Alvin's drums and trying to get the right sounds for him. That was a bit weird because Alvin played well.

Clive was Elton's genius live sound engineer and now he was producing too, so he wanted things to go well, and I gave all I had to give, and helped any way I could.

No sooner had we got settled at Super Bear than I came up with a couple of good parts for a song. Elton really warmed to me after that. The band started to gel and we were doing a couple of tracks a day with overdubs. Elton would do a guide vocal to hear the song and, man, he sang so good it was master quality.

A couple of times Elton and I sat at the piano after hours – there was nowhere to go in the studio/hotel, so we hung out a lot – and I would say to him, 'Hey, play "Levon" for me.' And he would and give it all he had. It was amazing. 'Now, play "Tiny Dancer".' He would go ahead and sing me those songs like it was a private concert. Elton sang every take live in the room, too.

For my part, I was very curious about his writing process. Elton told me that he wrote songs to the lyrics, not the other way round, which is what most people do. And while Bernie tells great stories, his lyrics are not really written from the standpoint of standard rhythmic cadence. They are phrased very strangely and are wordy as all hell, but Elton made them sound so smooth, like the song was always meant to be that way . . . a great team.

One night, I snuck down into the control room and Elton was all by himself in the studio. The lights were turned down, so he couldn't have known I was there. Someone had sent some lyrics over and Elton had not even seen them yet. He pulled the lyrics out and sat there at his piano. Then he put his hands on the keys and just started to sing the words he had never seen. A beautiful song was coming out. It was the most amazing creative thing that I have seen in my life. Afterwards, Elton told me that he had written the whole of the *Goodbye Yellow Brick Road* album, all seventeen songs of it, in two days flat. He said that he had just got on a roll. Elton is an otherworldly talent and one of the most insanely gifted songwriters in popular music. Further than that, he's also the nicest, sweetest cat ever.

Living in that house, there was nothing for us to do after a session but drink, or else go off to the casinos in Monte Carlo. I turned twenty-one while we were over there and hadn't been able to gamble legally until then. The first time that I did, I lost 500 dollars in a couple of minutes. I couldn't have been more like the goofy young American tourist if I had tried and, man, did the croupiers ever see me coming. I mean to say, I had travellers' cheques! Elton, on the other hand, would be led off into a separate room for the high rollers.

All sorts of practical jokes went on as well. I was a real picky eater as a kid – I mean real picky – and the staff would bring out duck to the dining table, but it would still have feathers coming out of it. I must have had a look on my face like I had just seen my grand-mother naked. Elton would also do things like put Comet cleaner in my hair. One afternoon, I hurt myself and went, 'Ow!' as you do, but something about the sound I made amused Elton. From then on, he would come up and kick me in the shins for no reason other than to hear me make it again. I would be like, 'Ow! Fuck, man!' and he would think it was the funniest thing in the world.

We got the entire record done pretty fast so Elton had us keep on cutting songs until he had enough for a second album. That would become *The Fox*. We never got credited on that record because the record executives Mo Ostin and Walter Yetnikoff were fighting and we were somehow caught in the middle. I was very upset as I was proud to be on that album.

Even after I flew back to LA, Elton had another couple of tracks that he wanted to get down and so we were all assembled again at Sunset Sound. At the same time, Van Halen were also in Sunset working on their *Women and Children First* record. One night, Eddie and Michael Anthony came over to our room to shoot the shit. I had borrowed an amp from Eddie as our gear was on its way to Japan for a tour. The three of us were holed up in the vocal booth together when Elton sidled over and pinched Eddie on the ass. It was all very playful and the rest of us thought it hysterical, but Eddie kind of got freaked out. I laughed and it was all in fun anyway.

At the end of those sessions, Elton called me and offered me a permanent position in his band. It was a great deal, too, a substantial amount of money and points on the record, but I couldn't accept it. I told him the guys in Toto were like my brothers, which he understood and respected.

One time, he turned up at an Easter party at my house. He happened to be in LA at the time and called. I told him we were having a bash and to come on over, not thinking for a second that he would. I had not mentioned it to Marie but it was she who opened the door to him, and she was so shocked that she screamed. Elton went and hid out in another room and Peter Frampton dropped by, too . . . oh, what a night.

Later that same year, I got hired to work on Boz's next record, *Middle Man*, which ended up being one of my favourite sessions I was ever involved with. David Foster had taken over the pianist and songwriter's seat from Paich and Michael Omartian, and at the time I was tight with both him and Boz. We cut at Studio 55 with the great Bill Schnee producing and Ray Parker Jr as my guitar partner. Ray and I were polar opposites as players, but I loved to work with him. We came up with very different parts that complemented each other, in a magical way.

Bill Schnee was getting killer sounds. I knew this was going to be great from day one. This was an important record and I was honoured to be there. One night Wah Wah Watson showed up and started in on Ray Parker, 'Get outta my chair, this is my gig.' We were laughing but it was weird.

At the time *Alien* was a hit movie and we all started calling Schnee 'Schnellian' and he hated that. Of course, he should have known better so Boz had T-shirts made with the words 'In space no one can hear you cream' and Schnee's face coming out of the egg . . .

Bill never liked the shirts.

I wish I still had mine . . .

Nowadays, everyone knows Ray Parker Jr from his *Ghostbusters* theme song, but that is a far cry from what he is really all about. That tune is still a money-printing machine for him. As a musician, he was the king of the parts. You have to understand, Foster was coming up with some of this shit on the spot and all that he would give us would be a chord chart. Every other bit of music you hear on that Boz Scaggs record was never written out. Ray would start to play something and I would find the exact counterpoint to it, so we were left speaker and right, trading off each other.

From the start, we knew it was going to be a big and special record. Bill's an amazing engineer and got great sounds. He would conjure up tremendous reverbs and perfect balance. Things got created fast and in one, two takes. Within any given six-hour period, we would cut and overdub a complete song, or maybe even two. Besides Ray and me, my old friend John Pierce played bass on 'Jojo', and Jeff, Hungate, Lenny and another favourite of mine, drummer Joe Vitale (I even have his solo albums), were also on most of the tracks. It was basically a very Toto-esque record and one that really sealed the deal on the 'LA sound' of the era. For lack of a better term, we had hit upon a winning combination of rock, pop and funk and with some really cool chords thrown in. These were not just power chords, but adult chords, as I like to call them. Once *Middle Man* came out, everyone in town wanted to use the same guys that had played on it.

It was also a milestone record for me because I had a bunch of solos on it, and on songs that became hits and were never off the radio. Every tune on *Middle Man* was touched by magic, and I had a big hand in writing one of them. Boz enquired of me one day, 'I need a rocker – what have you got?' So I worked up a riff, Foster had a great idea for substitution bass parts, Boz wrote the words, and together we came up with 'You Got Some Imagination'. Bill ended up getting a co-writer's credit on that, too. I think he added a word, so Boz gave him a cut of his part of the song.

With Toto, we mixed the *Hydra* record when I had finally finished up with Elton. In the interim we had put down some funkier-sounding tracks, such as '99' and 'Mama', but even still, if you had played either of those next to 'Hold the Line', you would never have said that they were the work of the same band. For some reason, Paich didn't want to have the guitars too loud on the record, so I was always fighting with him to turn my parts up. We started to run into problems in other areas as well. Since we were so concerned about our rock credibility, we wanted one of the record's more abrasive songs, 'White Sister', to be released to radio first, but Columbia opted instead to go with '99'. That song became a hit for us, sure enough, but once again we started to take a beating for being a pussy pop band. The album also went gold in the US (eventually platinum plus), but coming off the back of a triple-platinum record, it was perceived as a flop.

It's funny when some people say our records were a flop. Every single one has sold at least a million worldwide, so 'flop' is not the right word. The same people that say shit like that also say we were a bunch of drug fiends, when we were not only in our own band but also playing on most records that came out of LA. How could we be so messed up and do all that?

All of us were disappointed at the sales of *Hydra* compared to the first album, but in the short term we had the distraction of going back out on the road. The tour started in the States, then went to Japan. In Tokyo, we were met at the airport by hundreds of screaming girls and every night after that was an adventure. Even as recently as that, Japan was like an alien world to us and not Westernised in the slightest. There wasn't a McDonald's and women would walk ten feet behind the men. We ate sushi, drank sake and got taken out to bath houses. Truly, those were fantastic times.

The audiences went crazy. Then they would be silent. It was weird. They would scream again, then silence once more, and you could hear us walking across the stage . . . and us laughing.

In the States, we headlined our own dates and opened up bigger arena shows for more established acts. One night, we played with Rush and went down too well. Their crew pulled the plug on us. They vibed Paich out hard as he stumbled into their catering room by accident.

Another night in '78, we had the Ramones, of all bands, open for us. There were some strange bills back in those days. They were so bad that people threw shit at them. After their set, the four so-called brothers were so pissed with each other that they got into a fist-fight. We could hear them beating the shit out of each other backstage. In Cleveland, we stayed at Swingos, the famous rock-and-roll hotel. Cheech and Chong were staying on the same floor as us. Everyone flung open the doors to their rooms that night and I believe that all kinds of crazy shit went down. I don't remember much.

It wasn't the last time that this would be the case, but we didn't stay out on the road for as long as we should have done to push our new record. Jeff was a number-one studio guy and had this thing about not missing sessions. Same with Hungate, who also didn't like to party or tour. Hungate was married, meant to start a family and loved the life of a session musician. He didn't party at all, whereas I was also doing a lot of sessions and playing with Toto, and I wanted it all.

Not that I did waste all my money while living the dream. I sold our house, made a bunch of money and bought a nicer place up in the Hollywood Hills. It's my home to this day, but back then it was a big party house. If you look at the late seventies and read all of those Hollywood Babylon-style accounts of what went on, well, it was going on for most everybody in town. Let's just say the house is off Laurel Canyon and leave it at that.

We could never have made all the records that we did if we were that high, but we did do our share of hanging out, and the old 'sleep repellent' was everywhere that you went. We would go to our local Mexican joint in the Valley and order a 110-dollar margarita. That was ten bucks for the margarita and you can guess the rest.

I also got to meet some very colourful people through my association with Bobby Kimball, one of whom was a cowboy from Texas named Woody. He was a kind of dealer to the stars and the actors Gary Busey and John Belushi were among his regular clients. I do believe that I ended that decade holed up in my house on New Year's Eve, waiting for the 'Wood-man' to show. When he did, he drew out for me a big '79' on a mirror. Several Quaaludes later he went into my bathroom and ripped the shower curtains off and fell into the tub. He was huge, so trying to get him out was hard. Those were crazy times.

CHAPTER NINE

There are a lot of great venues that I have been fortunate enough to have played. The big ones would be the Hollywood Bowl, Tokyo Budokan, the Bercy in Paris, Ziggo Dome in Amsterdam and London's Royal Albert Hall. The Albert Hall, in particular, is awe-inspiring, for just being stood in the same mythical room where the Beatles, the Stones, Hendrix, Zeppelin, Cream etc. have all played before. When the lights go down in a big venue and the crowd roars, that right there is when you can bottle the mystique of rock-and-roll. Yet the one venue that is perhaps really special to me is that hole-in-the-wall joint down in Studio City in Hollywood, the Baked Potato, which became my training ground.

All through the late seventies, the Baked Potato was the place to be when the club hosted a resident jam band led by Greg Mathieson, the ace keyboardist, and also featured Jeff Porcaro on drums, the bassist Pops Popwell and Larry Carlton. Pops and Carlton had previously played together in one of the great fusion collectives of the period, the Crusaders. By the end of that decade, Carlton was the reigning king in the city. After his playing on

Steely's *The Royal Scam* and Joni Mitchell's *Court and Spark*, magic seemed to resonate out from him.

I got my shot to play with that band in 1980.

Carlton was on fire by that point, but maybe he got burned out from having such a regular gig. For whatever reason, he baled on the Baked Potato show the night of the gig. Mathieson called and asked me if I would fill in for him. To which my initial response was: 'Are you shitting me?' I was just twenty-two, making a bit of a name for myself, but it would require a great big pair of balls to walk in and take over from the great Carlton unannounced. It would be like going into the lion's den. I told Greg I would do it, but that I wouldn't play Carlton's songs. I didn't want to give people a reason to throw shit at me or make a comparison.

First night, I went down with two small Fender Deluxe amps and I cranked up my '59 Les Paul and decided to start the set with something really in-your-face from some of the jams we had written for that gig earlier in the day. I think the audience was expecting a bit more of a tasteful jam, but instead we knocked them back off their seats. It was more rock-and-roll than anything the Baked Potato had seen or heard before, but people dug it and we went down a storm, so much so that I was invited back the following week. That became a regular weekly thing for the next several years whenever Toto wasn't touring. I learned so much there from Greg Mathieson and made so many cool friends. All sorts of people would come down and hang and jam . . . Jeff was on fire . . . packed houses . . . jamming . . . the best of times. They used to throw us the keys and say, 'Lock up when you're done.'

The Baked Potato made me a better player. In the studio environment, what you played had to be very specific and sometimes simple. You were not there to crank it up and show off all that you had, whereas the Potato gig allowed me to improvise. The guys I was playing with were so good and that in itself was inspiring. Some nights, I couldn't believe my ears at the tangents that we were able to go off at, and that would compel me to go home and practise even harder. When you have to do two sets a night and at that rarefied level of musicianship, it does nothing but flex and grow your chops and enhance your musical ideas. Plus, I wasn't just playing rock-and-roll, so I could try out different things and began to develop my own style a little more. Up to that point I was used to doing eight- or sixteen-bar solos, but Mathieson would counsel me to take my time. 'You don't need to blow it all out in the first chorus,' he would say. I learned so much from Greg; his wife Barbara also cheered us on.

I would walk in through the back door and the place would be jam-packed. Jeff would already be sitting on his drum stool with a gin and tonic in hand. He would smile at me, get up and give me a big hug, a kiss on the cheek, and I would know that we were in for a great time. I remember a lot of nights standing there and thinking that it was the greatest feeling on earth. Everybody in that band's ears were so big, and so tuned in, that we could just go off to anywhere that we wanted and on the spur of the moment. Songs could end up being fifteen minutes long, or just as likely three. Sometimes we would stop in the middle of a tune and go, 'We don't want to do this one any more,' and crank out something completely different. Truly, it was a place where anything went and there wasn't another like it.

A lot of great people came by to sit in with us. Both Tom Scott and another great saxophonist, David Sanborn, who would sometimes show up to play with us. One night, Jaco Pastorius, shit-faced, had me up against a wall, his hands around my throat. All that he said to me was, 'I don't like guitar players, but you're OK.' I was like, 'Thank . . . you . . . Jaco . . . Let . . . go!' Allan Holdsworth would drop by and I would soil my pants as he watched me play. He was a great cat and we got to be friends. One night Mike Landau and I lost a drinking contest to Allan: he was fine; we were legless. Another night, by coincidence, David Gilmour and Jeff Beck were sat next to each other on the front row, a couple of feet from me. That was ever so slightly intimidating but we were friends and it was OK. On one memorable occasion, Sheila E, then playing with Prince, came down and sat in on drums. So many great people played with us at one time or another.

After we had been playing at the Potato for a year or so, we had Jay Graydon come down with a live truck, courtesy of childhood friend Scott Carlson who was working for Wally Heider, and record us. The record that resulted, *Live from the Baked Potato*, is a time capsule of that moment and has gone on to become a sort of collector's item. There was a real intensity to the way that we played and Jeff in particular was incredible. He used to jump up and hit the walls with his sticks, but would also get fatigued and none of us could figure out why. His arms would start to hurt and often during a second set, he would have to pull someone out of the audience to take his place – since the room was always full of other musicians that was never a problem. At the time, I never thought too much of it. He was still a young guy but then drummers beat on shit, so I presumed it was muscular.

As the decade progressed, the Mathieson line-up petered out and a new group evolved. I started to play with jazz-fusion piano player David Garfield, who was Carlos Vega's buddy I met in high school, and Lenny Castro joined us on percussion. Lenny suggested that we also call ourselves 'Los' something or other. 'Los Lobotomys' popped right into his head, and it was as such that we became the new Baked Potato jam band.

We wrote a bunch of tunes together and on 29 April 1989 went into Complex Studios out in Santa Monica and cut a self-titled disc in the room live. For that date, we invited a whole lot of people down to sit in with us and that record has three of the greatest ever drummers on it – Jeff, Carlos and Vinnie Colaiuta, who had made his name playing with Zappa and Joni Mitchell. That was a different band to the Mathieson thing.

The same thing happened with an even later group I put together, even though that was just a one-off. That one was called

Phux Snot and also featured Carlos, Castro, Landau, Will Lee and Eddie Van Halen. In 1992, we played a single-night stand at the Baked Potato. The word got out in advance and something like 4,000 people lined up on the street outside, trying to get in to a hundred-seat club. We did Cream's 'Sunshine of Your Love' and these weird versions of other standards. Eddie did the first set with us and then ran out. It was all too much for him.

Eventually, I had to take a break from the Potato. I got real busy doing other stuff and was going through a darker period in my life. I didn't want to be out in public that much. These last six, seven years, though, I have gone back to my spiritual home with a new band of musicians and we do a run of shows each Christmas time. The band's called Nerve Bundle, which is a clinical term for the head of your cock, so very childish as usual from me, but the music is deadly serious. It's a jam band with Jorgen Carlsson from Gov't Mule on bass and a couple of great studio cats, Jeff Babko on keyboards and Toss Panos on drums. (Google them . . .) People fly in from all over the world to see these shows.

To this day, there's still a vibe like no other at the Baked Potato. There's no dressing room, so you can't hide. You're inches from the audience. I'm able to ban camera phones from the shows, so everybody actually watches the band. Some things should just be left as, 'You had to be there.' It's the one place on earth where I can go play, talk and be nasty and be myself without feeling as if I'm being scrutinised under a microscope for the world to judge me.

The combined effect of my playing at the Baked Potato and on Boz's *Middle Man* was things were going very well. I ended up doing a lot of sessions with the great Arif Mardin. Whenever he was in town from New York he would hire us. Arif was a true giant of the music business. He had come to America from his native Istanbul in the 1950s and gone to work for his friends, Nesuhi and Ahmet Ertegun, at Atlantic Records. At Atlantic, Arif rose to being in-house producer and label manager and recorded everyone from Diana Ross, Chaka Khan, Roberta Flack and Melissa Manchester to the Bee Gees and David Bowie. Arif hired me for a couple of albums that he made with Aretha Franklin, *Aretha* in 1980 and the next year's *Love All the Hurt Away*.

Man, those were fun sessions. We cut *Aretha* at Cherokee Studios in Hollywood and with a band that included Jeff, Paich on piano, Foster on Fender Rhodes, Lenny Castro and the late great David Williams on guitar as well. That record was another that was cut live, in the room and with all of us musicians sat in a semi-circle and Aretha doing her lead vocals not three feet from us. The take would be whenever she got the great vocal, so you had to nail the parts every time, which made things just a little bit more pressured.

Aretha was lovely, but to hear that voice close up and unadorned was actually distracting. In the flesh, she sang even better than I had expected and the effect was nothing short of stunning. I had to force myself to stop listening to her, because I would lose track of the part. She also played grand piano on the date. For *Aretha*, we cut a funky version of a Doobie Brothers track, 'What a Fool Believes'. Oh my God, did Aretha sing the shit out of that!

There was a particularly funny moment, too. At the end of a day's recording, we would cut a few tracks and then go listen to them with Arif in the control room. Now, in those days weed was always smoked on sessions, but Arif was like an old-school gentle-man and really not cool with anything else. On this occasion, Arif and a certain musician had showed up for work wearing very similar jackets. As we were leaving, Arif picked up the wrong one. He put his hands into the pockets and pulled out a two-gram vial of blow. The culprit started spluttering and Jeff and I dove under the mixing desk, howling. The only comment Arif passed was, 'This is not my jacket,' but you could tell that he was disappointed. He had a look on his face that said, 'Really, you guys?'

Around that same period of time, Peter Frampton wanted to

cut what was essentially a live album but in the studio. Peter's a brilliant guitar player in his own right, but hired me to play acoustic and rhythm and so that he could concentrate on the lead parts and sing. Jeff was the best play-for-the-song drummer I've ever heard. He would get deep into what the artist was doing and trying to say. Jeff genuinely cared and I took that work ethic from him. You don't just turn up and collect the cheque.

We recorded Peter's *Breaking all the Rules* at A & M Studios and using a mobile truck. That record turned out to be one of those ideas that sounded great on paper, but was not so practical in reality. The problem was that the live monitors that Peter wanted to use leaked and made noise in the studio environment, which proved a logistical nightmare. Peter also took issue one day with his producer David Kershenbaum. We did a take that sounded pretty good to us and Peter shouted out, 'How was that, David? . . . David? . . . David!' Silence.

At that point, I think David might have had a pretty good buzz going on, if you catch my drift. We all walked over to the truck, opened up the door, and the cat was passed out on the desk with the tape still rolling. Jeff and I were once again roaring with laughter. Peter was not. I should add in David's defence that it was a Friday night, and things would always be liable to get out of hand at the end of a long week. And hey, in that era, it wasn't as if that kind of thing was an unusual occurrence.

CHAPTER TEN

The grand plan for the next Toto album was that we were determined to become an arena-rock band whether it killed us or not. While on other sessions, I had met Geoff Workman, who was the engineer for Roy Thomas Baker on all of the great Queen records. Together, they had also done the Cars and Journey, etc. Geoff seemed a perfect fit for us too as we had become good friends and we wanted to work with an English guy who understood how to make the kind of classic rock records that we loved. As it turned out, Geoff was not only a master craftsman in that respect, but also a true rock-and-roll character. Collaborating with him was a hell of a ride.

We made *Turn Back* in Studio A at Cherokee, which had a wonderful old Trident desk. Geoff had us cut live to tape and we made that record in three months. Considering there were only eight songs on the album, that was a long time for us but we took our time and tried lots of things that didn't work. Geoff would not let any of us touch the recording console. He would do things his way or no way. There was no midrange, and the drums were all room sound with the kick-drum pushed up for clarity. The record had a sound that was radically different, and we thought weird and different was good at the time.

This was pre-computers, so everything was done analogue, hands on the desk, and as an engineer Geoff was extraordinary. He was also one of the funniest motherfuckers on Planet Earth and a genuine one-of-a-kind human being. He would brag to us that he had never been to see a doctor in his life, yet his nightly diet consisted of two litre bottles of Jack Daniel's and coke and various other medicinal items. For breakfast it was barbecue potato chips. That intake didn't have any visible effect on him. He smelled of Gitanes cigarettes that he also habitually chain-smoked and the smoke filled the room. His assistant John Weaver was a great guy and a big help as well.

Geoff's teeth were a bit of a mess but he couldn't care less. He also bragged he never paid income tax, to which I would always say, 'They are gonna find you, man . . . I am telling you no one gets away.' Sure enough, one day many years later the IRS knocked on the door of his house. He ran for it. Jumped the fence never to be seen or heard from again until one day many decades later we played somewhere in the USA and he turned up. He said they never found him and he had re-married, got his teeth fixed and seemed set to live happy ever after . . . and then he died. RIP.

For me, *Turn Back* was a significant record because it was the first one on which I contributed a song that I wrote solo. Steve Porcaro had not long gone through a divorce and was living at the time at the house of another engineer friend, Reggie Fisher, who had recorded for Sly Stone, Bobby Womack and Randy Meisner of the Eagles. Reggie had a studio out in his house – this was before many people had studios in their homes – and we would go there to hang, record stuff and party. Up until then I had been nervous about competing with Paich, who is one of my all-time favourite songwriters, but he was very encouraging to me. One night, I went over to Reggie's and put down this track that I had got in my head. I played everything on 'Live for Today', guitars, keyboards, bass and drums, wrote the words and sang the vocal. The other guys liked what I had cut and decided to use the song for the record, which was a thrill. That tune convinced me that I could step up to the plate in terms of writing, in spite of it being so naive lyrically. I was twenty-two, what the fuck did I know about living?

I also co-wrote the title track with Bobby, who did the words. When we were in Japan on the *Hydra* tour, I had been gifted the first Roland synth-guitar. First time I plugged it in, I hit upon the 'Turn Back' riff. Each string was tuned to fifths, creating some interesting voicings.

Altogether we were proud of the eight songs on that record, but when it came time to mix, Geoff got very anal about things. He wouldn't let anyone else near the desk, and seemingly on a whim would choose to listen or not to our suggestions. There were a lot of arguments and it ended up being a very strange, dry and hollow-sounding record. Geoff took all the midrange out of the tracks, and they had a completely different feel to anything else that we had done to that point. The record company didn't really hear any singles but we put out 'Goodbye Elenore', Dave's fast shuffle and lead track on the album, and it rocked hard. Instead of doing a regular video for this and 'Live for Today', we insisted on doing completely live versions. 'Goodbye Elenore' got no play on MTV. We hated videos . . . we just wanted to play, but that meant the versions of our songs on video were not the same as the record. We thought it was cool; they didn't.

These days *Turn Back* has become a kind of a cult favourite among our fans, but some people really hated it when it originally came out because it sounded so different. Of course, the reviews were scathing. One in particular went: 'Turn Back? That's exactly what you should do when you buy this record.' It also got no higher than thirty on the American chart, then petered out and died. We didn't even bother to go out on the road behind it. The top brass at Columbia were bummed out. Their attitude towards us was plainly put: 'OK, if you don't make a hit album next time around, then it's all over for you guys.'

I was playing on a lot of hit records back then. One smash record I worked on during that year of 1981 was by Olivia Newton-John. Four years earlier, I had worked on a few things with Olivia and her Australian producer, John Farrar. John was also a great guitar player and songwriter, who back then wrote all of Olivia's songs. She, meanwhile, sang like a bird and was so beautiful that it made it hard for me as a wide-eyed kid to concentrate. Now, the pair of them had got down to work on a song by another Australian, Steve Kipner, for which they needed a guitar solo. John called me up and invited me out to Shangri-La, the famous studio in Malibu where Dylan and the Band, Clapton, and Crosby, Stills and Nash had all worked at one time or another.

John gave me directions to the studio but I got lost. Even now with GPS, that for me is by no means an unusual happening. I rolled up an hour late, which sucked, but John was cool as it was an overdub session, so I didn't hold anyone up too badly. There was a little partying going on and the vibe was very relaxed. He played the song for me and I just cracked up at the chorus, which went: 'Let's get physical, physical. Let me hear your body talk.' John took it with good grace and told me: 'I know, mate, but all jokes aside, this is going to be a big one, I think.'

He had me do three or four takes, no more, and from that comped together the solo that's on the record. John was spot on, too. 'Physical' went on and became one of the first huge things on MTV and sold more than two million copies in the States. That's a platinum single, which is a distinction I don't think even exists any more. Every time I heard that record, I would laugh out loud again. Some of the things that I have played on! It could be the coolest thing in the world, like 'Breakdown Dead Ahead' for Boz, or else 'Let's Get Physical', and it's the same guy. Me.

It was David Foster who recommended me to Quincy Jones, and so began one of the more important relationships of my career. Quincy was coming off the back of a huge hit with Michael Jackson's *Off the Wall* album and next up was doing a solo record, *The Dude*. The girl who booked all of his sessions, Janet, called me in for it and, on my first day, I showed up at Westlake Studios with excitement and anticipation. Quincy is assuredly one of the gold-plated names in music, and just the fact of getting that call sure helped my credibility and making a name for myself in the session scene.

Day one, we cut a song called 'Just Once'. I came up with a good part because all we got were chord charts and a road map, meaning the chord changes of the song and the form, and from that moment on Quincy was very appreciative of me. That was also the first day that James Ingram worked with Quincy. James had come to Quincy's attention singing on the demo of 'Just Once' that its two legendary songwriters Barry Mann and Cynthia Weil had made up for him. Funnily enough, James showed up to the session – really nice cat, funny, and we are still friends and have done many things together – but on that day he clearly hadn't realised that he was about to be made a star. Quincy otherwise had his own clique of guys that he used. On that session there was the now legendary JR, John Robinson, on drums and Louis Johnson on bass, who was a killer player and a nice but odd guy. God bless Louis, but I don't think I've ever met anyone who was more awkward socially. Greg Phillinganes, who I had known since I was a kid when he played with Stevie Wonder, was on keyboards. The session went great and Quincy asked me to play on the whole record, which I did, and that's how I met Rod Temperton.

Rod had been keyboard player in a funk band, Heatwave,

but couldn't read or write music at all. He had, though, just come off writing three hit songs on *Off the Wall*, one of which was 'Rock with You'. Quincy had subsequently signed him up to his publishing company and the two of them had become very fast friends. Rod heard whole records in his head and it was Quincy who gave him the wings to fly. Rod was very specific about what he wanted. When it came time to cut one of his songs, he would go up to each musician in the studio and sing the exact part that he meant for them to play. It was great ear-training, because not only were those parts invariably great, but they were also complicated. In any given eight-bar phrase, often as not one or two notes or a rhythmic figure would shift or change.

To Quincy, Rod was 'Worms' because he had been born in Worms in Germany. That was Quincy's thing. If he liked you, he gave you a nickname. His engineer, Bruce Swedien, was Swedish and so 'Svence'. Bruce would eat ice-cream pops all day long and get the greatest hi-fi sounds imaginable out of the top-of-the-line Harrison desk that they had at Westlake. Phillinganes was 'Mouse', because he was so small and young-looking. Greg's a little older than me but at the time he looked like he was twelve and, man, how he hated that name. Quincy is the only one allowed to use it. I, on the other hand, was truly honoured to get a nickname from Q. From that point to now, he has known me as 'Veets', which is my name almost spelt backwards and was partially what I had called my own publishing company.

Quincy is unique. Here's a guy who makes a record that he doesn't write, sing or play a note on, and yet it's still undeniably a Quincy Jones solo album. He's a great casting director and understands musicians and songs, which is half the battle. He would use different cats for specific things and always to the benefit of the song itself. As a whole, in my experience he created in the studio an environment that was entirely conducive to making great music. There was a lot of laughter. Quincy himself was hilarious, but also the consummate pro. He would order in great food and was appreciative of his players. Once, he sent flowers to the house for my then wife Marie with a note that said, 'Sorry to have kept him so late.' What's more, he paid very well.

One of the real highlights of making *The Dude* was that Stevie Wonder came in to play with us on a song that he had co-written, 'Betcha Wouldn't Hurt Me'. Stevie that day played the funkiest shit possible and it was one of those dream-like moments where I thought to myself, 'Can this really be happening?' I was working at the very highest level and with the greatest of the greats. I used to learn Stevie's songs as a schoolboy. From a composition standpoint and the voicings that he played, the very best way to be taught keyboards is through Stevie's songs. That's his genius and in the truest sense of the word. He was playing an early Yamaha CS-80, which I had seen as Steve Porcaro had one of the very first ones. But Stevie played it so funky and different.

Quincy and Stevie had an obvious rapport, and laughed and cartooned with each other back and forth. Stevie was very aware of everything else that was going on in the room, too. Some of my other favourite moments on those sessions would be when I cut a track with a full rhythm section. If I came up with an especially good part, Quincy would take out notation paper, write it down and then put it up on the desk. That was another of his great compliments. He would tell me that he loved the part and then sometimes have me come back later to refine it, with just the two of us sat together in the room and Svence on the board. Quincy meant for every bar to be locked down super-tight and so would have me play everything to a click track.

He also had these tiny, three-inch speakers called Auratones. If Quincy liked a take, he would shout out to Svence, 'Put it upstairs.'

That meant to crank it up on the big speakers so that we could all listen. Then he would go, 'OK, now let's put it on the radio.' That was Quincy's acid test. He would have just one of those Auratones set up on the middle of the desk and would play the track through it in mono. The volume would also be turned down low like a whisper. There is no hype at that level and that's when you hear the detail of the mix and all the parts. If a song sounds real good in mono and very quiet, then guaranteed it will sound great in stereo and loud.

The Dude came out in March 1981 and was a big success, and 'Just Once' was also a hit, making me valuable to other producers in the R & B genre. After that and in quick succession, I did one session after another with Quincy. The very next one was Patti Austin's *Every Home Should Have One* album, which was great because Patti herself was so beautiful and bubbly. We all loved her, still do. Quincy has a lot of kids but he was godfather to Patti and she also sang like an angel on his records. Also for Quincy, I did Donna Summer's eponymous album of 1982. Usually I was the only guitarist on a Quincy date, but on that occasion he also had Bruce Springsteen come down and play.

Bruce had written a song for the record, 'Protection', and showed up one day at Westlake. He's this humble, great cat, but the way that he made his own records was very different to the LA-slick version of recording that was in vogue at the time. Jeff was on that session too, and at first Bruce just wanted to jam a little bit on some old rock-and-roll standard or other. Jeff and I followed his lead, but it was as if he were giving a full-blown performance.

He had got his Telecaster slung on and was stood up, wrestling with the mic and throwing it down. Jeff burst out laughing and said to him, 'It's a session, man. You're working way too hard.'

Once he felt the vibe in the room was right, Quincy wanted

to cut the track. We started to play and Bruce abruptly stopped. He wanted to know what the banging sound was in his 'phones. When Quincy told him that it was a click track, Bruce shot back, 'But that's horrible. Turn it off.' We did a handful of takes without the click, but Quincy was after something that was so precise that he needed to hear it. He had to create a separate mix just for Bruce and then the rest of us did yet another to the click. I enjoyed working with Bruce. He was very soft-spoken and humble and so nice. I saw him recently at a Ringo Starr show and I said, 'Remember the time . . .' and he did. He worked with our brother Jeff Porcaro on the album *Human Touch*, one of Jeff's last sessions.

At another point on that date, Quincy asked Foster and me to write a song for the Donna Summer record. The two of us went on over to Quincy's house in Bel Air and wrote the song 'Livin' in America' in his music room. Donna came up to the house, too, and I at last got to tell her that I had played on a bunch of her disco records, including some of the hits. Donna was also a very humble and really nice person, and what a heaven-sent voice she had. Studio magic can make some people sound great, but Donna Summer was very much the genuine article. It was a cool song too, but when the record came out it was credited to four writers. I guess Rod Temperton helped finish the lyrics and melody.

Things could get even more punishing for us studio guys. Sometimes you would come up with all of the major parts of a song, or even rewrite it, and not end up with a writing credit or getting paid. As far back as the Wrecking Crew, Louis Shelton came up with the great guitar part on the Monkees' 'Last Train to Clarksville' that made the song, and his name's nowhere to be found on the record. (As it turns out, Micky Dolenz, his daughter Ami and her husband Jerry have been friends for decades – great family.)

There were exceptions to the rule, too. When Cheech and

Chong did their second movie in 1980, they hired Foster to write and produce a track and so I got the call. I had just taken delivery of a new Floyd Rose tailpiece, and Tommy Chong asked if he could record me messing around on it. The only instruction that he gave me beforehand was, 'Don't play too good,' so I just played about with feedback and using the whammy bar.

Now this all happened after we smoked a joint. I was not a big pot head at all but who would pass up a chance to get high with Cheech and Chong? I did and then we fucked around and recorded a bunch of noisy guitar bits with me showing them that the guitar would not go out of tune no matter what. I even threw a Strat across the room at full volume. Picked it up. Still in tune. Massive laughter in the studio. I didn't think any more of it until I went to see the movie.

In the middle of *Cheech and Chong's Next Movie*, there is a scene where Tommy goes into a music store and plays guitar. His fellow customers have their hands over their ears and scream at him to stop, windows get blown out, and they had used for that the part that I had recorded. I never knew they were going to use my humorous weed-induced guitar wanking and feedbacks. I couldn't believe it, but on the end credits it said: 'Guitar solos: Steve Lukather.' I was like, 'Wait, that sucked . . .' But it sucked on purpose. They never told me they were going to use it, but what I also didn't realise was that Cheech and Chong had been generous enough to put me down on the cue sheet as a writer of that noise. Over the years, I have made around 200,000 dollars off that fun.

Overall, I learned from Quincy so much about the art of making records and specifically from how he would listen to things. When Q celebrated his eightieth birthday in 2013, Nathan East was playing bass with Toto at the time and was Q's musical director, so Steve Porcaro, Paich and myself were asked to play 'Human Nature' with him at the Hollywood Bowl as surprise guests. It was so much fun, so many old friends. I saw the Brothers Johnson together again and it had been years since I had played on some of their albums too. I played with them again onstage that night during 'Strawberry Letter'. I was glad to see Louis Johnson again because he died not long after.

CHAPTER ELEVEN

The situation could not have been more cut and dried when Toto checked into Sunset Sound to make our fourth album. We had been signed up to a four-record deal with Columbia and now it was time to sink or swim, shit or bust. We knew that we had to stop second-guessing ourselves and go back to what had made our name in the first place, which was writing songs that married rock-and-roll with funkier grooves and hooks that sounded great on the radio. This was a do-or-die record for us.

To help us in that regard, we brought in our dear friend and legendary engineer Al Schmitt. Al has won something like 1,000 Grammys and is the easiest guy to work with ever. I learned a lot watching him work and we had a ton of fun too. At Sunset Sound there is a basketball court in the middle of the three studios where you can find someone shooting hoops any time day or night. We used to shoot hoops for 'treats'. Don't ask if you don't know. It *was* 1981.

Al had worked with Steely Dan and also produced Neil Young. His credit list was ridiculous in every style of music and every means of recording it, which was perfect for us, and we knew that he would record our stuff straight, no bullshit. A lot of guys get in the studio, start twiddling knobs straight away and never listen to the sound source, but not Al. He walked into Sunset Sound and to begin with just sat back and listened to what was going on in the room between the guys in the band. Based on what he heard, he would come out to the room, check out my amp sound, Jeff's drums etc., move the mics here and there and get the sound just so. Once he had settled on his set-up, he worked fast and that was also important for us. Whenever we cut, it was the first couple of takes that were the best and those that had to be captured. Al knew all that from working with us on hundreds of other sessions.

Sunset was a great place to pitch camp. We were in Studio Two. The Van Halen guys were in the front room working on their *Diver Down* record.

First thing we did was go to work on a tune that Paich had brought in with him. He told us that he heard it as a kind of Bo Diddley groove, but Jeff immediately had other ideas. There were two songs that we were listening to a lot at the time, which were 'Babylon Sisters' off Steely's *Gaucho* album and 'Fool in the Rain' from Zeppelin's *In Through the Out Door*. Both of those were slinkier kinds of shuffles. Jeff began to play something that was much the same but uniquely Jeff, and over the top of what Paich was playing. It changed the whole feel of the song at a stroke, and that was how 'Rosanna' started out.

Jeff and I had only just worked with Louis Johnson and, at that time, he was the king of that funky, thumb-slapped bass thing. Once we had established the groove, Jeff mentioned Louis's style to Hungate, who could play pretty much anything, and so that entered the picture. This all happened on the spot and came out of a jam between us that went on for just a minute or so, no more. The other thing we would always have to decide upon was who was going to sing each song. Bobby started off taking the lead on 'Rosanna', but the key was too low for him and so I stepped up. Paich then had the notion that we both sing. I took on the low part of the verses and Paich came up with a higher modulation for Bobby to come in on.

Hungate got a chord chart written up fast and went out and cut the track straight off. The first take felt pretty good to us, but we were still playing around with all of the various elements and the arrangement. The very next one we did that day is the take that's on the record. The tune was supposed to wrap after the second double-chorus, but instead Jeff led us into this whole other end jam with a Little Feat kind of groove and Paich on New Orleans-style, Dr John piano. That closing section was never rehearsed or even spoken of in advance, but Al was switched on enough to keep the tape rolling. Straight after, I overdubbed parts and did the middle solo on my '59 Les Paul, but the end is the live jam.

As far as I'm concerned, that eight-bar solo that Steve Porcaro conjured (with a little help from Paich) is one of the great synthesiser moments in recorded history, it was so perfectly composed. As a friend and as a musician, I was real proud of that one for him. It is a legendary recorded moment that few can duplicate. In my opinion, that track top to bottom really defines what Toto is musically. When asked, 'What song do you think best represents the band?', my answer is always 'Rosanna' as it has all the elements and we all get to shine on it.

Toto is a band. When I play the songs with other people, and most of us have, it never sounds the same. It is just the way we play together. It's always been that way. It's chemical.

In general, Steve was at the top of his game. By that same time, Paich had got a house out in Sherman Oaks and had built his own home studio there, which he christened 'The Manor'. For all intents, the Manor was a replica of Studio Two at Sunset Sound and Steve had pretty much gone and moved in with Paich. For the next several years and until Paich got married, Steve would work out at David's place in isolation and bring stuff in for the rest of us to listen to. He liked the solitude, I guess. Working with the earliest synthesisers in those days was also a time-consuming and detailed process, and no one else in the band was blessed with much patience. Our collective attitude was, 'Come on, man, what the fuck?', which over the years would drive Steve to distraction and even anger. We were all 'Let's get it done in one, guys' and Steve was not that guy. But he is like no other musician I have ever known so who am I to argue with results?

It was Steve who had indirectly inspired the title to 'Rosanna'. When I first met James Newton Howard, he had been married to a girl named Wendy who was best friends with the actress Rosanna Arquette. James and Steve had gone on to become close friends, too. Through their association, Steve had fallen in love with Rosanna and the two of them were now very much an item. Paich copped Rosanna's name and went with it for the song. As one half of a couple with Steve, Rosanna became part of our scene for a good few years. She was not hard on the eyes at all, and she and Steve had a very passionate but tumultuous relationship. After Steve and she had broken up, Rosanna went through a long period of denial that the song was about her, and ended up hating it because she became 'Rosahhhhhna'.

Then a few years back, I saw a TV show where she all of a sudden warmed up to it again. The show was about her and our song, and the Peter Gabriel classic 'In Your Eyes' that was supposed to be about her too. Funny how showbiz is . . .

Right after we had listened back to take two of 'Rosanna', Jeff announced to the room: 'I think we've got one here.' Within an hour, we had put together a nuts-and-bolts record with a killer hook. That was the song that popped the cherry for *Toto IV* and, after it, the floodgates were opened up. Everybody started to come in with songs and, in respect of that, there was a very healthy competitive edge to the sessions. You had to bring something good to the table, because it had to get the thumbs-up from all five other guys.

The ball got passed around. Paich had two other tunes, 'We Made It' and 'Make Believe', which got us into the groove. Steve arrived from the Manor with a song of his own, 'It's a Feeling'. I had one, 'Good for You', that Bobby helped me out on with the words. That got recorded 'cause Paich was late (a shocker, as we all know) and I was dicking around with the piano lick and the other guys jumped in and I wrote the bridge on the spot. I had the hook line, which when Bobby sang it sounded amazing. Then Dave walked in the back door and started playing a synth part I loved on his new Jupiter 8 synth. I said, 'Oh, man, you should play this piano part,' to which he said, 'No, you play it, it sounds good.' So that was my first piano overdub on a Toto record. I still crack up that it's me playing. I would do more later but I was honoured that they kept my part because the standard of playing in this band is very high.

And Paich and I came up with another, a rocker, 'Afraid of Love', that Jeff chipped into lyrically. I had also been goofing around with this one particular ballad since the *Turn Back* sessions. One night at Cherokee, I had lit some candles and, on the grand piano in the room. began to piece together 'I Won't Hold You Back'. When we cut it, I made Dave play my part because at that tempo you have to nail it and no one played ballads like Jeff and Paich. I wrote the bridge on the spot again. I thought the guys would not like the tune much because it was too slow and pretty, but everyone gave their all. When it came time for me to put down my lead vocal, I was in panic mode because all I had for lyrics was the chorus and the first verse. I only wrote out the second verse two minutes before I went into the vocal booth. Sometimes the good ones come quickly. I mean in song anyway.

Marie and I were married on 7 November 1981 at St Charles's church down the street in North Hollywood. Oddly, it was the same place my mother had her hands beaten by nuns with a ruler thirty-five years prior. As Marie was Catholic and wanted a church wedding, I had to go to these mandatory Catholic classes, including one on sex. Like we were all supposed to be virgins. I had a blistering hangover when I had to go to the sex education class and was howling with laughter, which did not go down well.

I was just twenty-three and Marie twenty-one, and truthfully I was scared to death. I can't even imagine now being married at twenty-three, but that's what you did back then. My parents would go on to me, 'Well, are you going to make it right here with this girl?' Marie's folks were much the same and I was led to believe that was how you did things: found a girl, fell in love and got hitched. Those were bat-shit-crazy times for sure. We did have some great times, and she gave me two of the most awesome kids ever, and we are close friends to this day.

Back in the studio, I overdubbed a soaring solo onto 'I Won't Hold You Back' and then Paich determined that we go big on the song. He was adamant all along that if this was to be our last album, then we should go out with a bang, balls deep, and spend every penny that we had on production. In this instance, that meant that Paich and James Newton Howard flew to England to get Martyn Ford and a bunch of the guys from the London Symphony Orchestra on the track. They also took along 'Afraid of Love' and 'It's a Feeling', as much as anything to justify to Columbia the cost of the trip. Dave and James arranged the parts with Marty, and they recorded with the orchestra at Abbey Road.

On 'I Won't Hold You Back' in particular, we were going for that epic feel that Elton John and Paul Buckmaster had got on a song like 'Take Me to the Pilot'. When I first heard what they came back with I was so thrilled that I had tears in my eyes. A lot of people have since made a point of telling me how much that song has meant to them. The only thing that Steve Perry of Journey ever says to me when we run into each other is that 'I Won't Hold You Back' helped him to get through his break-up with his girlfriend Sherry. That's a great compliment coming from Steve, and since it's the only one that he's ever given me, I'll take it. Whatever else, I wrote a song that touched a lot of hearts and

Me (on the right) on a Fender Jaguar, 1968. *(author's collection)*

My mother circled this and said that after the fall I was never the same. She was right! *(author's collection)*

A glimpse of what lay ahead. *(author's collection)*

Me, Dave Levy and Jimmy Nestor, 1972. *(author's collection)*

Todd Fisher, me, David Joliffe and Mike Porcaro, circa 1976. *(author's collection)*

An early band: Bobby Brown, Tony Rizzo and me, 1968. *(author's collection)*

(left) With Jay Graydon in 1977. (author's collection)

(below) 1977: with Boz. (author's collection)

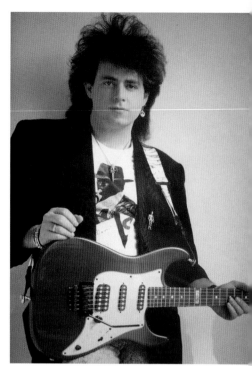

The mullet years, circa '87. (author's collection)

Toto, 1980: David Paich, Steve Porcaro, me and Jeff Porcaro. (author's collection)

Jeff Porcaro and Jim Keltner hanging in the late '80s. *(author's collection)*

'Africa' hits the #1 spot, 1982. *(author's collection)*

Jeff Porcaro shows us how it's done in a *Kingdom of Desire* session with Joe Porcaro in the background. *(author's collection)*

Elton John, Jonathan Moffett, me (channeling my best Pat Metheny) and Eric Clapton: live at the Hollywood Bowl, 1988. *(author's collection)*

Working on *Thriller*, 1982: *(left to right)* George Martin, Bruce Swedien, Quincy Jones, Michael Jackson, Jeff Porcaro, me and Paul McCartney at Westlake Studios.*(© 1982 Paul McCartney / Photographer: Linda McCartney. All rights reserved)*

Quincy Jones, Paul McCartney and Michael Jackson session followed by a Toto rehearsal! *(author's collection)*

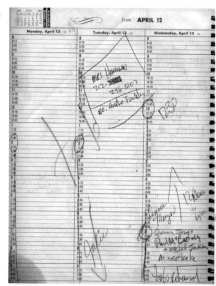

Jeff Porcaro, Tommy LiPuma, David Paich, Miles Davis, me, Mike Porcaro, Steve Porcaro. *(author's collection)*

George Harrison and me – tribute to Jeff Porcaro, 1992. *(author's collection)*

(above) Rick Allen (my next door neighbour for years), Phil Collen, Joe Elliott, Brian May, Vivian Campbell, Rick Savage and Tony Franklin. © *Robert M. Knight)*

(right) Randy Jackson, me, Richard Marx, Tommy Lee, early '90s. *(author's collection)*

At a Guitar Centre event honouring Jimmy Page: *(left to right)* Dweezil Zappa, Peter Frampton, Jimmy Page, Eddie Van Halen 1992. *(© Robert M. Knight)*

With Billy Sheehan, Steve Vai, Eric Johnson, Johnny A. at NAMM.
(© Robert M. Knight)

With Simon Phillips, Denny Dias and Donald Fagen: Jeff Porcaro tribute concert, 1992.
(author's collection)

(left) My son Bodhi with Swink our dog. *(author's collection)*

(right) Lily as backstage boss. *(author's collection)*

(left) My daughter Lily with the Stanley Cup at Billy Mumy's place. *(author's collection)*

(right) My daughter Tina and her husband Tony. *(author's collection)*

On vacation in Turks and Caicos with my new friend J.J. Abrams and my son, Trev. *(author's collection)*

(left) Four generation of Lukather men: me, Trev, my dad Bill and grandfather Lee. *(author's collection)*

(right) With Mike Landau – one of my oldest friendships (since I was twelve). *(author's collection)*

(right) Christmas Eve: a freaky double-exposure shot of my two grandmothers, both of whom had passed away. *(author's collection)*

(below) Lily the boss, Ringo and Mimi who has looked after our family for thirty-five years. *(author's collection)*

(left) George and Trev – when he was Batman. *(author's collection)*

(above) My kids Tina and Trev. *(author's collection)*

maybe even got a few people laid. I get told this by fans all the time for some weird reason.

When we were almost done recording, Paich arrived with one last tune. There are all sorts of paths that lead to a song and this one had grown out of a development deal that Steve Porcaro and he had got involved in with Yamaha. The two of them had helped with the design and testing of a prototype of a new synth that the company was bringing out, the GS1. They had even had to wear lab coats and sign confidentiality papers just to be able to handle this thing. Paich had hit upon some sounds when messing around with the GS1, one for brass and the other a kalimba, and that had subsequently inspired him to write the song 'Africa'.

Naturally, we found this last fact hilarious. Never mind not having gone there, I don't think that, at that time, Paich had even flown over Africa. He says he studied Africa in school. I don't know . . .

Paich came in and played us the outline of the song on the Yamaha CS-80. Almost instantly, Jeff leapt upon the idea of putting a percussion loop onto it. This was in the days when you actually had to make a loop and edit it together.

At the time there was no such thing as 'world music'. We were creating this shit from dust. Jeff called up his dad, Joe, his godfather, Emil Richards, who was another legendary percussionist, and also Lenny Castro, and got all three of them to come down. Emil was famous for his collection of African tribal instruments, Joe had marimbas and Lenny had shakers, congas and bells, and they brought all this stuff along with them. Jeff went out with Lenny and started playing the groove, just the two of them, and Jeff picked four bars for the loop. Now having Al Schmitt there was a blessing because he knew how to do all this stuff, and they edited the four bars together and started overdubbing with Joe, Emil and Lenny. We had those guys play to the outline groove of the song and filled up a couple of twenty-four-track tapes with just percussion instruments, and that was mixed and comped. Then Paich and Jeff played to the overdubbed loop, just the two of them, top to bottom. Jeff only came in with full kit on the chorus, and nailed that in one or two takes. Then we all started overdubbing and we were on that one for a few days. We filled up four twenty-four-track tapes because we all had ideas. It was fascinating to watch that whole process, because that song was literally built from the ground up. It was such a weird but amazing thing to be a part of.

We knew that the track was great, but there was the matter of the lyrics. Paich had the melody for the verse and a chorus lyric, but no other words. He and Jeff ended up thumbing through all of these geography text books for inspiration. To their credit, they did manage to get the word 'Serengeti' into a rock song, but I said to Paich: 'Man, "I bless the rains down in Africa"? What the fuck does that mean?'

Next, it was a question of which of us was going to sing the song and be able to get the words out. Paich took the lead vocal and Bobby sang the main melody in the chorus. I did the one under and all of us just started doing multi-layering of vocals on the spot on one full chorus. It took a long, long time. Bobby was having a real hard time with the high melody part and to triple it was crazy, so when we got a full one done we thought, 'How many more times are we going to have to do that for this song?' I had seen guys 'fly things in' to patch together a song and I believe it was Geoff Workman who had shown us how to do it. We did a pre-mixed background vocal balance, which took hours to do right. Then we flew that to two tracks from the half-inch machine. You make a mark with white grease pencil on the part where the section starts and try to hit play at the right moment, and if you get lucky it synchs up. It was not easy and it took a lot of punches. I did most of this with Al, with Dave and Jeff rooting me on. I had asked if I could do it as I had seen it done before and the guys said, 'Yeah, sure, go for it,' not really thinking it was going to work, but I got lucky and it worked, so I got the job for a while. This saved us countless hours and money for studio time and I got to like doing it. Now people just cut and paste and it takes five seconds tops. They're pussies.

That chorus vocal part was so high that we only got it out of Bobby once.

As with everything else we did on *Toto IV*, it was a case of do or die. The upshot was that the record as a whole ended up being the very best representation of what our band was all about. Even still, I told Paich: 'If "Africa" is a hit, I will run naked down Hollywood Boulevard.' No one would want to see that now. The song has had countless covers made of it. I have never been more wrong in my life.

The making of the album was also attended by more personal dramas. Right at the very end of the basic tracking sessions at Sunset Sound, David Hungate one day just upped and left the band. Paich, Jeff and I were in the room with him at the time and, out of the blue, Hungate picked a fight. It was brought to an end by him shouting, 'I can't take this bullshit any more,' and throwing his Precision bass across the room. After which, he announced, 'I quit,' and walked right out the back door. The three of us were stunned because Hungate just wasn't the kind of guy that ever showed his emotions like that.

As it turned out, he must have been plotting his exit for a good while. He had bought a house in Nashville and straight afterwards moved down there with his wife and kids. I think that he had calculated that he would do this one last album with us, make his mark on it and then get the fuck out of Dodge before he had to go out on the road again. Hungate had just got sick of LA, didn't want to raise his family there and was tired of being a touring musician. He had never shown the slightest interest in joining in with our crazier antics. It was a blow to us and we loved the guy, but Jeff didn't hesitate or draw breath. No sooner had Hungate disappeared through the door than he turned to Paich and me and said, 'Well, I guess my brother Mike is our new bass player.'

We lived in an era where people doing drugs was a fact of every-day life and everyone was partying, including the gardener. The first time somebody offered me cocaine, they said to me, 'You'll be fine – this shit isn't addictive, it's like having a cup of coffee.' It was easy to go with that big lie because there would be coke at every session. You could choose to do it or not, but it was still there. I'm not proud that I partook and wish now that I never had. Cocaine certainly brought out the worst in me. I made some of the most regrettable decisions of my life while high.

It was the night of 15 December 1981 that brought about Bobby's arrest and subsequent downfall. He did a stupid thing and got set up. Out where he lived in Toluca Lake, there was a Mexican restaurant that he used to hang out at, drinking and doing whatever else. Being the loud personality that he is, all of this would be very obvious and out in the open. When Bobby walked in the room, you would know right away that he was there.

Bobby was arrested on suspicion of selling cocaine to an undercover cop. The way I was told it, he was accused of getting four ounces of coke. That's like ninety grams of cocaine. Nine-Zero! Most every other guy would buy a gram at a time, but Bobby was accused of getting his hands on much more. I had found out from my mom. She called me at six o'clock the next morning, terribly upset. It was on the TV news, so now we were all in the middle of a shit-storm. Jeff in particular was furious. And when Jeff got pissed, none of the rest of us would have to say a word. We were just left shaking our heads at how Bobby could have been taken for such a fool. From that moment on, the word 'cocaine' attached itself to our band. For starters, I hadn't wanted my parents to know that I did drugs. My dad gave me the hairy-eyeball treatment, and I was an adult, living in my own house and married. He actually said to me: 'How much drugs are you assholes doing?' If nothing else, it really shook the rest of us up and made us look at ourselves.

When it came time for the Grammy nominations it all came back to haunt us. We got labelled the blow band, like no one else in LA was doing it. Jesus, it pisses me off, when anyone could see from our band and collective session careers that we couldn't have done all that and been high all the time.

I was a far cry from an angel but I did not destroy my band with it. I fucked up my personal life, but more on that later . . .

Bobby, I'm sure, regrets his transgression to this day. At the time, he obviously felt terrible and was scared. Possession of coke with intent to sell: that was a heavy felony and if convicted he was looking at serious jail time. The press was all over the story. It would also be months before the case went to trial, so Bobby had that hanging over him. In the meantime, we had an album to finish and a tour booked. It wasn't the time for us to kick our lead singer out of the band, so we gave the brother another chance. And then another, and then another . . .

The very first time we played *Toto IV* from top to bottom, Don Henley was in the room. Henley was hanging because we are all friends and most of us worked on Don's solo records sometimes. He was also working on a new album with our engineer and soul brother Greg Ladanyi, who I had brought in after we had both worked on a Peter Cetera solo song called 'Living in the Limelight'. Greg's sounds were insane, huge, and I had convinced the other guys in the band to bring in Greg to help mix our tracks. Al was awesome but not a real rocker and I thought fresh ears on what we had been working on for months would be a great idea, and Jeff and Paich knew him anyway and agreed. Greg was part of the Sound Factory gang and had recorded Jackson Browne and Warren Zevon. Greg brought a more aggressive, rock-and-roll feel to the party and his final mixes sounded incredible.

We turned the lights down and Henley came and sat down on the couch in front of the console right in between the big speakers. As the last echoes of the closing track, 'Africa', faded away, nobody really said too much except Don. He popped up out of his seat, smiled at us and said, 'Wow, that's a really good record, guys.' Henley could be a harsh critic, too, so coming from him that meant a lot. He was real supportive of what we were trying to do and knew about the hurdles we had encountered.

It was our good fortune that the guys at Columbia also flipped out when they got to hear the finished record and wheeled out the big guns to sell it. They gave us what was called 'independent promotion', which was one of the great euphemisms of the music business. Back then, radio play was crucial to having a hit record and there were two ways to get it: someone at the station could like your record, or else you indirectly paid them to play it through an independent radio promoter.

That payment could be made in the form of money, vacations, gifts or whatever the fuck someone was into provided it could be used for promotions. These stations would then report their play-lists and it was from being on those and actual sales that your record would be shot up the Billboard chart. It was a shabby game, but everyone played it and it was legal. God knows how much was spent over the years on our behalf, but it always came out of our pockets in the end.

In the case of *Toto IV*, though, we didn't really have to arm-wrestle anybody. We had begged Columbia to release 'Rosanna' as the first single and people just instantly dug that song. We were all over MTV with the video, which had a kind of *West Side Story* vibe and was shot by a guy named Steve Barron. A couple of years later, Steve would cause a stir with a part-animated clip that he directed for the Norwegian pop band a-ha's breakout single 'Take on Me'. Steve also shot the video for 'Africa', and when that came out the record went off like wildfire. That's the silliest and most oddball song of our entire catalogue, but it truly hit a nerve. Off the back of 'Africa', *Toto IV* became a triple-platinum smash and now that song's like herpes. Every time you forget about it, some-one else samples it and it breaks out all over again.

I can't wait to see what Seth MacFarlane has in store for us next as he just licensed 'Rosanna' and the rights to make cartoons out of us. We love Seth and he has had his way with us before to the point where Paich's name on the hotel rooming list used to be Peter Griffin. People think we don't laugh at ourselves. They obviously don't know us at all.

The tour we did behind *IV* was a victory lap and got pretty wild. In Japan we sold out the Budokan, 11,000 seats, for three nights. On one of those nights, as I went into my end solo on 'Rosanna' the crowd went absolutely nuts. I was thinking to myself, 'Man, I must be tearing it up tonight.' Then I looked up and standing there next to me was Stevie Wonder. He had a big smile on his face and proceeded to blow some killer harmonica and sing his ass off. The place erupted, and we just followed his lead.

In London 1982, we did the Hammersmith Odeon in London and Jeff Beck, one of my favourite guitar players, came along to see the show with Bernie Marsden, another legendary blues player who was in the original Whitesnake line-up. Gary Moore was there, and Cozy Powell, who I worked with some years later . . . So many of my heroes as a kid, which was a real trip for me.

Mark Hartley had been to Harrods on the day of the gig and brought back with him a gigantic fish, which he had put makeup and panties on, lipstick and all, and left in my room tucked into my bed. It was nicknamed Betty and I took it with me to Hammersmith. The first time I got to meet Beck, I was cradling a dead fish with bright red lipstick all over its mouth; I was pouring shots of booze into the fish's mouth and offering it to all . . .

We sold out everywhere that we went and the band was playing great, but it wasn't a long enough run. Once again, Jeff didn't want to do a big tour. We could have cleaned up doing arenas in the States, but we passed up the opportunity and went home instead. It was also the case that Bobby's problems got even worse on the road. He would be great one night, and not so great the next, and that had really started to bug Jeff and all of us. Bobby also made a dumb-shit move when we were playing in Nashville and broke his leg. Towards the end of the set, he tried to jump over a monitor, missed his landing and hyper-extended his leg. He managed to haul himself up and sing the last song of the night sitting on the edge of the stage. Bless his heart, he must have been in excruciating pain. He was rushed off to the hospital immediately afterwards and had to do the next show in an automatic wheelchair, and with his leg raised up horizontally. He came out on stage and proceeded to roll around the stage like Dr Strangelove. The rest of us were laughing hysterically, but the humour wore off because it was so silly. He ended up singing behind a keyboard for the rest of that tour.

Bobby made the grave mistake of starting to smoke the shit, and 100 per cent guaranteed that will make you lose your fucking mind. The poor cat got strung out. There were a lot of all-night hangs on that tour, but if you're the lead singer it gets increasingly apparent if you've stayed up until dawn. As a guitar player, I could get away with it and still be able to perform.

CHAPTER TWELVE

I believe we went to work on *Thriller* the very same month that *Toto IV* came out, which was April 1982. It began for me with a phone call at eight o'clock one morning. This was during a period of my life when every one of my friends would know that a hang was always likely to be on at my house. The phone by the bed rang very early. I snatched it up when it rang. A high-pitched voice said, 'Hello.' I went, 'Fuck you,' and hung straight up. I figured that it was one of my friends who was still up and fucking with me.

The phone rang again immediately and the same distinctive voice said, 'This is Michael Jackson.' I said, 'Fuck you, Michael Jackson,' and again hung up. He called back a third time. On this occasion, I asked, 'Which one of my idiot friends is this?' He said, 'No, no, it is me.' The voice was very familiar and that made me pause. I had never spoken to the cat before and so couldn't be sure. Previously, Quincy's office had always called to book me for his sessions.

My solution was to start grilling the cat, which is to say that I asked him a succession of trivia questions about Michael

Jackson's music, the musicians he works with, etc., all of which he answered correctly while sounding amused at me grilling him. I asked him what kind of idiot would call a musician at that ungodly hour and informed him that if he really was Michael Jackson, then he would ring back at a more sensible time of the day. Then I hung up once more. Three hours later, I got a call from Quincy. He told me that it had indeed been Michael on the phone and that I had better get back to him. I called the number Quincy gave me and, sure enough, Michael answered. I apologised profusely for my being a bit of an asshole, but he said: 'Oh, it's OK. That happens to me all the time. No one ever expects me to call.'

The first track we did for *Thriller* was Michael's duet with Paul McCartney, 'The Girl Is Mine'. Jeff, Paich and I got the call to come in for that one.

We were expecting something different than what was put in front of us in terms of what kind of song it would be, but we were very excited to be working with some of our heroes. I was tripping as this would be the first Beatle I would meet – they were my reason for playing music. I was nervous and wanted to play really well that day, and hoped that Paul and Michael would have a good time, and we knew that Quincy was counting on us, so we gave it all we had. Q had hired us to take this simple, very poppy track and come up with cool parts for it.

We went along to the session at Westlake and that turned out to be a truly surreal scene. A camera crew arrived and a very strange group of people showed up along with them. Among these was Dick Clark, the host of *American Bandstand*, and an assortment of child TV stars from the seventies. Michael came in and was carrying around in his arms Emmanuel Lewis, the little kid who was the star in the sitcom *Webster*, like an accessory. We were cracking up. Then into the room walked Paul and Linda McCartney, George Martin and the Beatles' engineer, Geoff Emerick. That was humbling. The greatness in the room was palpable. You could feel it. It was a pinch-me moment for sure. These guys had changed my life . . .

I had met George Martin a couple of years previous at Cherokee Studios, and hadn't forgotten that encounter in a hurry. I was on a session and my demented sense of humour reputation preceded me. I was still just a kid at the time. When I showed up, someone had left a present for me, knowing I was coming in the next morning. Hung up in the hallway was a big, blow-up sex doll, naked and with 'her' mouth wide open. Around the neck was draped a sign that read: 'Welcome Luke.' I pulled this thing down and kicked it as hard as I could along the corridor. At that precise moment, the main Studio One door opened and out walked George Martin. To my horror, the doll hit George full in the face. He was George fucking Martin! Legend, hero, and I had just kicked a sex toy in his face. I was on my knees apologising. Fortunately, he took it with his usual good grace and laughed it off.

The amount of security that day at Westlake was insane. This was less than two years since John Lennon had been shot and, according to Quincy, McCartney was very nervous about meeting new people. At some point beforehand, I think we had all had to be vetted. On the day, the plan was for Michael and Paul to sing live in the room. As we were getting set up, Paich started to play a Stevie Wonder song, 'I Was Made to Love Her'. The rest of us leapt in with him. Jeff was on drums, David Foster on electric piano, Louis Johnson on bass and me on guitar. When we hit the groove, Michael started to sing along and then Paul jumped in, too. You could see the whole control room light up. And, man, it was roasting in the 'phones. That jam set the tone, and also the pace for the day as a whole.

As much as anything, it made Paul feel more comfortable. He visibly relaxed after that, as if he were reassured that the band was good, and we got right on down to the tracking. We hadn't learned the tune right off the bat because we knew from experience that in all likelihood Quincy would want to try it a thousand different ways. The thing is, though, that when you have got a roomful of cats with that level of musicianship, magic can always happen. Sure enough, we nailed the song on the first few runs.

After the session, Jeff, Paich and I and a bunch of the guys sat in an adjoining room and did what musicians did back then after the work was done, meaning we sparked up a joint. We were just kicking back when the door was flung open and in walked Paul with Linda. He stopped, sniffed the air and announced: 'I smell musicians!' The two of them came in and hung out, and that was another special moment. At one point, Paich struck up the last chord of 'A Day in the Life' on the piano. Paul cracked up and said, 'Hey, not bad,' and then told us the story of how all four of the Beatles hit that last chord on the *Sgt. Pepper* record. We were looking at each other like, 'Is this really happening?' Not long afterwards, Jeff and I got a call from Paul's office in London to go work with him on his *Give My Regards to Broad Street* project.

Michael Jackson was just like any other great artist in that he knew exactly what he wanted. He didn't play anything per se, apart from a little keyboard, but he heard songs in his head. He would make up demo tapes of song ideas where he would use his voice as all of the instruments. His singing voice was otherwise pristine.

In the studio, Michael's body language said a lot. Whenever he got excited about something, he would start to dance and do that Michael Jackson thing, and you would know that you were on to something good. Of course, he was also a very striking-looking guy. We were the same age, as it turns out. I tripped on how long he had already been doing all this and what a pro he was. He had just had his nose done for the first time, but I didn't pay it too much attention. So, he'd had a nose job, no big deal. When I met up with him again a few years later, it was an altogether different story.

The second track we worked on was 'Beat It'. There were two versions, which is why some people claim to have played on it when they didn't. There was a version that got sent to Eddie Van Halen's house. Quincy had the master-reel first-generation twenty-four-track tape with Michael's lead and backing vocals done, plus on that same reel was Eddie's first-generation solo along with Michael playing two and four on a drum case, which presented Quincy with a problem. Eddie and Van Halen's engineer, Donn Landee, had independently cut the tape because Eddie wanted to play his solo over a different section of the song than planned. When Quincy got hold of Eddie's tape, he found out that the SMPTE code wouldn't sync back up to his master track. He called Jeff and me and asked us to fix it with an engineer, Humberto Gatica, at Sunset Sound while he and Michael were at Westlake working on another track. We were in touch by phone all day, old-school.

Jeff went in first and put down a fake click track with his sticks to match Michael's hitting of the box on two and four. There was nothing else on the track but air. Jeff nailed it in two takes and it meant that I would have something to play along to. I then did the basic guitar riff and the bass part. Since Ed was on the track, I quadrupled all the guitar riffs through a double stack of Marshalls. Quincy and Michael weren't in the room, of course, so I sent it back to Westlake. Quincy told me he thought it was fantastic, but added, 'Except it's too rock. I've got to get this song to cross over to pop and R & B radio. Do the same thing again, but use one of your little Fender amps this time.'

Once I had done that, Quincy had me come back down to Westlake to work with Michael and him on the rest of the guitar parts. Michael sang out for me the four-bar guitar part that he wanted for 'Beat It'. However, I told him that that alone running through a four-minute piece of music would be too monotonous. I suggested to him instead a change-up, putting in that signature 'duh-duh-duh-duuuh' part, so that it became an eight-bar phrase. I played that for him and he started to move, so I knew that he and Q were digging the slight change-up in the figure.

Thriller was no different to most other albums I worked on in respect of the fact that what we were given was just a broad sketch of the tracks. There were no parts or arrangements written out for us. Take 'Human Nature', for example, one of the other tracks we did for that record. That one is basically a Toto song, written by Steve Porcaro and with an arrangement credited to me and the guys – thanks, Q. I came up with the main guitar part, which is kind of the glue that holds the song as a whole together. If you take that part out, it's a completely different tune.

Quincy had said to me that he loved the track, but that he needed it to be funky. Or to be more accurate, he got inches from my face and urged me, 'Come on! Make this funky for me!' It took me just a few minutes to come up with the part and to put it down. It just popped right into my head and I started to play along. Quincy was like, 'That's great – great!' It was just him and me and Svence in the room. Michael wasn't there for that one. I perfected it over a take or two, and was plugged directly into the console – there was no amplifier. It has a very unique sound for that reason and I double-tracked it right away. I thought Steve would dig it too when he heard it, but he hated it. Once it was a hit, he said, 'You know, that guitar part is not so bad after all. Ha-ha.'

During the course of those sessions, Quincy would play us other stuff from the record. One day when I came in, he put up 'Billie Jean' for me to hear. He told me that it was going to be the first single and a huge hit. Coming off the back of *Off the Wall*, Michael was poised so that pretty much anything that he did next was going to be a hit. Even so, I think he put a lot of pressure on himself making *Thriller*. It's hard to have that kind of success twice, and he did, bam-bam, back to back, and with *Thriller* going on to be even more massive. For my part, I knew all along that there was something special going on with that record. The songs were great and as a whole it was undeniable. Now, I'm not saying I foresaw that it would be the biggest-selling album of all time, but it was a great honour to have had a hand in that success.

When *Thriller* swept the Grammys in 1984, we were invited to present an award as we had won Album of the Year the year before. Seeing as I was divorced, I took my little sister Lora along with me and introduced her to Michael. He was very cool with her, perhaps because he found me amusing. That night, the band and I got to present the Producer of the Year award to Quincy and Michael. The funny thing was that we were stood right behind the two of them when they made their acceptance speech, and they thanked everybody who had been involved in the record but us. It had been the same thing when 'Beat It' took off all over MTV. It was made to seem as if that song didn't exist except for Michael and Eddie. There was no mention of the guys who had done all the heavy lifting.

Often we would be called in to save something or had to sign an agreement saying we would never say we played on certain records. That is a book in itself. I played on a track on Cheap Trick's *Dream Police* album and got no credit, but Rick Nielsen was very cool and gave me a gold pick and a platinum record from Tom Werman, their producer. Rick can play so I guess they wanted a different flavour that day. Rick and I had just done an Alice Cooper record, *From the Inside*, together and he played on one of the songs I co-wrote. We got on well and I was honoured to be on Cheap Trick's 'Voices'. The rest is all Rick. Great band. Nice people.

From 1981 and on through 1982, you could not have thrown a rock in a Los Angeles recording studio without hitting Jeff, Paich, Steve P and me. Between the four of us, we got all the calls and doing sessions from daybreak to dawn became our everyday life. The downside was that I got to be so busy that it started to have a detrimental effect on my personal life at home. Marie was alone a lot of the time and I felt bad about that, but when you're riding a wave like that, you just don't say no. Equally, I don't do so good when I'm not occupied with work. I used to go on vacation, and would then need a vacation from my vacation.

I did a lot of sessions with Jeff, including that first solo album by Don Henley, *I Can't Stand Still*. Don had Danny Kortchmar and Greg Ladanyi producing him and had written a bunch of great songs with Danny. Henley's one of the great voices of all time, but the Eagles guys had a reputation for being very intense in the studio and that gave me cause for concern because I am the exact opposite. That isn't to say I'm not a serious musician, but I am a silly man.

Don, though, was very relaxed and I guess that Jeff and I contributed to his good mood because we worked fast and had a good vibe, and there was no tension in the room at all. We would always roll up early to a session and be very open with each other. There was a lot of laughter and hugging. The first track we cut with him was the song, 'You Better Hang Up', which had one of Kootch's famous riffs. It was done live in the room with Kootch and me on guitars, Bob Glaub on bass, and Don and Jeff played double drums. That was a gas and we nailed it pretty fast.

Danny and Don next broke out 'Dirty Laundry', which Don had cut a demo of with a drum machine. He wanted Jeff to over-dub live drums, which I watched him do in one take, as usual.

Kootch then came over to me and said, 'Joe Walsh is taking the middle solo on this, do you want to do the second one that's at the end of the track?' Walsh was a guy I had stood in line to see when I was a kid – he is one of my all-time musical heroes and now a friend – so I was thrilled beyond words even to be asked to play on the same record as him. Kootch could have played on the song himself but he wanted me to do it. Don was very positive as well because the vibe was great and everyone was having fun and a lot of work was being done. Ladanyi set me up with a monster guitar sound and they rolled the tape. Everyone was staring me down and Jeff was looking at me like, 'Bring it, man, bring it,' and he always knew how to get the best out of me. I think I nailed it in one take.

That was another surprise for me about Henley. We had all heard about how painstaking those Eagles records had supposedly been to make, so I was anticipating being asked to do endless takes. On the contrary, Don was happy to let us fly. He must have dug our vibe, because he also had Steve P figure out how to make that wonderful Farfisa organ part and sync up and work on 'Dirty Laundry'. It went on to be a big hit for Don and he sent us gold records, which was real nice of him.

Danny Kortchmar: The solo that Luke put down on 'Dirty Laundry' was absolutely brilliant and yet he knocked it out real quick. Right off, he sounded amazing. As a whole, that was an incredibly great time to be a musician in LA. The studio scene was jumping like mad and everyone knew everybody else. Even if we weren't on a gig, we would just go down to the studios and visit each other. At the time, A & M Studios had four or five big rooms and visiting there was like going to Harvard and being on campus. It was that much of an incredible learning experience, because even if you weren't on a date, you could go round, stick your head in the rooms and see what the other cats were doing. Everyone learned from everybody else.

In the same timeframe that I did Don's record, I also got a call to work on Joni Mitchell's *Wild Things Run Fast*. I was deeply honoured with that, because it was a known fact that Joni had the most brilliant musicians and I was a huge fan. We were based at A & M Studios and I put down my tracks as part of a trio with Vinnie Colaiuta on drums and Larry Klein on bass. Joni is an incredible artist. She would sit at the piano or play the guitar, sing note-perfect and every take would be good enough to keep. That one was a bit more of a rock-sounding record for her, and afterwards she asked if I would join her band for the tour. Once again, I couldn't, this time because of Toto. My brother Mike Landau got the gig and did the tour, and he also worked on overdubs on that record. He was the right man for the job.

Those were heady times. Another stellar session that I did around then was for Jimmy Webb's *Angel Heart*, produced by Fred Mollin and Matthew McCauley. Jimmy, of course, was and is a remarkable songwriter and that album was a deeply personal record. Leland Sklar, Dean Parks, Glaub and Freddy Tackett were also on the date, as I remember, and all of us showed up for work each day at Sunset Sound knowing that what we were doing was going to be great because Jimmy had all of these brilliant songs. With people like Joni and Jimmy, I would catch myself going, 'I can't believe I'm in the same room as these people.' How could I not? I wouldn't have had a soul if I didn't.

Jimmy's charts were a little more detailed than the norm, but there was still room for freedom of expression and he worked fast. In a six-hour period, we would do two tracks, the overdubs and that would be the day. I loved it when guys like that knew what they were after, but it wasn't always the case. Some people also refused to believe that one or two takes was enough. They assumed that if they kept on pushing you, things would get better, whereas more often than not the reverse was true. All the life and passion would get sucked out of the room and there would be nothing left to play off. Spontaneity and angst is what made so many of those records from that time great, and sometimes you had to keep something that was a little bit rushed or out of tune because it was all done to tape. With digital technology, there is nothing that can't be recalled and fixed. Records are like plastic surgery nowadays, where everybody is cut to look and sound the same.

Anything that Foster was doing at the time, I would play on. I was part of his team then and he was good to me. Back then, it was still all about the music with him and he got hired to help resuscitate the band Chicago, whose powers had been dwindling. Some of the band's fans ended up hating how he changed their sound on the resulting *Chicago 16* album, but Foster was brilliant in his own way. He called me in to help him out and, as a huge Chicago/Terry Kath fan, I was honoured. Jimmy Pankow from Chicago had played trombone on 'Rosanna', and we are still friends.

I felt a little uncomfortable going into that situation because Chicago already had a fine guitar player of their own named Chris Pinnick. Foster, however, pretty much took over the band at that point and told everybody where it was at. When we cut the basic tracks, I played along with Pinnick, but Foster didn't keep much of his stuff and had me come back in and overdub all the solos. The guys in the group were a little pissed off because Foster basically dismantled everything that had made them famous in the first place, which is to say their musical dexterity, and hung everything instead around Peter Cetera and his voice. There was, though, no doubting the fact that he put them back on track and brought the hits.

Foster did much the same with the Tubes. We were already fans when we were at school and Paich played on one of their early records, but they didn't write hit songs and couldn't get on the radio. Foster got the job of producing their 1981 album, *The Completion Backward Principle*, and along with the band's singer, Fee Waybill, we wrote the signature song for that record, 'Talk to Ya Later'. The bass player Rick refused to play on the song because they didn't write it so I played bass on that too as well as all the guitar parts. It was a bit of a weird vibe as we showed up in the morning with nothing and wrote the song on the spot. I had the opening lick and we were off. Done in an hour. That became the Tubes' first radio hit, so the record company wanted the same team to help them follow it up.

Besides Fee, who's a great cat and one of rock's best EVER frontmen, I'm pretty sure the other guys in the band weren't too pleased to have me back for the next album. The vibe had been a little bit thick when I had turned up for work on *The Completion Backward Principle* and my credit on that record had ended up being so small that you would have needed a jeweller's eye to find it – even though Prairie Prince, their drummer, Foster and I cut the basic tracks while the other guys were not even there. The first thing I came up with for the new album was the riff for the opening song, 'She's a Beauty'. Foster, Fee and I took it on from there and it became an extravagant production and very Toto-esque, because Foster also had Bobby Kimball do a backing vocal. Once again, I don't think the rest of the Tubes were happy aside from Fee and Prairie.

'She's a Beauty' went on to be a huge, top-ten hit for the Tubes. Afterwards, Fee invited me on a couple of occasions to come out and play the song with them at shows in LA. One of those nights, their guitar player, Bill Spooner, gave me a bunch of shit for not recalling a guitar part that by then I had written many years ago and had never played since. I don't know what he expected me to say. I wrote his band a smash. You know, sorry. I didn't know I was going to play that night and I forget everything as soon as it's recorded.

There were other cats who would be just as reluctant to use any of us from Toto. Jimmy Iovine said to me once, 'I didn't want to hire you Toto guys because I don't like Toto but, man, you guys can play.' In 1982, he called me in to play on some rhythm tracks for Stevie Nicks's *The Wild Heart* album and even got me back in to do the main guitar parts on the single, 'Stand Back'. He was looking for a Billie Jean-style clean, funky lick. Dean Parks had given it a go, and Jimmy had even got hold of David Williams, who had also played the real part on *Thriller*, and he wasn't able to give him what he wanted either. I plugged in, listened to a few bars of the groove and came up with the part on the record in one take.

Stevie called me up afterwards to say thank you and how much she dug the part, which touched me. Not a lot of people did that. What I didn't know was Prince was the keyboard player on that track as I was overdubbing.

Iovine must have been impressed as he later hired me for a bunch of stuff and I also got along great with his engineer, Shelly Yakus.

Together, Jeff, Paich, Lenny Castro, Nathan East and I did Randy Newman's *Trouble in Paradise* album. The five of us played and sang backing vocals on that record's hit single, 'I Love LA', and I took the solo. Typical of Randy, rather than being a love letter that was his piss-take on LA. Even still, the local basketball franchise, the LA Lakers, made it their theme tune. Good news for me, because every time the Lakers won a game, they played it and I got a cheque. That record was a lot of fun to do and it was the first time I had met Nathan. It was one of his first big LA sessions and we all dug him right away.

Randy is hysterical and his sense of humour is dry as a bone. There was one time that Toto was on the road and in Amsterdam. We were feeling a little restless one night after dinner and so went out around the red-light district. We wandered into this particularly seedy place and who should be there but Randy. All of us sat up on the balcony, from where we were able to look down upon a live sex show. Randy spied a guy on the front row who was sporting a Viking helmet and cheering the copulating couples on. He observed: 'Will you look at that fucking idiot?' I did and informed Randy that it was our drum tech, Robbo. 'Well,' said Randy, 'that figures.'

Jay Graydon and I were best pals at that time (and still are). He was working at the time with George Benson, who was doing a greatest hits record and wanted to have a couple of new tracks to go on there. Jay asked me and also Bill Champlin from Chicago over to his house to see if we could come up with something for George. I happened to have a piano riff that I had been working on, so played that for Jay and it started out the song. Bill came over and then we were dicking around trying to hit upon a lyric. At one point, Jay announced that he had to go take a shit. He came back into the room ten, fifteen minutes later, shouting, 'I've got it!' And then he sang, 'Turn your love around.' We pissed ourselves laughing at the whole way it came about.

Later that night I called Paich and Jeff. Jay had Jeff drop by and program the Linn drum machine, as that was the sound of the era. As Jeff had foreseen, by then everybody was starting to use one of those things. Here he was, a maestro who could nail a part in one take, reduced to pushing buttons on a box. At midnight, I called up Paich and he also came over and played a rip-roaring synth-bass part à la Stevie. Jai Winding played my piano part properly; Jerry Hey and his horn section killed it; essentially we finished up the whole song in just that one night. Next thing you know, 'Turn Your Love Around' was a hit record for George. And Jay, Bill and I, three of the whitest motherfuckers you have ever seen in your life, got nominated for a Grammy for Best R & B Song that next year.

CHAPTER THIRTEEN

By the end of 1982, I felt as if I were sitting on top of the world. All of us in the band did. *Toto IV* had rescued our career. We had the number-one record in America with 'Africa', 'She's a Beauty' had been a top-ten hit for the Tubes, 'Turn Your Love Around' was number one in the R &B and Adult Contemporary charts . . . and *Thriller* was the number-one album all around the world. It was like getting everything that you had always dreamed of and also heart-stoppingly scary all at the same time, because when you're on that much of a high, where else is there for you to go but straight back down? That dawning realisation brings with it a whole new kind of pressure.

We were still coming to terms with such things when the nominations for that year's Grammys were announced. I got a call from our managers to tell me I wouldn't believe it, but that we had been nominated in all of the major categories. While personally I was up for Best R & B Song, which for me was jaw-dropping, we were up for Album of the Year, Record of the Year, best this and best that. In fact, alongside Paul McCartney and Stevie Wonder, we had been the artists recognised the most. Also, we would effectively be competing against ourselves because one or other of us had played on something like forty or fifty of the records nominated overall. Our ascendancy at the Grammys even made the cover of the *Hollywood Reporter*. Being in the film and TV business, my dad had the *Reporter* delivered. Everywhere he went that week, he would show his copy to people and say, 'See, that's my kid.'

Right before the Grammys ceremony, we got offered the cover of *Rolling Stone* magazine, our nemesis. That was another of the things that people ticked off on their check-list in terms of having made it as a successful musician, and we turned them down. Old Jann Wenner apparently got his underwear in a bundle when the news was relayed to him, but right then we thought it was the most punk-rock move that you could ever do. With hindsight, I would say it was a bad career move for us. Even if it would have been a hatchet job, we would still have had that status symbol. That, though, is me talking from a distance of thirty-five years.

At the time, we were just so sick of them beating up on us in print at every opportunity. Even when *Thriller* came out, the *Rolling Stone* review had remarked how unbelievable it was that Quincy Jones had managed to get the members of Toto to play with some degree of taste. To us, it was like squatting over a wood-chipper, balls first.

The Grammys went ahead at the Shrine Auditorium in LA on 23 February 1983. We had been asked to play at the event, but Jeff hadn't wanted to do it, in the main because of Bobby. Kimball could blow hot or cold. It would be impossible to predict if he could pull it off vocally and in front of a television audience of many millions. It seems counterintuitive, but the fact is that a proper PA system in a big hall can be very forgiving of an off vocal, but with something much reduced, every imperfection is magnified tenfold coming out of a six-inch speaker (i.e. your TV). Jeff and Paich also had a bug up their ass about performing on TV in general, which I think they had inherited from Irving Azoff and the Eagles. Irving had said that rock-and-roll should never be put on television, because it makes everything look small. Our decision to pass did not go down well with the Grammy organisers.

There were a couple of other more minor glitches about the evening. The host for the event was to be John Denver, which stirred up in me a discomforting memory. When I was fourteen years old, my aunt and uncle on my dad's side had taken me on a skiing trip and every third song on the car radio had been 'Rocky Mountain High'. I had spent most of the trip pissing and moaning about this guy Denver and his infuriating song. Secondly, Hungate decided to join us at the ceremony. We were still on good terms, but Hungate had left right after doing the basic tracks on *Toto IV* and had next to nothing else to do with the making of the record. Mikey came along with us too and had fit seamlessly into the band, so that situation was a little weird. They denied Mike his Grammy even though he did the tour and played on some of the record. That was fucked up . . .

It was only once we arrived at the Shrine that I started to enjoy the occasion. I looked around the room and there was Elton, Quincy and all of these other people who I had worked with just recently. We also discovered that we were sitting in the second row, which was a jolt. Truly, we didn't turn up on the night with any expectations of winning a thing. For Album of the Year, we were up against Donald Fagen's *The Nightfly*, which Jeff had played on and I thought was a shoo-in. To me, that was the album of the year and it is still one of my Desert Island Discs. Stevie Wonder with 'That Girl' and Marvin Gaye with 'Sexual Healing' were among the other nominations for Best R&B Song, so neither was I holding my breath on that one. It was nice just to be there, but it soon turned out to be one of the most surreal evenings of my entire life, which is saying something!

To begin with there were what's called the pre-show awards, which are handed out before the start of the TV transmission. One of the first of those was for Best Engineered Record and Greg

Ladanyi, Al Schmitt and David Leonard won for *Toto IV*. I didn't get to hold that Grammy in my hand, but it was one for the team. Next up was Best Instrumental Arrangement, which 'Rosanna' won, and Jeff, Paich and Jerry Hey (who did the amazing horn parts) got to go up. In truth, it was a group effort. The event was in full swing by then and they announced the nominations for Best R & B Song. I leaned over to the guys and said, 'No chance in hell.' When they read out, 'Jay Graydon, Steve Lukather and Bill Champlin for "Turn Your Love Around",' it was as if I were sleep-walking on acid. Champlin was stuck in traffic and not even there to accept the award, but I was so caught up in the moment that this fact barely registered with me. I could have been struck down by lightning right there and then and it would not have mattered to me.

Producer of the Year we had never even considered winning. As a band we were nominated against Quincy for Donna Summer's record and everything else he was doing, Gary Katz, who had recorded all of those Steely albums that we so loved and was up for *The Nightfly*, Foster for *Chicago 16* and John Mellencamp and Don Gehman for Mellencamp's *American Fool*, which had been another of the year's big hits. We felt sure that Foster was going to win. I think he did, too. On the night, he was talking like he had a speech ready prepared and how he was going to make a crack about my playing keyboards. It was the legendary Herb Alpert who presented that award and even he looked to be in shock when he opened up the envelope and read out, 'Toto.'

The first person I locked eyes with in the audience was Foster. I shrugged my shoulders and mouthed to him, 'I don't know.' I thought in all fairness that he had deserved to win and felt a little uncomfortable, but not that it would be a big deal between us. In his acceptance speech, Paich acknowledged Foster and also Gary Katz and thanked them for their inspiration. Paich also went on to thank the music critic of the *LA Times*, Robert Hilburn, for all of his support. In the lead-up to the Grammys, this asshole had written that if we won a thing then he would quit and various other threats, and that crack got a good laugh in the room. It was Foster, though, who appeared to me to hate the fact that we had won the most and I have always felt that that one award brought about the end of our friendship.

Even that night, Foster started to rail on us. He went up to Katz and others and said, 'Can you believe those guys won? That's bullshit.' I would guess he might have been pissed off that guys like Hungate and Kimball had been honoured when they weren't genuinely involved in the process of making the record, having effectively left the band.

Here's a guy who has won armfuls of Grammys and yet he turned on us over just the one. He stopped calling me as a friend, let alone for work, and that hurt very deeply, because I had thought that the two of us were close. I didn't need the work. I needed the friendship. I guess there never really was one. That hurt the most. Success, ego and money, it changes people, fucks with their heads, and some more than others. It broke my heart at the time, but I feel sorry for Foster now.

We went on that night and picked up the Grammys for Record of the Year for 'Rosanna' and Album of the Year and between us and the rest of the gang we won a total of nine. After the ceremony was over, Marie and I were sitting in back of a limousine in the underground parking lot at the Shrine. We were helping ourselves to cocktails and I spotted Quincy walking over to his car. I hung my head out of the window and shouted out to him. He started to laugh and strolled over to our vehicle, whereupon he reached in through the window, grabbed my nose between his thumb and forefinger and squeezed just as hard as he could. 'Congratulations, man,' he said. It was sweet of him and meant a lot to me.

That night turned into an epic party. The guys were at one house, while Marie and I came back to our place, which was full of our close friends and family. We went back and forth on the phone to each other all night long and raged until the next morning, when we were due to sign a new contract with Columbia.

Once *Toto IV* took off, the record company hadn't been able to get a new deal in front of us fast enough, and claimed that they had never been serious about all of the threats they had made to dump the band. To which our parting line was: 'Fair enough, then make us an offer we can't refuse.' They did.

They sent a car to take me from the remnants of the hang at my house and round to our tour manager Chris Littleton's house down the hill. Everyone was still up from the night before, party still raging. It was 10 a.m. by then, but seemed to me like the crack of dawn. All of the guys in the band, our wives and girlfriends were still frothing from the night before. To be sure, it was an interesting state of mind to be in and have to deal with a retinue of lawyers, but by the time that meeting concluded we had signed up for another four more albums and at a million dollars a pop. Our legion of detractors had taken their best shots at us, but we had flipped them all off.

Soon after the Grammys, Jeff and I flew to London to begin work on McCartney's *Give My Regards to Broad Street* soundtrack album. We felt a little uncomfortable because at the ceremony *Toto IV* had beaten Paul's *Tug of War* to Album of the Year. As soon as we met up with him, Paul said to me, 'You know, the Beatles never won a Grammy.' Of course, he was fucking with us, but succeeded in making me feel both a dick and embarrassed for having won. As I found out only later, it also wasn't true. *Sgt. Pepper's Lonely Hearts Club Band* had won Album of the Year in 1968, as it should have.

Paul's original idea was to cut the soundtrack record live on the film set. In case that didn't work out, and in advance of shooting, he had also arranged for us to put down our track at EMI's studios. We were doing a version of the old Wings tune 'Silly Love Songs', but funkier than the original and in part because Paul had also hired Louis Johnson from the *Thriller* sessions. Paul played keyboard, Linda sang backing vocals and was on a Mellotron and George Martin and Geoff Emerick respectively produced and engineered. Paul, George and Geoff were quite a team and it was fascinating just to watch how they worked together.

The filming was done at EMI Elstree Studios on the outskirts of London. First day on set, Jeff and I arrived at Elstree to be told by the production manager that we would need to be fitted for our wigs. The two of us were baffled. We asked, 'Wigs? What do you mean – wigs?' The guy patiently informed us that everybody, including Paul and Linda, would be wearing not only wigs but also full kabuki makeup for our scenes. That was the first we had heard of it and I still have no idea as to why that was the concept. What's more, it was going to entail three hours of painstaking makeup and not one person was going to realise that it was me and Jeff in the movie.

When we at last made it onto the set, all of the instruments and amps were plugged in and ready to go. In spite of how well the date had gone at EMI, I think Paul thought we might put down something else that was interesting and different once the cameras were rolling. Like I said, though, once you have done thirty takes of a track, inevitably the very earliest will prove the best. In total, we spent two weeks working with Paul. During that time, we had lunch almost every day with him, Linda, George and Geoff Emerick. Linda in particular was lovely, laughed freely and could not have been nicer. Their kids were really young at the time, but there was no nanny or help as such. Linda was a hands-on mom. Once during a break on set, she leaned over to me and said: 'Everybody hates me because I'm in Paul's band. Oh, I read the papers, but it's Paul that wants me to be in the group, not me.' I had a laugh and she was so nice to me. I will never forget her kindness and humour.

All of us in the backing band were told in no uncertain terms beforehand that whatever we did, we were not to ask Paul about the Beatles. On set, I was stationed next to Linda and we struck up something of a friendship during the hours of idling around while the lights and gear got sorted out. I mentioned this Beatles ban to her one afternoon and she said, 'What? That's ridiculous.' I thought I would test out the theory about not talking the Beatles and proceeded to play the intro to 'Strawberry Fields' on her Mellotron. To which Paul, a bit startled, smiled at me and said, 'You did that pretty good,' and then launched into a few stories about the Beatles and that song. Then I just said, 'Fuck it,' and went for it and played 'Please Please Me'. Paul jumped in and so did Jeff Porcaro. It was magic and I shall never forget it. At the end the entire crew applauded.

After that, I felt liberated to be able to ask Paul every obnoxious question. He was so kind and was not afraid to tell details he remembered. I asked how they recorded this or that. Geoff and George Martin would tell me stuff, too . . . I was in heaven.

I thought of every Beatles-geek question that I could. He was an amazing person to be around and even better to work with than I could possibly have hoped. The thing that came across most to me was the way that he would light up whenever he would talk about John, George or Ringo. Often as not his stories would begin with, 'When me and the lads . . .' and it was immediately apparent just how much they meant to him.

Still, not much more than a couple of years had passed since John's death and that had obviously hit him hard. The only time that the atmosphere got weird on set was one day when we were messing around playing Beatles songs. I started out with 'Get Back' and everybody joined straight in with that jam. Next, I went into 'Dear Prudence', one of John's. Paul instantly looked up at me, straight back down at the piano, and then got up and walked off set. I went to Linda, 'Uh-oh.' She said, 'No, no, it's OK. It's not your fault. It's just that he misses John.'

We did a lot of jamming on Paul's Beatles songs, but Jeff and I were mortified to discover that Louis didn't know any of them. When I had initially struck up 'Please Please Me', Paul joined in on piano and began to sing his part, so I took on Lennon's, wishing I sounded like him. And Louis just sat there. I simply could not understand how that level of ignorance was even possible. All of the other funk players I had worked with had their Beatles thing down. Look at Otis Redding and Aretha. Everybody covers the Beatles because those songs are so perfect that you can adapt them to any style. You would have to be Helen Keller not to have heard at least one Beatles song.

However, something in general wasn't wired right with Louis, God rest his soul. With the experience that I have had as a parent of an autistic son, I would now guess that he was somewhat autistic, or else had Asperger's. At the time, I just thought he was very peculiar. He compounded his Beatles oddity by only ever addressing any of us in Japanese, and bad Japanese at that. On set, Paul would go, 'Hey, Louis,' and Louis would shoot back at him a garbled, guttural, 'Hai!' Understandably, that would confuse the fuck out of Paul. It was funny on the first occasion, but Louis kept it up for the whole time that he was with us.

There was one other tale from our time in London that pretty much summed up my life at that point. David Gilmour, who also worked on *Give My Regards to Broad Street*, wanted Jeff to play on his second album outside of Pink Floyd, *About Face*. The two of them arranged to go out to dinner one night and so I pleaded with Jeff to introduce me to David. I was a huge Floyd fan and Gilmour's one of my favourite guitar players of all time. As it happened, he was very keen to come back to our hotel and hang.

Jeff ended up going to bed and I stayed up the whole night with Gilmour, picking his brain. The two of us emptied my mini-bar and had a million laughs. However, 5 a.m. came around fast and I had a wake-up call to be back on set at Elstree. When I fell into the car with Jeff, I was still blazing. We had a two-hour drive. At one point, I rolled down the window and stuck my naked ass out at people in traffic. The only other thing that I could hear was Jeff laughing at me being still drunk from the night before, and saying over and again: 'Chill out, man! Chill out!'

CHAPTER FOURTEEN

Everyone with a long career behind them will have their own should've-would've-could've moments, and I'm no exception. It's just that so many of mine, and also by extension those of the band, happened to occur in the immediate afterglow of *Toto IV*. In the first instance, after the Grammys, we ought to have gone back out on the road to capitalise on our success. Jeff instead wanted to stay home, do sessions and for us to go straight in and make another record. Jeff could be very persuasive and intense when he felt a certain way about how things should go down, and 90 per cent of the time his instincts were bang on. He made a couple of judgement calls that, looking back, were not the right ones, but nobody ever knows this shit until afterwards. That one in particular was the wrong decision and because of it we blew our main chance to be a US arena-rock band.

Jeff was a homebody after he had his son Chris. In the old days, when not working, he always had cats hanging around. He had an interesting set of characters that could be at his pad at any given time, some living there for short periods. Jeff had aspired to have a figurative white picket fence, be married and have kids, and he got to have all of that, but also, I think, a little more than he might have bargained on. Not long after the Grammys, ABC News set up a story on the band. They wanted to do a story on us, and we were out at dinner at Chasen's restaurant, where I used to park cars. The cheapness of the idea was enough to make you roll your eyes, but the reporter they sent along to do the interview was a girl named Susan Norris and it was immediately obvious that she had made an impression on Jeff. He asked her out that very night and within a matter of months they were living together, but as I suspected at the time, there was an agenda with her. First was to get rid of all his old school friends and all the freaks who would just show up and hang: she didn't like us much at all.

Susan, of course, got to know Jeff in ways different to us, and he was totally different around her. He bought the whole conventional family life thing, just like in the old American sitcom *The Adventures of Ozzie and Harriet*. However, there were other aspects of Jeff's character and his past that she didn't understand at all. Jeff liked to be in control, that was true enough, but also to get a buzz on. There were a few funny nights of drinking out with the boys when he used to say 'Juiceheads are the lowest', then proceed to get shit-faced, but they were rare times. He liked to party but low-level, keep-it-together kind of partying. In Susan's mind, the rest of us were forever after cast as bad influences.

Bobby's physical and mental state made Jeff reluctant to tour. Bobby had deteriorated to the point where he simply would not have been capable of bringing it home every night. What our managers should have done, in hindsight, was hold everything up and force Bobby to go into rehab. They did step up and get him out of the mess that he was in on the intent-to-sell-drugs rap. That May, Bobby was cleared of those charges in court and escaped jail time. If they had also helped him to clean up, we would have been able to go on the road with him. Paich, though, had got a handful of great songs together and work began at the Manor on what would end up being, way more than a year later, the *Isolation* album.

To this day, Bobby goes around telling people that he cut a lead vocal for every track on that record. The truth is that we managed to pull just one out of him. That was for the song 'Lion', which was actually one of my favourites on *Isolation*, and it was painfully extracted over a period of weeks. Yet again, and to be fair to Bobby, Paich had written it at the very top of his range, but in general we had a tough time just getting him to turn up at all to the sessions. Once more, he would disappear for days at a time when we were supposed to be working. (Remember that there were no cell phones back then.) When he did show, more often than not he wouldn't have a voice to do anything with and we ran into a brick wall.

We had given Bobby countless chances. We had sat him down and told him that he had to get his shit together. We weren't saying that he had to be a schoolboy, but if he couldn't sing then he wasn't any good to us. Bobby was not an evil man, but blow is a very addictive drug and it had damaged him. It was Jeff who finally pulled the plug on him. He got up in the room one day and announced that we needed to get a real singer, one who would show up, do the gig, be able to deliver every night. 'We're going to have to let him go,' Jeff concluded.

That was a hard thing to do. It's one thing to bitch and moan about a guy behind his back, but a whole other deal when he is stood in front of you and you're about to take his livelihood away. Bobby didn't see it coming. He was stunned when we told him that the situation had gone on long enough and that it was over between him and us. To this day, he comes up with every possible excuse. It was the monitors, it was the headphones, or this or that. He can't admit that he had lost it and couldn't sing like he used to. It was tragic.

Nevertheless, Bobby's departure was also a body blow for us

as a band. We were at the height of our career and it really knocked us off course. The record company were aware of the problems that we had been having with Bobby, so weren't surprised at the outcome. They also knew that we still had two other lead singers in the ranks. I had fronted hits for the band and Paich had sung our biggest one of all, 'Africa'. However, our momentum was stopped dead. Before we could carry on any further with our new record, we had to find a singer who could hit Bobby's high notes. In the interim period, we made another off-the-wall call, which was to get ourselves involved in a film.

At that moment, rock and pop music was starting to creep into the world of film soundtracks, and all of a sudden to have a song featured in a blockbuster movie would be a very good career move. Two things were offered up to us. One was *Footloose* and the other a sci-fi movie, *Dune*. *Footloose* was clearly going to be a big film and we had the opportunity to do a song for it, but David Lynch was set to direct *Dune* and his offer was for us to write the whole score, which would be more orchestral than rock-and-roll.

Being an artsy-fartsy fuckhead, when I heard the words 'David' and 'Lynch' I was sold. I was obsessed with Lynch's films, especially *Eraserhead* and *The Elephant Man*, which had moved me greatly. I had also read some of Frank Herbert's *Dune* books as a kid. They had their own peculiar language and a bunch of other strange shit going on in them, so that you would have to read each three times just to make sense of the story. I had no idea how they were going to be translated onto film, but *Dune* was pitched to us as being the next *Star Wars*. To me, that was a way cooler prospect than a disposable teen flick such as *Footloose*. Paich was also desperate to compose for film and, since it wouldn't require a singer, it would buy us precious time.

We worked really hard on that job, too. Honestly, it was pretty much Paich's baby, but we all jumped in and wrote for it, and he was very gracious in spreading the publishing around to make it worth our while. I played a little electric guitar on the sessions, but mostly it was written for orchestra. David Lynch would come and sit in with us while we were recording the music, and he and I hit it off. I got to love hanging with Lynch. He would wear the exact same clothes every day: khaki pants, a white shirt buttoned up to the neck and a brown fleece flight jacket. This was in the middle of summer, a hundred degrees in the shade and there he was dressed for winter. He didn't seem to mind the heat and never even broke a sweat.

Lynch was a creature of habit. Opposite to his films, I never heard him swear, not even once. He told me he hated the smell of food being prepared and so would not cook in his own home. I ate lunch with him every day for three months and in the exact same place. He would only ever go to Bob's Big Boy, a fifties-style diner down in Burbank. They had an old-fashioned drive-thru and he loved that place. Every lunchtime without fail, Lynch had the same meal, which would be a Bob's cheeseburger and fries. He's a staunch vegetarian now, which I find hilarious looking back. We are still friends. I like him very much and we would get to know each other well through my brother Miguel Ferrer, who was in *Twin Peaks*, as was Kyle MacLachlan from *Dune*.

Lynch was clearly a brilliant man and could spin a story. I talked to him a lot about his work. Two years before it even got made, he gifted me the working script for what would be his next film, *Blue Velvet*. There was some really weird shit in Lynch's original version. In one of the most memorable scenes in the film, Dennis Hopper's character, Frank Booth, is sniffing oxygen through a face mask and talking a bunch of shit. That was disturbing enough as it was, but Lynch had intended for Hopper to have been inhaling helium as well and to then spout all that weird, demented gibberish in a high-pitched voice. I think the studio ended up convincing him that since his film was already off the chain this would be a step too far. For myself, I thought it was genius.

Matter of fact, Lynch ended up adapting another mad idea that I'm sure he got from me, but he won't admit it. One time, I told him a story about how my high-school buddies Mike Landau, John Pierce and I used to make comedy tapes on Mike's Teac four-track machine. We figured out that if we flipped the tape over, spoke backwards and then played the recording forwards, what you got was a very comical version of English. Next thing I knew, *Twin Peaks* had come out and one of the characters was a dwarf that talked backwards. Coincidence?

To put down the strings for our score, Paich and his dad flew to Austria and recorded the Vienna Symphony Orchestra. That escapade was another fiasco. We had pre-recorded all of our tracks onto two-inch tape and tuned to A 440. When Paich and Marty got to Vienna, they found out that the orchestra tuned to A 442. The orchestra refused point blank to tune to us, so Paich and Marty had to use this thing called a Variable Speed Oscillator to painstakingly and very finely tweak our two-inch tape until it was compatible with the strings' tuning. That was also required for a hundred-plus separate orchestra cues.

My job was to go to the sound mixes for the whole movie and represent the band while the other guys were playing catch-up finishing more cues to be added to the mixdown of the movie. I would be sat between the sound effects guy and the guy who mixed the dialogue, and Lynch would be there, too. The entire operation was run to strict union rules, so no one but the designated engineer was allowed to touch the board. Fortunately for us, the cat mixing the music, Steve Maslow, was an old acquaintance of ours from our old Sound Factory days and was very cool and liberal about allowing me to have my say. However, the sound effects guy was an asshole. There was one scene for which Paich had composed a very stately, beautiful piece and in it there was also a dog panting. This dude wanted the mutt to be louder than the music. Let me say that again: the dog's panting! We had some words about that one.

Ultimately, the movie didn't turn out the way that Lynch had envisaged. We were invited along to the premiere and almost hid under our seats with embarrassment. To rub salt into the wound, when *Footloose* came out it became the number-one movie in the country and the soundtrack album sold ten million copies. (Ironically, I played on that as well.)

Among ourselves, we refer to *Dune* these days as 'Doom'. To be sure, for anyone who was involved in it that was not a shining moment. In 1991, we played the Rock am Ring festival in Germany and Sting was due to go on directly after us. Infamously, Sting had taken one of the lead roles in the film and for the duration of it had been attired in what looked like spray-painted Speedos. We came off stage and I was cradling a bottle of German schnapps, which I had taken a big dent out of during our set. Sting was stood right there in the wings. I flung my bottle arm around his shoulders and said to him, 'Duuuune.' Sting just shook his head and intoned, 'Oh God.' It was the one time that the two of us have met and those were the only words that ever passed between us.

I worked on another soundtrack that year, for *Staying Alive*, the sequel to *Saturday Night Fever*. That was directed by Sylvester Stallone, who had spotted his lead actress, Cynthia Rhodes, when she starred in our 'Rosanna' video. (She later married my friend, Richard Marx.) It was a fun thing to do and I played on almost every song that got used. Afterwards, I took a call from Stallone himself, who asked me to teach him how to play the guitar. In that instantly familiar voice, he said to me: 'Yo, Steve, Sly here. I wanna get some guitar lessons.' He didn't play at all, so I told him I didn't think I was the right guy to help him from scratch. I said that patience was never a big virtue in my family, which made him laugh, and suggested that he start off with the basics. I gave him someone else's number. I don't believe Sly ever called that person, or that to this day he can play so much as a note on the guitar. Sly was very nice and it was cool to get a call from him.

Paich, Jeff, Steve and I also got called in to work on the Jacksons' *Victory* record – Paich and Steve were writing and producing some of it – which was positioned as the follow-up to *Thriller*. The whole thing had been agreed before *Thriller* went supernova, and since Michael hadn't yet toured his album, I think the idea was that he would go out as part of the Jacksons and for the brothers to get a big payday too. Paich and Steve wrote a couple of tracks for the record and I have a triple-platinum disc for *Victory* in my garage, but it was certainly no *Thriller*. Michael didn't appear to be as into it as the others were and it was a challenge to lock him down to perform anything. Michael was also meant to be producing the record, but every once in a while would sneak off and we would find him hiding out at the Manor, Paich's house and studio. Then again, a lot of people would vanish to Paich's place.

Other than very briefly at the next year's Grammys, I didn't see Michael again until I was asked to do something for his *HIStory* record in 1994. I was flown out to New York to put a bunch of acoustic parts down on one track, which at the time he liked but didn't end up using, although he used my surf guitar bits at the end. Before the arrival on the scene of the goon squad that Michael had latterly acquired, I worked with just Bruce Swedien, who was manning the desk. Quincy was not there. They had three studios going at once on this thing and, at one point, Michael came over from one of the others to ours. The lights were turned down low and he came into the room in a surgical mask. He took it off after admiring some humorous filth I had written on Swedien's computer, forgetting that Michael was going to show up. His appearance completely unnerved me. His face had totally changed from when we had last met, and somewhat terrifyingly so. You might think a member of his family, or someone else who was around him, would have challenged Michael about what he was doing to himself. I can only surmise that after having had all of that success and exposure, he had completely isolated himself from the rest of the world. He was a great-looking guy. He didn't need to do that. That's just my opinion, of course. But wow . . .

I did one more, ill-fated session with the other Jackson brothers for their 1989 album, *2300 Jackson Street*. Post the *Thriller* tour, they had money to burn and they made that album out at Tito's house where he had built a studio. At the time, I had a 1984 red Ferrari, like the one Tom Selleck drove in *Magnum PI*. I pulled into the driveway of Tito's place and the dad, Joe Jackson, was stood out there with his arms folded across his chest and scowling. I got out of the car and he barked to me, 'Where'd you get the car, boy?' I hadn't even said hello and he actually called me 'boy'. Now, Joe Jackson's reputation preceded him, but genuinely he was a very scary man. Get close, and you could feel the evil radiating off from him.

The scene became even more twisted once I got into the actual studio. For one thing, Don King was there, also scowling. I realised I was the only white guy there aside from the second engineer. There was a huge submarine sandwich laid out on a table and I said, 'Ah, I'm starving.' I was told that I couldn't have a bite until after I had played my part. Tito, who was always cool with me, revealed to me later that this was on the express orders of Jermaine, who was evidently in charge of things. I had stepped outside for a smoke and Tito followed me to bum a cigarette. He said to me: 'Don't tell Joe, man, cos he'll kick my ass.' This was his house and he was thirty-something years-old, but his old man was still going to beat his ass for having had a cigarette? Really?

Back in the studio we were cutting live with some cats I didn't know, and they had me put down a live solo on one track. They weren't using the regular guys, like Louis Johnson and JR, and from what I could glean nothing stunning was occurring. I did a take and a pretty good solo. At the end of it I said, 'I think that's the one, guys.' At that point, my confidence level from doing so many sessions was high and I would say if I thought something was right. Jermaine piped up, 'Do another one.' I can't recall how many takes he had me do in the end, but Jermaine bagged on me all day long and acted like a complete jerk. The whole experience made me feel very uncomfortable and sick to the stomach. When he finally released me, I went to have that sandwich and found it smothered in mayonnaise. And mayonnaise is like kryptonite to me. I fucking hate mayonnaise!

As usual, at the end of the session I signed the W4 form and split. You were then supposed to get your money within a couple of months, but after using me unusually hard, that motherfucker never paid up.

CHAPTER FIFTEEN

All of the time that we had spent on other people's music, we really should have been making our own record. However, the combined effects of *Dune* and Bobby's departure served to hijack our career for a year. Added to that, the movie had bombed. To many people, Bobby was the famous voice in our band, even though Dave and I sang on hits too. Hell, I sang on more hits than Bobby – 'Georgy Porgy', '99', 'I Won't Hold You Back', and we both sang 'Rosanna', 'I'll Be Over You' and 'I Will Remember – but Bobby had 'that' voice and when it worked it was great. But here we were now at the height of our career, and in shambles.

All those things combined were tantamount to being disastrous, but we were perhaps over-confident from having had the biggest record of the year and won all those Grammys. We thought that people would accept whatever we did and with whoever, because it was the band as a whole that they dug.

When at last we began to audition singers, it was almost a re-run of the Michael McDonald situation from our first record. Richard Page was the first guy who stood out. He was already known to us from the session circuit and an old friend, and came in and killed it. We offered Richard the gig, but he declined as he had a deal on RCA for his band Mr. Mister. I wanted a guy named Eric Martin, who I thought was awesome. Kootch produced his solo record and I played on some of it. To me, Eric had more of a Paul Rodgers swagger and sound, but we tried out quite a few other guys. Great singers. But no one fit.

Jeff had heard about another guy, Fergie Frederiksen. Fergie was then fronting a band called LeRoux. He had not long written that band a minor hit single, 'Carrie's Gone'. More important to us, he was a skinny rock-star-looking guy, which we thought was a plus, he sang super-high and was a very nice guy. We brought Fergie down to Jeff's studio, 'The Villa', to try out and he sang himself into the job.

Meanwhile, I was going crazy. *Dune* was a great one-time experience but I am a rocker and missed records and touring. I was antsy as hell to get back to the follow-up to *Toto IV*.

Work soon cranked up again on *Isolation*. We meant to recover any ground that we had lost, but were going headlong into a period of upheaval.

From the outset, *Isolation* was a different kind of record to *Toto IV*. Fergie had a similar range to Bobby's but a style very much of his own, so at a stroke that changed the sound of the band. It was also the first whole record that we had made with Mike Porcaro, who fit brilliantly. We set out to expand our musical vocabulary and once again not to repeat ourselves. Everybody also wanted to contribute more to the songs. For one thing, we had all realised that there was a lot of money to be made from songwriting and especially in those days of multi-platinum records. I'd had a hit with 'I Won't Hold You Back' and the money from that and all the other songs I co-wrote was a lot more than just being in the band. We all felt it: it was nice to have some money. Paich, Jeff and I started to come up with a lot more stuff together. Fergie wrote melodies and words with

Paich, but the music was by us. Steve was isolating himself more and more at Paich's house. He was, though, doing high-quality work and literally24/7.

As the sessions progressed, it began to feel as if the band was splitting into different camps. Steve was off on his own mission working on his special touches no one else could do. Paich would also be at the Manor with Fergie doing vocals. Jeff and I were at Record One with Greg Ladanyi and overseeing the mixes. Jeff now had the Villa, and had spent a lot of time and money putting together what was effectively a miniature version of Record One, with the same make of console and speakers.

Jeff was so happy and proud of his studio. He had always wanted one. We did a lot of work out there, so we were saving a lot of money too. He was proud that the band was using his place, but Susan wasn't so keen on having us around and then she wanted to start charging us money. Jeff rather sheepishly came in one morning and told us we were going to be charged for the studio, even though we as a band had paid for a lot of the gear in it. Look, I get it . . . the extra electric bill, sure. I understood that, but the real problem was Jeff's interesting stoner friends, some of whom were very weird, freaky cats. People would jump over the property fence in the witching hours and be in the studio when Jeff woke up. Once they were married and had their first child, Christopher, Susan wasn't about to tolerate that shit. She wanted to clean house and started on her plan to move him away from all of us.

That period was life-changing for me because Marie got pregnant while we were recording *Isolation*. I was beside myself with excitement about becoming a father and Jeff was one of the first people I called with the news. Jeff was already by then a super dad and was the happiest I had ever seen him – he was ecstatic around Christopher. He invited me over to the house to celebrate.

Paich was also having difficulties of his own and with Fergie. It was proving really difficult to put the vocals down and Paich had to ride Fergie hard take after take. It was weird because Ferg could sing great live but put a pair of headphones on him and his pitch was not good. As ever, Paich had written insanely high melodies and it took a lot of time, patience and takes to realise them. There was no magic about the process, that's for sure. We were all freaking out under the pressure of realising deadlines, but the more that Fergie struggled, the harder it became not to fear the worst and for the rest of us to think: 'Oh no, here we go again.'

At the same time as we were completing *Isolation*, Eric Clapton was also in LA wrapping up his *Behind the Sun* record. Eric had done most of that album with Phil Collins producing. However, his record company wanted him to put down a couple more commercially minded, singles-type tracks and he had to go back in with Ted Templeman and Lenny Waronker. Jeff got the call to do that date, and it was the only time that I ever asked to be on a session. I really wanted to meet and play with Eric. I was helped by the fact that the contractor for the date, a great old friend named Ivy Scoff, had once worked as an assistant to our original managers and the two of us had remained friends. I called her up and said: 'Ivy, what do I have to do to get on this Clapton record? I will do it for free. I just wanna be there and play.'

I knew Ted and Lenny from working with them on a Michael McDonald solo record, plus Rickie Lee Jones and Randy Newman things we had done together. They asked Eric and he said yes. I was very excited so they were happy to have me come down. They had assembled a great band to cut with Eric. Aside from Jeff, there was Nathan East on bass, Lenny Castro on percussion and on keyboards both Greg Phillinganes and Michael Omartian.

We were booked into a place called Lion Share Studios and when I arrived for the date, Eric was there to greet me at the door. His introduction to me wasn't exactly conventional. He pulled me to one side and asked to see my hands, which he took into his own, and he then proceeded to poke around at my fingers. After a moment of this study, he proclaimed: 'You don't have any callouses.' I had to tell him, 'Eric, I've just got out of the shower, but if you give it a minute they will be back.' I felt like 'Uh-oh, I failed test one.' He then told me a very sweet story about how he liked my solo on the end of 'Rosanna', which tripped me out as Eric is a huge influence and a hero to me. I was star-struck. That usually did not happen to me, especially at that point.

This was a period when all of us guitar guys would travel around to dates with monster racks made by my old friend and genius innovator Bob Bradshaw. There were walls of gear and cases of guitars at every session. The cartage guys were making a fortune. By contrast, all that Eric had was a Strat and a Fender amp and yet he had the most amazing tone.

The first time he plugged in and played a blues lick, I got shivers down my spine. I was in the room with Eric and he was playing and we started jamming a blues to get warmed up and get a feel for how the band would sound. Eric threw me a solo but I did not want to start playing fast and trying to over-impress him. I laid back and played a pretty simple solo. He was really checking out all my gear and I offered to let him try mine out. He dug it and was laughing, 'There's so many buttons.' Then he ordered a custom one for himself from Bradshaw.

The first song that Ted, Lenny and Eric hooked up for us was 'Forever Man'. I was meant to be doubling Eric on rhythm guitar, but it was one of the very few times that I got star-struck on a session. In my defence, this was a guy whose records I had spent hour upon hour listening to in my childhood bedroom, lifting the needle on and off so that I could learn every note of his solos. Now that I was in front of him, I sort of fell apart. All that I found myself able to do was strum along and stay out of the way musically and play the riff, which was most unlike me. Eric was very gracious on the day, but whenever I listen back to that track, I hear a hundred different things that I could have added to it but didn't.

I desperately wanted to have a second chance at playing with Eric, but that wasn't to be. Right after that session, he hired Nathan and Greg for his touring band. I was playing one night with Los Lobotomys at the Baked Potato and Nathan brought Eric down to the club. As always, the place was jam-packed and there was a guy on the door who refused to admit Eric. What kind of moron doesn't make room for Eric Clapton? No one in history has ever turned away Eric, except for this one guy. Fucking moron! This was before anyone had a cell phone, so I didn't get to find out what had happened until the next day when I got a call from Nathan. I tried without success to get hold of Eric to apologise and repeatedly asked Nathan to tell him how sorry I was, but that one incident seems to have put me on his shit list and I have not seen him since.

When *Behind the Sun* came out, I went along with Eddie Van Halen and his then wife Valerie to see Eric play at the Universal Amphitheatre. I got the tickets and passes, and before the show Eddie wanted to meet Eric so the three of us went backstage. As it turned out, only Eddie was allowed in to see Eric. I was left standing out in a corridor with Valerie and I was feeling rather defeated. That Eric appeared to blame me for something that I had no prior knowledge of still eats at me. There's not much I can do but say I am sorry, Eric.

Isolation ended up being a record that we were proud of, but it was painfully obvious that it didn't sound like the work of the same band that had made *Toto IV*. The omens for it were also bad. While we were still mixing the record, we had the idea of asking David Lynch to design an album cover for us. David had become a good friend of ours and was into doing it. He came up with the notion of building a conceptual piece that would be symbolic of the record's title and hired a team of people to help him create it, and also to make a short film of the entire process. Since both Paich and Jeff had regularly had their fathers work on our records, on this occasion I thought it would be fun to have my dad be involved, and got him hired as Lynch's assistant director. I didn't take into account the fact that my dad was genetically conditioned not to be impressed by anyone or anything.

My father was like a glorified bag man. Some directors and producers would hire him specifically to deal with temperamental stars. Hours on a shoot could be lost with the crew sat around waiting for a star to come out of his or her trailer, so my dad would be the one who would go break down the door and, if necessary, physically remove them. The star would then have Pops fired, but all of the crew guys would applaud him off the set. Then my dad would be re-hired for something else. Putting someone as no-nonsense as that in charge of a budget being spent by a maverick like Lynch was nothing but a recipe for disaster and, sure enough, the whole thing was a failure.

Lynch had this elaborate design of his made up on a Hollywood sound stage. It was meant to be an expanse of space peppered with black holes from one of which a human head would protrude. Every day of construction, Dad would call and tell me, 'This guy is out of his mind and he's spending your money like crazy.' And I would tell him back that David Lynch was a genius and not to worry. When we finally went down to see the finished work, it was not good. Jeff, our resident artist, was the most disappointed and it was obvious this was not going to be the cover. Dad stood there with a knowing look on his face and said, 'Well, here it is. This is what cost you twenty-five thousand dollars.' I felt terrible that we wouldn't be going with Lynch's idea.

In the end, when we were mixing at Record One, a guy brought down several things for us to look at and Jeff picked out an image that was even more surreal, which became the cover of *Isolation*. The good news is that David Lynch is still friends with myself and the guys.

The record company liked *Isolation* when they heard it, but then we started to argue with them about what the all-important first single should be. We had a new singer who we wanted to introduce and felt pretty strongly about a song Fergie had taken the lead vocal on, 'Endless'. They, on the other hand, wanted to go with something more familiar-sounding and specifically that Paich had sung (because 'Africa' had just been number one). To that end, we had a catchy little tune called 'Stranger in Town'. It was more of a synth-pop thing and that was also the sound that was just then all over MTV.

It was 'Stranger in Town' that got chosen and for which we also made a black-and-white video that was influenced by no one as much as David Lynch. The storyline was a take-off from a British movie of the sixties, *Whistle Down the Wind*, and we even had one of Lynch's regular actors, Brad Dourif, play the central character, a Jesus Christ-like figure. The band didn't appear in the video much and altogether it was a weird, quirky affair. We spent a shit-load of money on it and no one ever really saw it. By then, MTV had become all-powerful and could make or break your record. 'Stranger in Town' went top thirty, but that wasn't what anyone was anticipating from a band that had last had a number-one smash. The irony is it was nominated as video of the year by MTV.

From there, things spiralled from bad to worse. Before we had even finished the record, we had been booked to do a major arena tour of the States. Since we had previously been selling out theatres, it seemed at the time like a natural progression to move to arenas and we spent another 350,000 dollars of our own money on pre-production and rehearsals. However, ticket sales were slow at home and we lost our shirts. We had simply waited too long to go back out there and, what's more, were doing so with a new guy up front. By the time the dates rolled around, some places would be packed but others half-full or worse. To look out on a 10,000-seat arena and see just a quarter of that number of people was brutal. The venues would find ways to curtain off the empty seats and once the houselights went down it didn't matter to me – I always play the same way for ten people or 10,000. If anything, the band as a whole dug in that much harder to put on the best show that we could. We had the legendary Clive Franks mixing us live out front, giving us stunning sounds. He was Elton's guy and he made it sound like a record out front. We had a great tour . . . just not enough people showed up because we booked too big and waited too long.

A three-week break had been scheduled into the tour for when Marie was due to have our baby, but she was late. We tried everything conceivable to hurry the birth along, but to no avail and I had to re-join the tour, by which time my morale had sunk. We made it as far as Wyoming and the last song of our set, when I believe it was Bob Bradshaw who told me, 'Your wife is in labour. The plane is waiting.' We didn't even do an encore that night, but someone told the crowd I was having a baby and they cheered and were cool. Some of the guys had chipped in for the plane to take the financial heat off me and so they could see their families. We rushed straight from the stage to the waiting Lear Jet.

When I finally made it to Cedars-Sinai hospital in LA, I rushed in to see everyone, all excited, and things seemed to be going normal. Then the foetal heart rate plummeted, and so did Marie's. I was kicked out of the delivery room and in pieces. I was given no idea whether or not either my wife or unborn baby was going to pull through. It transpired that the umbilical cord had got wrapped around the baby's neck. Our baby doctor was this old guy Susan turned us on to but the second-in-command saw what was up and pushed him out of the way, got up inside and cut the cord. After that, I was allowed back in and the birth proceeded as normal. We didn't know if it was a boy or a girl. When they handed me my baby girl, I lost it, spilling tears of joy. When I think about it now, it still brings tears to my eyes. I had never loved anything as much in the whole wide world as little Cristina.

I just couldn't believe that I'd had something to do with this most beautiful creation.

Since Marie had such a tough time with the birth, I was given the baby and I insisted on her sleeping with me that first night. I don't think I slept much trying to care for them both. I was also horrified I had to leave in two days for another five weeks.

I cried my eyes out leaving the hospital and with having to return once more to the tour. For the next five weeks, I would call home every day and have Marie put the phone up to Tina's ear. That period of being apart from the two of them was excruciating and every day would feel to me like a year. There was some compensation in the fact that our record had done rather well outside of the States, and most especially in Japan. The Japanese shows were selling out but by then Fergie was having a tough time. He would have a couple of good nights and then start to lose his voice, which would force us to cancel shows. He was freaking out and under so much pressure that cold sores started to break out on his lips. Not that he got much sympathy from the rest of us. Each time that he got a sore, I would whip out a jar of strawberry jam and we would all smear it around our mouths just to taunt the poor guy. He was such a good guy he took it well. In his defence, some of these songs were just way high in key.

Isolation went gold in the US, sold more than a million overseas and went triple platinum in Japan, but back then that was thought of as a disappointment, and particularly coming off the back of a multi-million-selling record. The record company came down to see us play at the Ventura Theatre in LA and rather apologetically presented us with our gold discs. Between us in the band, we felt we had failed. Fergie took the brunt of it, which wasn't fair. It wasn't his fault, but we started to feel that we had made a mistake with him. After the tour, we also fired our booking agents in a rather shitty way, but really we were trying to pass the buck. Danny and Fred at Monterey were good to us and it wasn't their fault. Sorry, guys . . .

If it were possible to know how to be successful, no one would ever fail. However, if you have one hit, then you're automatically expected to able to do it every time. People were obviously waiting for us to serve up the next 'Rosanna' or 'Africa' like we were magicians.

CHAPTER SIXTEEN

After the *Isolation* tour ended, we were due to go to Europe but Jeff really wanted to stay home, do another record and keep doing sessions. I was busy all the time, too, so that's what we all did.

It was back to the drawing board and we hurried into the studio. Yet if we thought that burying ourselves in a new record would be the end of our troubles, we were soon to be proved otherwise. The big problem was with Fergie. Most of the time we would write, then cut the basic backing tracks, and then write lyrics and melodies afterwards. Quite quickly, we had a set of tunes, as everyone was writing at this point.

One of the first songs for what became the *Fahrenheit* record was 'Could This Be Love', a song of Paich's and for which Fergie came up with a lyric. Unfortunately, he had one hell of a time trying to actually sing it. Essentially, Fergie would get very nervous and not be able to stay in tune.

When it's not going well in the studio for a singer, it's a form of mental torture for them and in my experience often as not they deteriorate even further. For the rest of us, there was the growing frustration of yet again not being able to get a performance out of our lead singer. We did take after take at the Villa or the Manor. Fergie struggled to no avail. Jeff would be throwing up his hands and Paich sat slumped over the console. It was a fraught situation and one exacerbated by the fact that our previous record hadn't done the *Toto IV* numbers.

With nothing to show for our efforts, the record company eventually began to ask what the hell was going on and that ultimately did it for Fergie.

A group decision was made to cut our losses before things could get any worse. In our minds, we had found ourselves back at square one and so had no option but to let Fergie go. Unlike with Bobby, I think he knew that it was coming, but that didn't make it any easier for the rest of us. The most painful thing was that Fergie was one of the nicest cats you could ever hope to meet and we all liked the guy. Nobody in the band wanted to be the asshole who told him he was out, so we had our managers Larry and Mark deliver the bad news. He was obviously hurt, and I don't like making people feel bad. There was no bad blood and we stayed in touch. He even got up and sang with us years later at a gig in Minneapolis, and we had fun. Tragically, he passed away a few years ago now from cancer. I spoke to him right before he died.

Here we were once more, in the middle of another record and having to find a new lead singer. We had all kinds of people in to audition. James Ingram's brother, Philip, was one. Another was a guy named Max Carl (Gronenthal) who I had known from the Alley Studios days. Max had played keyboards and sung with the ex-Deep Purple guitarist Tommy Bolin and is now fronting Grand Funk Railroad. He showed up and sounded great, but didn't fit with what Paich wanted. There were more but they were unknown for the most part.

I again lobbied hard for Eric Martin, who was at the time leading his own band and would go on to sing with Mr Big. I thought Eric had the perfect voice for our songs, so we had him fly down from his home in San Francisco to try out.

However, right from the beginning the scene was not set fair for Eric. The morning that he arrived, I had been up all night. Our then tour manager Chris Littleton and I picked him up from Burbank Airport and I had a twelve-pack of beer on me. We went straight round to Paich's house and Paich wanted Eric to sing 'Could This Be Love'. Eric, though, didn't want to do the song in the key that Paich had written it and heard the hook phrased differently. Paich started to get very frustrated, so we called a halt and went out for a few drinks. Poor Eric proceeded to get plastered and then somehow rubbed Jeff the wrong way, which completely blew his chances. To me, it was really hard on Eric. He had just let his hair down, but Jeff was adamant.

Between us, we even had a brief conversation about where Bobby might be at. The answer was out on the road and using our name to sell tickets. People in Butt-Fuck, Nowhere, would see 'Tonight – Toto' billed at a little club, go along and it would just be Bobby up onstage. That was the first time that we caught him ripping off our name, but by no means would it be the last and we immediately scratched him off the list.

Out of the blue, Joseph Williams's name popped up. Joe was known to me from high school and through his elder brother, Mark, an excellent drummer, writer and all-around great cat, and we had played a lot together in high school. Jeff got hold of a cassette of new songs that Joe had written. These were really well-produced demos and Joe's singing was great. Around the time of *Toto IV*, I had worked on a solo album that Joe had made, which had my bro Jay Gruska as producer. Joe was still the same funny-assed little dude I recalled from childhood, but put him behind a microphone and he was like a machine and quite brilliant. He came along to the Villa and nailed everything that we threw at him, one impeccable take after another. Paich was ecstatic. Joe was also a real musician. As well as a singer, he's a keyboard player, songwriter and producer. Add in the fact that he could party but still show up bang on time the next day, and we were high-fiving each other at our good fortune in hiring him. We all loved the guy and his personality fit like a glove. He was family instantly.

In the midst of this latest lead-singer drama, Steve took a call about doing something with Miles Davis. Miles was recording an album of pop songs, *You're Under Arrest*, and wanted to cut a version of Steve Porcaro's song 'Human Nature', which had been a huge hit for Michael Jackson. It was arranged that Miles would come over to Paich's place and that they would put down some bits and pieces with him. The band was gathered at the Manor and we got word that Miles would be arriving imminently. Sure enough, at 10 p.m. precisely Paich's gate bell rang out.

In the hallway of his house, Paich had mounted a stuffed German shepherd dog in an attack position, and it looked very real. When the front door was opened to you, it would appear as if this great big, snarling beast was about to leap out and bite. We in the band had all of us walked by this thing so many times that we had pretty much forgotten about it. Miles knocked at the door. He was accompanied by his producer, legendary Tommy LiPuma, one of our dear friends and a cat we had worked with many times. Miles was decked out to look like everyone's idea of what Miles Davis would look like in person: red leather suit, long hair and with huge square dark sunglasses, even though it was ten at night.

The instant the door was swung open to him, Miles jumped back and freaked out. It took us a split-second to realise what was happening, but then all at once we started shouting, 'Whoa, Miles, the dog's a fake!' There was a moment of silence before Miles slowly walked into the hall, crouched down, lifted his glasses over his eyes and peered intently at Paich's dog. Then he announced in that fabulously rasping voice of his: 'I got some shit on me make that dog come *aliiiive*.'

As an opening line, that totally broke the ice. We were on the floor, laughing uncontrollably. Miles settled in and began to regale us with stories about the old bebop guys in New York, including how the drummer Philly Joe Jones had once spent all of his hotel-bill money on smack. He had to jump out of a two-storey window and broke his right leg, which is a pretty big drag for a drummer. Philly couldn't afford to have a doctor put his leg in a cast and what's more had to play a gig that night. According to Miles, Philly did the whole show left-footed and presumably dulled from the pain.

We were just enthralled by Miles. Here he was, the very hippest of cats, hanging out with just about the whitest motherfuckers in all of Hollywood.

Paich already had a germ of an idea for a Toto song Miles could play on, and I had jumped in to write the bridge so we had a tune that became 'Don't Stop Me Now', which was written in the vein of Miles's *Sketches of Spain* period. We had put down a pre-recorded track we cut at the Villa – it was very simple as we had no idea if Miles would do it or not – on the off chance that we might be able to persuade Miles to blow on the track.

We were egging each other on to ask him, but it was Paich who finally stepped forward and said, 'Miles, we've got this other song . . .' In his living room, Paich had two grand pianos lined up in tandem. Miles said, 'So let's hear it.' Paich sat at one piano and I sat at the other, and together we played this tune for Miles. After we had done, Miles said, 'That's cool, but what are you guys, Ferrante & Teicher?' They were a cheesy pop piano duo that had a couple of hits in the sixties, and we all cracked up.

They ended up going over to Jeff's house to cut the music because he had a bigger room and was going to overdub drums on to Miles's 'Human Nature' while Steve was working on his bits. Only a mad genius like Steve could come up with the mad intro he came up with. I think Paich helped him with it as well.

Once Jeff had done his take, we turned Miles's attention back to 'Don't Stop Me Now'. We had all our gear set up ready and we played it once live, but we knew it wasn't right because Miles suddenly wanted to change everything on the spot. As he would: no one tells Miles Davis what to play. To save time and not lose his interest, we asked him to blow whatever he wanted over the backing track. Miles said, 'Roll the tape,' and straight up put down the most unbelievable take. He was out in Jeff's studio blowing up a storm and we were in the control room screaming and pounding the floor, not able to believe what we were seeing or hearing. At the end of the track, Miles kept on playing and we left the tape rolling. That wound up being the last thing people heard on the *Fahrenheit* record, Miles Davis's horn blazing off into echo.

After that, it didn't really matter to us what the critics said about our band. You can't get any cooler than having Miles Davis dig what you do. Matter of fact, a couple of months on from that session I got a call from Miles. He wanted me to fly out to New York the following day and join up with his band. I asked him, 'Why me?' I mean he had Mike Stern, John McLaughlin and all these other legends on guitar in his band. His answer was, 'I like that rock-and-roll shit you do.' As it happened, I was leaving the next day because Toto was about to go off on the huge, sold-out *Fahrenheit* tour of Europe. I told Miles how deeply honoured I was at his offer, but that I couldn't possibly bale on my brothers the night before. He understood, but I hung up the phone thinking, 'Fuck, I just said no to Miles Davis.' The truth is, Miles being Miles, I might have been with him for just the one day and he could have fired me.

Miles also took a unique form of payment for being on our record. Both he and Jeff shared a passion for art. Jeff had wanted to be an artist even before he took up the drums and Miles happened to see a figure drawing that he had done. Jeff had called it *Martini Man*. I had it tattooed on my right arm after Jeff passed. Miles said to him, 'I want that drawing, but I'm going to make you one first.' He sent out for some pens and paper, and sat and did this sketch for Jeff. Miles was a hell of an artist, too. He wouldn't take any more for the track than Jeff's picture. When

David Foster found out Miles had worked with us, he tried to get him to play on one of his records. Foster was no doubt expecting a similar arrangement, but when he called him, Miles snapped: 'Fifty grand, man.' We heard about it and cracked up. Like I said, there was no one hipper than Miles Davis.

Every now and again, and when he was hung up on something, Foster would still call me. One of the last times that I worked with him was right around that same period, in late 1985, on a Neil Diamond record called *Headed for the Future*. Foster was producing that one and booked me in for a live date, where the band and Neil would be playing together in the room. The session was out at Village Recorders in Santa Monica. We got there, set up and, even before we had played a note, Neil walked in and sparked up a jazz cigarette. To the other musicians I was going, 'Yo, dig the Diamond, man!' Neil, who was such a nice man, looked around and said to the room, 'Does anybody want a hit of this?' Nobody else replied, but I piped up, 'Fuck, yes!' I wasn't about to pass up the opportunity of having a hit with the Diamond. I only took a couple of puffs, but Foster seemed pissed for the rest of that day and I felt it was because I'd had the balls to smoke on his session. It didn't affect me as a player. Once the tape was rolling, Neil was a total pro, very appreciative of the musicians and every vocal take that he put down was pitch-perfect. I was honoured to be there. It was the last time Foster ever called me for a session, which was fine as I was winding down as a session guy. I started saying no a lot.

I had one other memorable diversion during the time that we were cutting *Fahrenheit*. Mister Udo is Japan's version of the late, great promoter Bill Graham, but the son of a samurai and the sweetest man alive.

A legendary promoter, he had brought the Beatles over to Japan and he and I have been dear friends since Toto's first visit to his country in 1980. He called me to ask if I would like to do a one-off show in Japan with Jeff Beck and Carlos Santana, and I almost dropped the phone. Jeff Beck, Santana and Lukather: it sounded like something I might have dreamed up myself as a teenager.

Udo's proposal was that I would sit in with both Jeff's and Carlos's bands and then the three of us would jam together as a finale. Rehearsals went ahead at SIR, a studio on Sunset Boulevard. I was a little nervous, since I had effectively been thrust upon both Jeff and Carlos. I had also heard on the musicians' grapevine that Jeff could be somewhat difficult if he didn't like you.

When I showed up, Jeff asked me what I wanted to play with him. As I knew all of his stuff, I told him that anything he wanted to do would be cool with me, which I guess made him relax a little. We began to play and it was like I was living out a fantasy from junior high. I was stood next to Jeff and looking around the room at the rest of his band, every one of whom was a world-class musician. He had Simon Phillips on drums, Jan Hammer from the Mahavishnu Orchestra on keys, Doug Wimbish, who went on to play with Living Colour, on bass and Jimmy Hall from Wet Willie to sing some of his old blues stuff. We had a blast and all through that day I was living a dream.

Jeff warmed up to me, as did the band, and rehearsals went well. My sense of humour has carried me through many an uncomfortable situation. I was being self-deprecating and made Jeff laugh a lot. It also helped that I could play. Jeff, meanwhile, played his Strat through a little rat fuzz tone and a Marshall amp, and sounded positively godlike.

Carlos showed up for about ten minutes of the rehearsal. He had written a one-chord shuffle in E for us to jam to and so each of us would be able to throw solos around the groove. He was another childhood hero who turned out to be very nice. Who knew that one day I would be in a band with his original keyboard player, Gregg Rolie, who is a dear friend?

In Japan, we were sequestered at a luxury mountain golf resort called Karuizawa. It was a hundred miles from Tokyo and pretty much in the middle of nowhere, but the gig was to 15,000 people and being filmed for national TV. The whole thing ended up being pretty loose. I kind of bullshitted my way through Carlos's set as no one told me what to learn. I knew a bunch of his music as a fan and I knew a lot of his musicians – man, they were good. I was able to find a little pocket in each of his tunes and took a solo whenever he pointed at me.

It was the same deal with Jeff's band, and they came out and killed. Jeff had his *Flash* album out at the time, which for him was more straightforward, but he was also doing some of the amazing instrumental stuff from his brace of classic seventies records, *Wired* and *Blow by Blow*. As an encore we did 'Johnny B. Goode' with Carlos, and Beck also had Buddy Miles of Hendrix's Band of Gypsys fame come out to sing with us. Buddy was a groover and he told me a bunch of Hendrix stories. When I first met him, I started playing the song 'Who Knows' from the *Band of Gypsys* album and he smiled at me and we became pals after that.

That was the loudest show I have ever done. Monitors were strung right across the front of the stage and there were huge side fills and monitors all around the back, too. I had never seen anything like this before and this was for a primarily instrumental band. In total, there must have been 125 decibels pumping out onstage. When everybody came out to play together at the end, the sheer volume got to be unbearable for me. Jeff motioned for me to take a solo and I had to jump over the front monitors because the sound pressure had got so great that it was like having my head in a vice.

That one move has followed me around like herpes. As the show was televised, it has since ended up on YouTube and count-less people have bagged on me for looking as though I were raging on cocaine. I'd had a couple of cocktails, yes, but not blow. They would throw you in jail and throw away the key if you had hard drugs on you in Japan. I wasn't high or trying to hot dog anybody, but just desperate for some sonic relief. I was in pain.

To add insult to injury, and due to the need for the analogue tracks on the tape machine, they only recorded one half of my guitar system, which subsequently made it sound like it was all effects and no original guitar sound. This was to be a one-time TV event. But thanks to the miracles of YouTube, I have been shit on for decades for the sound and performance of that. You don't get paid for insults. I've suffered from tinnitus from that night in '86, and I've not heard silence ever since. In musician speak: it's triple D above middle C 24/7. In other words pretty fucking high . . .

That aside, we thought the show was a great success and afterwards we went partying to celebrate. I was in my twenties so I was still bulletproof. I ended up engaged in a sake-bomb drinking contest with Jeff's road manager, Al Dutton. Al was a nice guy, but he looked a little like Jeff. He had the exact same haircut and people would stop him and ask for his autograph. The hotel bar we were in was split between three levels. Al and I were on the top level, and Jeff and the others were sat down at the bottom. At one point, I drank down a sake bomb in a single chug; I leaned back on my chair and kept right on going. I went down three flights of stairs, flipping over backwards one, two and three times. It was like a circus trick. Like an acrobat, I landed on my feet and announced to the room, arms up like an Olympic gymnast, 'I am absolutely fine.' Not a mark on me. I got applause, and also disbelief. Had I not been shit-faced, I would have broken every bone in my body.

In every sense, *Fahrenheit* was a hell of a record. Joe sang his ass off. He could not have strayed out of tune if he had tried and we blazed through the tracks, which was a source of enormous relief. Henley also came in and sang on a song of Steve's, 'Lea'. We considered it a great gift that Don would agree to show up. He could sing the alphabet and it would be incredible. The funny thing was, he flat-out refused to sing one line in the song, which was, 'Lea, my concertina.' There was just something about that word and the rhyme that got to him. Steve ended up saying, 'Look, Don, do whatever you want.'

I also started to work with an outside writer on that record, a guy named Randy Goodrum. It was my mom who introduced the two of us because Randy lived directly behind her, and we hit it off immediately. Randy's a great musician and had written songs for so many people in so many styles, and all Steve Perry's hits off his first solo record. He also had his own studio where we were able to make lush demos. One of the first of these was for a big ballad we wrote together, 'I'll Be Over You'. Having written for the Tubes and George Benson, I had meant to give it to someone else and played it to the guys just to see what they thought of the tune. Jeff in particular pushed for it to be my song on our record, and as a kind of follow-up to 'I Won't Hold You Back'. They even arranged for Michael McDonald to come down to the Villa and sing a great part on the song.

Towards the end of recording, Columbia had started to put together the soundtrack for the movie *Top Gun* with Giorgio Moroder supervising things. Paich and I went along to an advance screening of the film and it was obvious to us that it would be a big hit. Since we had missed out on *Footloose*, we were determined to make amends. We were told that the producers were looking for a love song, a ballad, and so Paich and I went back to the Manor that same day and wrote and demoed up a tune called 'Only You', on which I sang. We were convinced that we had hit a home run with that one.

The two producers of *Top Gun*, Don Simpson and Jerry Bruckheimer, came out to Paich's place to listen to what we had. Simpson was infamous for his ego and the first thing that he said to us was, 'Who's got the red Ferrari outside?' He had the same car and was kind of pissed that I had one, too. Paich and I excitedly played them the song. Their joint response was, 'Uh, it's OK. Have you got anything else?' The only other thing we had that fit the bill was 'I'll Be Over You', so we played them the rough of that and they started to effuse about how it was great, a hit, and this and that. 'We'll get back to you,' Simpson said and they split. Not long after, our management got a call to say that they were going to pass on the song. We saved 'Only You' for our next record. They did, though, have another song that they wanted us to cut. It was by Moroder and even though we told them we didn't do outside material, they sent over a demo of this track, 'Danger Zone'.

We cried with laughter the first time that we heard that song. It was made up of just one chord and pure cheese. In the end, though, we did go to work on it, added some chord changes, did a spot of rearranging and made up a demo of our version. All along, I kept on telling the guys, 'Remember, if this thing is a hit then we'll have to sing it for the rest of our lives.' It would be like handing our critics a baseball bat with nails through it to beat us over the head. We submitted our take on 'Danger Zone' and got a call back to say, 'It's really good, except we're just going to use Joe's vocal and bring in some studio players to do the other parts, but it will be a huge hit record and really good for you guys.' We just went, 'No.' Columbia was furious with us, but we were deeply insulted. They were going to bring in studio players? We *are* A-studio players. We were pissed and insulted that we had polished this turd and got no love.

When 'Danger Zone' subsequently came out, Kenny Loggins was singing our arrangement of the song. Kenny's a good dude and would have had no idea what had previously gone on, but we were furious. Those motherfuckers stole from us. And, of course, the record went to number one and Kenny still has to sing it every night.

Altogether with *Fahrenheit* we thought that we had salvaged our situation. It sold millions worldwide, Joe was on fire and we had a number-one hit with 'I'll Be Over You'. The record company put it out first because a ballad was safe territory, but it further cemented our 'soft rock' status (a term that tightens my sphincter) in radio and critic land.

We went out on tour around Europe and that was a sell-out smash. I felt as if we were back on track and it felt good to be on the road worldwide with a hit. We were getting soccer chants every night. It was good for my bank account as well. When *Fahrenheit* came out in the summer of 1986, it gave us other hit songs, including one of Paich's that I also sang on, 'Without Your Love', which Tommy Chong directed. A bunch of the guys were pissed off because we had an unbelievable singer in Joe and he was grossly underused. When it came to the singles, Steve's song 'Lea' was a hit in certain parts of the world but wasn't released as a single in the States. He was getting even more angry and frustrated, and he was slowly pulling away from us.

Marie had got pregnant again during the period that we were making the record. I found out I was going to have a son when we were doing the TV show *Solid Gold* in 1986. I was thrilled as I was the last Lukather in the family and I needed a son to carry on the name.

Unbelievably, at the birth we had the same freak-out with the umbilical cord getting wrapped around my son's neck, but on this occasion it was corrected right away and we had the sweetest baby boy, Trevor. It was another of the most joyous moments in my life. I had a son! (A son who is now my best friend.)

I was on a high. I couldn't possibly have known that we were going to be hit with one hammer blow after another.

CHAPTER SEVENTEEN

Our world spun so fast that it would take your breath away. One minute you might have your head in the clouds and the next your ass on the floor. It got to be so that I took nothing for granted and had no expectations, except that anything could happen. That was never truer than during the next five whirlwind years of our lives, when I enjoyed some of the best of times, but then again endured the very worst. There were days of pure ecstasy and as well periods of being in a deep black hole of despair. None of it killed me, so I guess it must have made me stronger, but I acquired scars that will never heal. In the end, I hurt someone I loved and I had little kids who were everything to me . . . I was at a crossroads in my life. I was more lost than anything.

With *Fahrenheit* having done well, our services were as in demand as ever. Most of the band worked on Jon Anderson of Yes's solo album, *In the City of Angels*. That was an honour and a joy because I had stood in line to see Yes on their *Close to the Edge* tour in 1972. Jon was very nice to us and one night endured me asking Yes-geek questions. He laughed and was cool about it.

An even bigger trip for me was playing on Cher's self-titled album of 1987. I hadn't seen Cher since I had followed her around on the *Chastity* film set all those years ago and it was like coming around full circle. My surname is pretty unique, so sure enough she recognised me. She pretty much gasped, 'Oh my God, it is you!'

Cher's unbelievably talented and I went on and did a bunch of her records. We got on well and I even dated her best friend Paulette for a brief time. She was real nice, and Cher was real nice – not fake nice. It was good to be around her. She treated me very well. I played on a bunch of her hits like 'I Found Someone' and 'If I Could Turn Back Time' etc.

It was around this time I was becoming friends with John Kalodner, who was the guru of radio and A & R at the time, and he had me on most of what he was doing, no matter what. We had a friendship. He was a one-of-a-kind man. Through the Cher album I also got to work with songwriter Diane Warren, who is always very involved in her songs, and Michael Bolton, who is a nice cat. Then I produced a track on Cher's *Love Hurts* album, which went gold. The track was Gene Simmons's song 'World Without Heroes' and I did a massive production/arrangement on it, way different than Kiss. Gene came down to a mixing session at A & M where we were working and he loved it..

Jeff also had a session right around then with a couple of friends, Billy Payne of Little Feat fame and George Massenburg. (Paich and Steve P were totally into Billy as a keyboard player.) I had previously done a bunch of sessions with Billy, loved him, and worked with George on Earth, Wind & Fire's *Faces* album. Billy and George made a point of lobbying Jeff to produce our next record. Jeff was open to the idea, and thought those guys might light a fire under us. We would get some fresh new music and we needed hits. We had a meeting, hit it off and they got the gig. It turned out to be a great idea. We had got on like a house on fire. George and I were like two demented souls meeting in the night, and this was proved a million times during the sessions for Toto's next album, *The Seventh One*.

At that point, we were on a roll with our songwriting and in large part driven by a positive sense of one-upmanship. Paich was particularly prolific, and I had built a small studio in a guest room at my house so was able to write a lot more with Randy Goodrum. Randy and I came up with a ballad, 'Anna', that everybody in the band loved. It turned out to be one of my better songs and the band's productions, if I can say that without sounding like a dick. Paich put down a track called 'Pamela' that immediately sounded like the heir apparent to 'Rosanna'. Then Paich and I together worked up what seemed like a sure-fire hit, 'Stop Loving You'. Joe was also coming up with all sorts of great stuff. It felt as if we were going in to make this next record armed with a lot of classic Toto-style songs, but then Steve Porcaro dropped the bombshell that he was quitting the band.

There were a number of factors that influenced Steve's decision. For one thing, he had embraced the latest technology and the rest of us hadn't. He would come up with all of these intricate, brilliant parts, which would invariably end up getting buried on our records, and that led him to fight with his big brother, Jeff. In fairness to Steve, he also wasn't as well represented with his songwriting as he might have been. Altogether, he was hurt that his voice wasn't being heard in the band and felt undervalued. In addition to all that, there was a lot of 'self-medicating' going on. I was drinking way too much. There was too much bullshit going on within the band and that had blurred everybody's thinking.

I never thought Steve would really leave. I thought he was just on a rave or something, and we all have bad days. I was crushed at his decision, because had it not been for meeting him at high school, my life would have been very different. His parts, sound and touches really help make Toto special to my ears.

It turned out to be the weirdest departure from a band in the entire history of rock-and-roll. He went right on living over at

Paich's house and also continued to contribute to what became *The Seventh One* record. He wouldn't, though, be party to any other band business. We paid him as if we were hiring him for a session. He wouldn't do interviews or be in photographs, but ended up going on tour with us. He left, but he didn't.

George Massenburg was insistent that the band make the record at his studio, the Complex, in West LA. All of our gear was moved down there. Both George and Billy thought that we were missing a rocker, so in the main room we jammed up an epic piece, 'Home of the Brave', that later we had the great Jimmy Webb come in and write some of the lyrics for. It has become one of the staples of our live show. George was brilliant, and had engineered some of my favourite-sounding records by the likes of Earth, Wind & Fire, Linda Ronstadt, Little Feat, etc, but we tested his patience to the limit and especially when it came to the mixing.

By that stage of the process, we had already spent months meticulously doing overdubs. We devoted at least two days to mixing each song, getting them to sound just so. The level of detail was ridiculous microscopic shit, and with Jeff, Paich and me riding George, there were also a lot of chiefs in the room. George got to be pulling his hair out. Eventually, he stuck up pictures of us on the wall above the console and brought a blow-gun with him into the studio. Whenever any of us would make a suggestion, he would yell out, 'No!' and blow a lethal dart right at a picture, right between the eyes.

Billy, on the other hand, was much more of a laid-back, straight-ahead guy. He had lost Lowell George, his close friend and co-founder of Little Feat, to a drug-induced heart attack at just thirty-four. The rest of us would stay at the studio until three in the morning and it would be rather obvious what we were up to, but Billy didn't want to know about that kind of shit. That was apart from one occasion that we were holed up doing illicit things in the bathroom while waiting for something to get fixed, and Billy marched in and ripped into us. He shouted us out: 'What the fuck are you guys doing? You've got to stop with this shit – it killed Lowell, man!' He had tears in his eyes, too. We just stood there frozen to the spot and open-mouthed.

An after-hours club sprang up at Paich's house as it was right on the way home from the Complex. As well as Steve, Joe had basic-ally begun to live out there too. In fact, Joe soon enough let himself go a bit and his voice got somewhat ragged (I should talk). It was all too easy for me to stop off at Paich's on my drive home, and often as not I would stay all goddamn night long. Paich had a housekeeper, Patti, who would come in at seven in the morning and slam open the studio door. We would still be in there, like vampires, and she would berate us: 'Don't you people have homes to go to? Get the fuck out of here!'

I would have drunk so much that I had to call a cab. Indeed, the Ferrari spent so much time abandoned outside of Paich's that he was going to get me a personalised parking space.

The difference from my younger years was that I was married with kids and my lifestyle was beginning to crumble my relation-ship with my wife. Of course it was, because while I was off raging, Marie would be stuck at home with two screaming kids. That was a tough job. Regularly, the phone would go at Paich's house and I would hear her ask: 'Where's my fucking husband?'

The Seventh One came out in early spring of 1988. We thought it was one of our strongest records and Columbia was also thrilled. In America, 'Pamela' was the first single. The president of the label, Al Teller, swung the full company muscle behind it, so that it seemed as if we were going to have an 'Africa'-sized hit – top ten or even better. We even went to dinner with Teller one night to celebrate how the record was doing. The very next week he left the company. It then took an age for him to be replaced, and with no one at the helm 'Pamela' stalled at eleven on the *Billboard* Hot 100 and fell away. That was the moment that our star dwindled in America and it would take years for us to recover momentum.

Thankfully, it was a different story elsewhere. In Europe, 'Stop Loving You' had been the lead-off song and gone on to be a number-one to top-ten smash in most countries. In its wake, the album went gold to multi-platinum in regions across the continent, and we did a sell-out tour of arenas. Steve P joined us for the dates and, for the first time, we were joined by our new English tour manager, Martin Cole, who was to become my great friend and co-conspirator. Martin's reputation as an outstanding tour manager and accountant preceded him. He was also a great hang.

I nicknamed him 'Tay' or 'Martay', like the guy from the Eddie Murphy movie *Trading Places*. I loved the man and still do.

The tone for Martin's time with the band was set one night in Germany on that tour. Our German promoter Ossie Hoppe took us out to dinner. During the course of the evening, he had trays of a quite lethal drink brought out. ApfelKorn shots were ice-cold, sweet schnapps that went down way too easily, like cold Martinelli's apple juice, but had a kick like a shovel in the face at full speed with no warning. Most everyone got a massive buzz on from this stuff, but Martin in particular. At a certain point in the evening, he scooped up a platter of mashed potato and was going to throw it over our manager, Mark Hartley, and me. I warned him, 'Martin, if you do this you will live to regret it,' but he nevertheless took aim and fired. Dollops of potato splattered all over the two of us and a full-on food fight ensued. In the midst of the chaos, I swore revenge.

Whenever we were on the road, Jeff would always draw caricatures of what we had got up to the night before and have them Xeroxed on to the next morning's call sheets. Jeff had a real flair for bringing out people's worst features and so I asked him to draw me a picture of Martin. Tay's uniform was a suit jacket and T-shirt, and Jeff sketched him in that, but from the waist down rendered him in leather panties, fishnet stockings and heels. He drew him holding hands with a cherubic English schoolboy who had in his other hand a balloon. Underneath this picture, Jeff inscribed, 'Martin Cole for Parliament' and various other, unprintable things.

I called up our European agent and friend Alec Leslie in London and asked to have thousands of seven-by-four-foot posters of this cartoon made up, and for them to be distributed all over London. The bill for this ran to 4,000 dollars. The legendary Hammersmith Odeon was the last date of the tour and when we arrived by bus, I asked Martin to have the driver detour by the venue so that we could scope it out and dig the sold-out signs. As we drove through the underpass immediately before the Odeon, the unsuspecting Martin saw the first poster of himself in leather panties. 'You bastard!' he shrieked in his upper-crust English accent and stared me down. Howling ensued. As more and more of these posters popped up along our route, Martin turned a vivid shade of puce, but it was one stuck to the side of Harrods that tipped him over the edge. 'My mother shops here, you wanker,' he snapped at me. He swore never again to go into battle against me.

Such moments of levity were a very welcome distraction from the darker side of that tour. Joe had got himself caught up in the rat wheel. He had sounded a little rough in rehearsals, and that had given us cause for concern. To make matters worse, the first show was in Amsterdam and to be broadcast live on national radio. Since infamously you can get whatever you want, day or night, in that city, we cautioned Joe not to party too hard beforehand. Joe didn't heed our warning. When we hit the stage, it fast became apparent that he had helped himself to something debilitating. Joe opened his mouth to sing the first note and not a sound came out. Panic-stricken, he turned to us and mouthed, 'I've got nothing.' Holy fuck, this was the opening night of a five-week tour and it was a disaster. We were furious with him. And it went out live on the radio.

Joe's voice didn't really recover after that. We had to add songs to the set that Paich or I could sing, or else have Warren Ham, who we had brought along to play sax and sing back-ups, come out and cover for Joe. That was still like putting a Band Aid over an amputation and all of us turned on poor Joe. We tried to banish him to his hotel room and forbid him from seeing anyone in the hope that he would sleep and get well. It was all so sad. We were all partying way too much considering what was going on, like it would make it go away or something. I wish we had done things differently.

Paich and I would get pissed at him, but Jeff was seething and more unforgiving. Mikey, who was always so laid-back then, tried to see both sides.

I loved Joe and didn't understand why he couldn't get himself together, but he was also hurting from being ostracised by the rest of the band. That only made him anaesthetise himself all the more. In truth, we had all kind of lost the plot, but it was Joe who had got himself into the deepest hole. When you're still pretty young, as Joe was, you think that you're bulletproof. The toughest thing is finding out that you're not. At the end of the run, Jeff convinced the factions in the band that we should cut Joe loose and rethink things all over again. These days Joe is back and singing better than he ever did.

CHAPTER EIGHTEEN

Towards the end of *The Seventh One* tour, the escalating problems with Joe had caused tension to spread all through our ranks. By the time we came off the road, we needed more than anything else to get away from each other and from being in Toto. We all felt thoroughly deflated by Joe's loss of voice, no more so than he. Joe and I had been friends since we were kids, and he was getting the cold shoulder. I tried to play both sides but Jeff was a strong force and when he went off on you, you knew it. It's the old rule: 'I don't care what you do as long as you can still do the gig great.' I shamefully admit that Joe was getting vibed even from me. I loved the guy and he still is one of the funniest cats ever. I always believed in him and his talents but he fucked up . . .

I think Jeff himself was considering whether or not he wanted to continue with the band. He'd had another child, Miles, and was missing his kids while also under pressure from his wife. Jeff was still two different guys. One around us. One around her. He still wanted to be Ozzie and Harriet at home, but he could be like a little Ozzy Osbourne when she wasn't looking and he was on the road. We were sworn to secrecy.

If my brother was happy, that was cool with me, and I felt for him. I really dug his kids and was excited to have two of my own. I know what missing your kids is like. I have four and I've experienced thirty-plus years of it.

He missed his kids, he was pissed at Joe and the band wasn't sure where it was going. We did great everywhere else, but we were only doing OK in the States, and that was to become a mantra. The session scene at home sounded more inviting, yet he loved being on stage too. He was torn for a bit. So was I.

The break was viewed as more of a hiatus and nobody came out and said that they meant to quit, but I was the first of the guys to jump into doing something else.

As the dust settled, I started to get the sense that Toto might not be put back together so wanted to see if I could establish a career outside of the band and make a solo record. In the first instance, I was determined that it would be a real rock-and-roll record. I was so desperate to be taken seriously as a rock guitarist, which in retrospect I find ridiculous. I am what I am, but at the time I was hanging out with some of the flashier and more heavy-metal-type players.

Marie had been patient with me doing sessions, touring and partying all the time but it couldn't last. I thought I could stay mostly at home in 1989, make a solo record and see how the guys felt after a nice long break.

Since I had written some hits for the band, the record company gave me a good budget and I jumped right into the studio. At the same time my marriage was falling apart.

It was an album that I made with my friends. Firstly, I had hit it off with Steve Stevens, Billy Idol's guitarist, and the thought of writing and recording some tracks with him was exciting. I wrote a couple of songs with him, 'Darkest Night of the Year' and an epic piece, 'Fall into Velvet', for which Cy Curnin from the Fixx wrote the lyrics. He was a nice cat and said he took some 'shrooms before he wrote the trippy lyrics. No doubt. I loved them. We cut both tracks at Right Track studios in New York with Jan Hammer, Thommy Price on drums, my brother Will Lee on bass, Steve and me on guitars and Cindy Mizelle on additional vocals. It was a psychedelic jam with all solos live, and it was a great experience. We did some hanging, it was a lot of fun and we got some great music out of it. I love NYC.

I co-wrote another track, 'Twist the Knife', with Eddie Van Halen, for which he also came in and played bass. I had been bugging Ed to do something with me. Getting to work with him was a real coup for me because he very rarely operated outside of Van Halen, except on *Thriller* and an early eighties track that he had done with Brian May of Queen.

I also asked his brother Alex to play on the album. He said, 'No,' because he *never* plays on anything outside of Van Halen. He was really not happy about me working with his brother on recorded music, either. Al and I are still great friends but he called me to let me know he didn't want me to use Eddie's name on the record. My heart sank a little because I knew that having Ed on my record would give me the rock credibility I so desperately still wanted after taking so much shit from the press that Toto was a pussy pop band.

I said, 'OK, Al,' rather bummed. I told Ed I would use a fake name for him.

For that date, it was just Eddie, Carlos Vega on drums and me. Shep Lonsdale was my engineer, and a few others worked on the album, while Greg Ladanyi mixed it for me. Shep and Greg did a killer job for me and I was mortified when the album came out and their credits had been left off.

We holed up at One on One Studios in North Hollywood, where at the same time Metallica were making their 'Black Album'. Ed had a jam pretty much written and I wrote a melody and the lyrics. Not surprisingly, the finished track ended up sounding rather Van Halen-like. Ed was famous for coming up with weird harmonics and for the sheer strangeness of his tunings, both of which I had to grasp. He had me put a low bass string on my guitar, tuned it to an A and then tuned the whole guitar up a step. Even for a guitarist, this was weird stuff.

Nobody ever called in my high-school buddy Carlos to play rock-and-roll shit, so he was thrilled. He was playing with James Taylor at the time, which he loved but that couldn't have been more different. I asked Carlos to unleash his inner Keith Moon and he did just great. We did a bunch of different takes, all of which ripped, and it was obvious that 'Twist the Knife' was going to be side one, track one of the album. The three of us hung out after the session, listening back to what we had cut. Ed must have liked the song because in the end he said, 'You can use my name.'

It turned out to be a great day for me to remember Carlos by. Ten years later, on 7 April 1998, my dear friend Carlos took his own life at forty-one. Man, how that one hurt. Carlos was an incredible drummer and also the sweetest, funniest guy, never without a smile on his face or a sarcastic barb.

I never saw it coming. Carlos had talked to me about the fact that there was depression in his family, but I didn't think too much about it because he appeared the happiest cat alive. Also, everyone has depression in their family (I have it), just like everybody has an alcoholic, a drug addict, a gambler and a gay uncle or aunt etc. Carlos was the minister of good vibes. He had a loving family, beautiful kids and a great gig with James Taylor. By that time, he was also playing in a band called Burning Water with our other great friend Mike Landau and Mike's brother Teddy and David Frazee, and they were starting to make some noise. All of us who knew Carlos were speechless when he took his own life. I don't know if you ever get over such a thing.

Nobody can ever really know what makes a man go there. His doctors gave him something for his depression, which I think gave him a negative reaction. He was also suffering with sleep deprivation and something inside of him just snapped. I never knew he even had a gun. He went missing from the house one day after not sleeping much. His wife Teri went out to where he would ride his bike in the hills and saw the coroner's truck there and lots of activity . . . it's everybody's worst nightmare.

Carlos's was a horrendous loss, and it brought home to me that some of my closest friends could die at any time.

Also for my first solo record, Richard Marx came over to the house and wrote a great track with me called 'Swear Your Love', which he co-produced. Rich and I go way back and he is a great singer-songwriter and a great producer. We had a million laughs doing that track.

I had been working a lot with legendary songwriter Diane Warren and we hit it off in humourland. I had played on some hits for her and I wondered if she would write something with me. Diane does few co-writes so this was an honour for me, and we came up with 'Lonely Beat of My Heart', which became the first single off the record, produced by Richie Zito and me. Paich came and played a killer organ part à la Procol Harum for me. Richard Page and Richard Marx did some killer background vocals.

Danny 'Kootch' Kortchmar co-wrote and co-produced two songs for me. We had a blast at the Complex for a week. That was where I met Stan Lynch, the original drummer with Tom Petty and the Heartbreakers. He was with Kootch and Ivan Neville from Keith Richards's band was there too . . . Anyone who came by ended up on the record.

Stan and I were to become great friends and we also wrote a lot of music together later on. Kootch is a magical cat and a great musician and songwriter. He got some great stuff out of me. I have a mad respect for him in every way.

Randy Goodrum and I wrote what I would say are more pop-rock songs – things like 'Anna', 'Turns to Stone', 'I'll Be Over You', 'These Chains', to name a few – for the record to round it out. I have always loved working with Randy. He's great at everything he does and we did most of the work at his place. It turned out great and Lee Sklar played some killer bass on the tracks. I wrote a cool tune with Mike Landau and also a tune with Tom Kelly and Billy Steinberg.

My record had a dark aspect to it, too. More than anything else it was a break-up record, because my marriage to Marie had deteriorated beyond repair. As we fell apart, we were fighting like cats and dogs, and a lot of ugly things were said on both sides that could not be taken back. I had gotten into a bad place with boozing and was still partying hard, which only served to amplify our problems. At the time I was trying to finish making my record, I had also had to move out of our house and into a place called the Oakwood Apartments.

You could rent month by month, and it came furnished, with plates and everything. It was a shithole. Out-of-town musicians on tour, actors the studios didn't want to put up in a hotel, divorced guys and coke dealers lived there, so there were many poker games and plenty of sleep repellent and beer. I was a mess and bleeding out emotionally. It was thoroughly depressing.

I missed my kids so bad there was a huge hole in my heart. I missed my house and I missed my life. The marriage was over. It was a sad time for all and the kids didn't understand. They were too young. Tina was just four at the time and Trev only two, and I was destroyed that I was not living at home. I would drop by to see them.

I was anaesthetising myself more and more. The Oakwood was nearby to the Baked Potato, where I became a fixture. I would get so drunk that guys would have to carry me out the place. I never failed to show up to work the next day, but after hours I was trying to drown my sorrows.

Work always was the best and safest distraction for me. As the band's situation was unravelling through *The Seventh One*, I had thrown myself into doing some sessions again.

There was a memorable date on David Crosby's *Oh Yes I Can*

record, which I was on with a bunch of the Section guys, Kootch, Lee Sklar and, I believe, Russ Kunkel and Craig Doerge.

I am a huge fan of Crosby and like me he has a demented sense of humour. We were at A & M Studios and almost done for the day. We cut some great stuff. Kootch wanted to go hang at his pad post-session, but as we were getting up to go Croz said to me, 'Hey man, would you just do a solo for me on one more tune?' I looked over at Kootch and he was itching to leave, but I said to Croz, 'Sure, throw it up.'

Croz said it was just an eight-bar solo, so I told him I wouldn't need to hear the track beforehand. If he gave me the key that it was in I would just go for it. Maybe I was being a little bit cocky, and kind of winking at the other guys. Croz started to laugh, too, and said something like 'OK, big shot – go for it.' Croz gave me two bars and counted me in, and I started to solo. At the end of the take, Croz shouted out: 'Fuck you! That was great. Now, get outta here.'

Danny Kortchmar: *That's how sharp, intelligent and perceptive Luke is as a musician. He understood the DNA of the song, put his headphones on and was able to play a great solo in one take. There's no question that he worked hard to be that good and studied like crazy, but there's also an element he had that you can't learn. He was able to feel those kinds of things instinctively. His instincts were what made him even greater than he would have been had he simply been a student. Studying only gets you so far.*

Richard Marx was a guy I had first met when he was very young and David Foster's assistant. At first, I hadn't known how talented he was, because Foster would just boss him around. Gradually, though, David brought Richard onto the scene doing background vocals and co-writes, and when his first album came out in 1987, it was a smash. A few years later, Richard booked me to play on his follow-up, *Repeat Offender*, which also went on to be a huge seller. The two of us became good friends, but what stood out for me about that date was that I also got to meet Tommy Lee of Mötley Crüe. Richard had Tommy come in and drum for him. Randy Jackson was on bass . . . Yes, that Randy Jackson, dawg. Great player, great cat. This was way before *American Idol*.

It was blatantly apparent from the start that there was no difference between Tommy's onstage persona and his actual self. He has boundless energy and an infectious joy for life. I dug that cat right away. He played his ass off too.

After the session, which went great, Tommy said to me, 'Me and you have got to hang, bro!' And hang we did. Invariably, we would get up to no good and into trouble. We had a night out and consumed many cocktails and Tommy took me along to his tattoo guy on Sunset Strip. I picked out a little devil figure to go on my left arm, which Tommy swore looked just like me. For a while there, the two of us were inseparable, but I haven't seen him in a long time now. Sometimes in our world, friendships come and go like the seasons. You get busy all over again and move off into different scenes, but if I happened to run into Tommy again tomorrow, I know for a fact that it would be as if nothing between us had changed.

More bittersweet was an all-too-brief reunion that I had with Boz Scaggs. He was making his *Other Roads* record with Bill Schnee producing, which was the first he had done in eight years and a kind of comeback. Bill wanted to recapture the sound that Boz had got with us guys on *Middle Man*, but also to have some fresh blood in there. It was a rite-of-passage thing. Jay Graydon had told me many years before that very few guys got to be studio players for life. If you were lucky, you got to have a ten- to-fifteen-year run. You would then need to advance to being an artist, producer or songwriter, because the next generation of cats would be hurrying along to take your seat. I had done that.

But in my case, a young cat out of Nashville by the name of Dann Huff came to LA. I was getting out of the studio scene at the time. Dann played a lot like me back then. So much so, that there were a couple of records he was on where I actually went, 'Whoa! Did I play on that?' I was flattered to have a sort of semi-impersonator. Bill initially called Dann in to play the basic tracks on *Other Roads* with Paul Jackson Jr taking the Ray Parker Jr role.

Jeff was on the date and I pressed him, 'Dann Huff? What did I do wrong?' Jeff told me that Dann just showed up with no warning. I found that strange and I never really believed him – I think he was trying to be nice to me. Later in the sessions, Bill did have me come down and do some overdubs and it went well. I always wanted to give my best to Boz.

It was around that point that I started to wind down my session career for real. I had hit the wall as a session man. I could not go any higher and I was starting to get impatient and weird, and I didn't like that about myself. I had been given a great gift as a session man.

I knew it was time to move on. I wanted to be an artist either with the band or without.

I had intended to call my first solo record *I Hate Every Bone in Your Body Except Mine*, but the record company wouldn't let me. It became just plain old *Lukather* instead, which was a minor disappointment compared to what happened when I turned it in to the label. Columbia had just appointed a new president. In my view one of the most awful, maniacal pieces of living shit on Planet Earth, Donny Ienner. He was big, tall and goofy-looking with a fake smile, and Mr Ed's teeth. I thought this guy was a tool. And he refused to put my album out. I had just spent six months of my life working on this thing, but Ienner didn't want people on the label to be doing solo records. There were three or four other bands on Columbia who also had guys doing their own records, and he shit-canned us all.

It was like someone had taken a sledgehammer to my heart. My marriage had gone down the drain and now it seemed to me that my career was heading that same way. I was humiliated and also terribly embarrassed about what I was going to tell all of the guys who had worked on the record. The only upside was that people at the label outside of the States loved what I had done, so the album did come out in Europe and Japan . . . everywhere else but the USA.

Mister Udo also offered me a solo tour of Japan with Jeff Beck and a new band called Bad English that Neal Schon and Jonathan Cain of Journey had launched with the singer John Waite. I put together a group with a couple of my oldest friends, John Pierce on bass and Joey Brasler on second guitar and vocals, with Jeff Daniels on keyboards and vocals, and John Keane, who played drums and sang, and would go on to score the *CSI* shows on TV.

By then, I had become friendly with Jeff Beck, I knew Neal Schon well and I played on Jonathan Cain's first solo record in 1977. I knew almost everyone so the hang in Japan was great. Jeff was also touring on the back of an acclaimed record, *Jeff Beck's Guitar Shop*, and selling out arena-size shows. He had yet another world-class band with him with Terry Bozzio on drums and Tony Hymas on keys. I had the privilege of opening up the dates for my first solo tour. I was excited and nervous. Beck and Neal can really play, and we watched Jeff from the wings almost every night.

The whole tour was a blast and that included, for very different reasons, a couple of shows for which the late Chuck Berry was booked as the headline act. What went down at those was some of the weirdest and funniest shit I have ever witnessed on a rock-and-roll stage.

Right then, no one in their right mind would have wanted to have gone after Jeff Beck. He was playing at the very top of his game and every night did a ripping set with his killer band.

Chuck would insist upon using pick-up bands, which he never rehearsed. The idea was that Terry and Tony from Jeff's group were going to play behind Chuck. On the first show, Chuck showed up and he had got this weird, shitty-sounding amp he had to have or he wouldn't play, and he didn't want to run through his set at all with Terry and Tony. Just before he was due onstage, Chuck also demanded 5,000 US dollars in cash or else he wasn't going to play. Mister Udo managed to rustle up a bag of USA cash, but he was fuming. (One of Udo's main staff, Tack, was my Japanese hang and always has been. I really truly love the cat.)

Chuck walked out onstage. Terry and Tony were already up there waiting for him. He snarled, 'Where's my bass player?' Tony put up his hand and Chuck started to play, except that his guitar was horribly out of tune. He riffed for thirty-five seconds and then called a halt to the band. At which point Chuck began to rant about how he needed some musicians. 'Where are all the musicians!' The crowd had no idea what was going on, but Neal Schon and I took this to mean that Chuck wanted some back-up players so we had our guys bring out our amps and plug in. The two of us came out from either side of the stage. The crowd went mad, but Chuck just glared. He stomped over to me and said, 'I don't play with other gee-tar players. Get off my stage.' Then he turned and did the same to Neal. Next thing, he fired Terry and Tony on the spot. Terry threw his sticks up in the air and stormed off. Things went from bad to worse.

Chuck was now by himself on the stage and the crowd had started to boo. Eventually, he made a slap-dash attempt to play three or four tunes, like 'Johnny B Goode', with a guy John from my crew on drums who couldn't navigate anything but the most basic beat, before stalking off. It was hilarious and sad, as the crowd was booing, but it was something to see.

Next night, Chuck made it clear that he wanted to have an all-black back-up band. Finding a bunch of brothers in Japan was something of a challenge, but once again Mister Udo came through. A group of guys were over from the States doing top-forty covers at a local club, four sets a night, and he hired them for the evening. On this occasion, we all knew what was going to go

down and so made sure to be in the wings to watch. Mister Udo
had got Chuck a bass player, keyboard player and drummer. No
sooner had they gone into the first tune than Chuck stopped them
and flew off the handle about how they were doing his song
wrong. The cat was completely insane.

One at a time, Chuck again started to fire each of these guys in
front of a full arena. The bass player was the last man that he got
to. 'You're fired!' said Chuck. 'Fuck you,' said this cat. Then he
walked to the front of the stage, dropped to his knees and broke
into a Louis Johnson-style thumb solo. The crowd went wild and
those of us at the side of the stage were roaring with laughter.
Chuck had finally shit his own bed and that was the last that we
saw of him. He appeared to vanish, though in fact Mister Udo had
arranged for him to be spirited from the venue to the airport and
out of his country. I, meanwhile, returned home to find that
Donny Ienner wanted to meet with Toto. I feared the worst.

CHAPTER NINETEEN

Donny Ienner would hold court at a bungalow at the Beverly Hills Hotel and the arrogant asshole summoned us to meet him there. He told us that it was high time that we wrote another 'Africa', and that only once we had would he put some money behind the band. He made it sound as if it would be as easy for us as clicking our fingers, and so began what was all at once one of the most bizarre, infuriating and soul-destroying periods in our collective history.

The one thing that we agreed upon with Ienner was that we should put out a 'Best of' record to buy ourselves time. We'd had enough hits worldwide to justify such a release, but Ienner was also insistent that we conjure four new songs to go on this compilation and make it more appealing to our fans. Once again, Bobby's name came up. We were at least on better terms with him. By then I had gone to see Bobby play a couple of times at local shows and at each had got up with him to do 'Hold the Line'. After all that we had been through, going back to square one also didn't seem like the worst of ideas.

Paich had a song that ironically he had written with Joe, 'Goin'

Home'. It was the kind of big track that would suit having a multiple lead vocal, like 'Rosanna' or indeed 'Africa', so we asked Bobby to come and sing. It was apparent that we were right back where we had left off just as soon as we had got him into the studio, but in only the worst sense. Bobby had a really tough time of it putting down that vocal. Nevertheless, the finished song itself sounded to us like vintage Toto and so we handed it over to Ienner, who promptly told us that he hated it. In fact, his exact words were: 'I want "Africa" and this isn't a hit record. This is shit.' Patently, a rethink was in order.

Ienner had appointed as his new head of A & R a cat named Bobby Colomby who used to play drums with Blood, Sweat & Tears. I had worked for Colomby on a Pages (Richard Page's band) record many years before. Ienner next had us meet with Colomby and there were two things that came out of that summit, only one of which proved to be any good. Colomby sold us on the notion that we needed the help of a co-producer and floated the name of James Guthrie. James was Pink Floyd's engineer and looking to break into producing records himself. I loved that idea. He seemed such a wild card to work with us that the prospect was genuinely exciting. That, at least, was borne out.

Colomby's other idea was for a singer. He knew we were missing someone who had a high voice once again. He had come across a guy from South Africa, who he said might be very interesting for us. The first we saw of Jean-Michel Byron was a publicity photo and a video that he'd had shot. He was an exotic-looking guy, as opposite to us as was possible. Colomby also played us a demo of a song that Byron had written, 'Love Has the Power'. It was catchy enough, for sure, but Jeff was bowled over by just that one tune. Byron sang high, too, but for real did not have a rock-and-roll voice. Put simply, he sounded more like Michael Jackson than Bobby Kimball.

We decided to allow ourselves a few days to mull Byron over, after which Jeff called me. Jeff was ever persuasive and his line of reasoning was that maybe we really needed to make a left turn. He said maybe we had do something crazy and go for it, and see what happens. I was a bit more 'No, no, not again.' 'It's for a greatest hits album,' he reassured me. 'If it doesn't work out with this guy, nothing is lost.' That made sense and I figured the least I could do was to give this Byron dude a shot.

I should have known what was coming down the pipe. Right before we met with Byron, Paich, Mike and our wives got an invite out to Colorado for a sponsored celebrity ski trip. That was as weird a scene as it sounds and with a really eclectic bunch of people. Ray Parker Jr was also along for the free ride and so too were Rita Coolidge and Mary Wilson from the Supremes, and Kool Moe Dee. Mikey had never skied on snow before and the very first day, he fell off the ski lift and snapped his right leg. He was screaming in agony and came back from the hospital encased in a plaster cast from foot to thigh. It ruined his trip, and his wife's too, but he was well sedated and after a few cocktails offered up pearls of sarcastic humour that only he could deliver.

We had Byron flown over to LA from South Africa. He seemed nice enough on first impression, but I suspected that Colomby had already told him that he had got the gig. Jeff was totally won over, and as he could coerce the rest of us into doing just about anything, Byron got his shot. We were under such a tight deadline from the label to work up the new songs that we didn't even try the guy out singing something like 'Hold the Line' or other Toto rock songs. It was a ridiculous situation that we had gotten ourselves into, but that's what being put under pressure will do.

We wanted to work outside LA and the location we chose was Bearsville Studios in upstate New York. This was a legendary rock-and-roll studio, just west of Woodstock, which had been established in 1969 by Bob Dylan's then manager, Albert Grossman, in what looked like an old converted barn. Since then it had become more synonymous with the Band and Todd Rundgren and that whole rural folk-rock sound. To record at Bearsville was indeed to live in the country. It was surrounded by lush woodland and our accommodation was log cabins with a creek out back. The main studio was fantastic. It was set in the middle of the forest and had a huge, high ceiling and vintage Neve desk. It had also snowed when we arrived and as such was not the ideal place for Mike with a handicap to have to go to work.

The living quarters were called Turtle Creek. There were three buildings so we split up. We had been told Turtle Creek was haunted so I, of course, went to work on 'the new guy', as we all did. In fun . . . it started that way anyway. In the middle of the night, we scared the shit out of Byron by sneaking into his room with these weird old African masks and turning the light on . . . Byron screamed like a little girl. It was hilarious. In his defence, we had all known each other since we were kids, so he didn't expect that kind of shit. It was funny for everyone except for Byron.

One night, Mike was coming down an outside flight of wooden stairs to dinner on his crutches. We had probably all had a few glasses of wine as an aperitif and there was a big puddle of mud right at the foot of the stairs. Mikey led with his left-side crutch and slipped. Not wanting to damage his leg any further, he sort of lurched forward and flung himself face first into the mud. It was freezing outside and he had mud dripping from his face and clothes. The rest of us scrambled to pick him up, but Mike was inconsolable and also in a lot of pain. He began to rave at us: 'Fuck this shit. Fuck all of you. And fuck this band.' I'm one of these guys who has a nervous reaction to seeing someone hurt themselves, which is to laugh. When I was a kid, this caused me to almost get my ass kicked many times, but I couldn't stop laughing then or now and that only made Mike all the more angry.

At all events, I was just then feeling particularly low. My heart was still broken from the collapse of my marriage and at not being able to see my children as often as I liked. Marie had filed for divorce and once the lawyers got involved, the situation between us turned even uglier. She was hurting, so was I, and we were very antagonistic to one another. While we were at Bearsville, the phone calls between us got to be both more frequent and more toxic. I would be in good spirits and then Marie would ring, and after that I would disappear into a black hole. It got so bad that whenever the phone rang, Jeff would admonish me: 'If you pick that up again, I swear that I will kick your ass.'

Marie and I did at least come to an arrangement over the house, but it cost me. Effectively, I bought our home back off her and she was able to go off and get a nice place at the beach for herself. In order to have that happen, I needed to get my hands on ready money fast and so Mark Hartley arranged for me to sell off my early publishing rights for the hit songs I had written and all the rest.

In Mark's haste and my own desperation, that ended up being a horrible for-life deal, with no chance of getting the rights back. The consolation is that I'm still living in the same house and that my kids got to grow up there.

At the time in Bearsville, I was so bummed out that I wrote a maudlin six-eight ballad called 'Out of Love'. Byron wrote the words with me, but they were an accurate reflection of my state of mind. That became one of the new songs that went on to the *Past to Present 1977–1990* album alongside Byron's 'Love Has the Power'. They were some really great tracks and the band was having fun. We were trying to make Byron feel comfortable but it was so very obvious he was not one of us in any way. He was reading the George Michael book, for fuck's sake. He was A; I was Z: that far apart. Our keyboard tech JJ (John Jessel) and I got up to a lot of fun after hours. I needed to loosen up I was so stressed out. Byron, on the other hand, pretty much kept to himself.

Cutting those tracks finally gave us the opportunity to hear what Byron could do, because so to speak we had bought the car pretty much sight unseen. A couple of times, James had suggested to Byron that he put a guide vocal down, but he had demurred, saying that he was still working on his lyrics. He had sung pretty good in the room at rehearsals, but sure enough, once he got the headphones on and in front of a studio mic, things went wrong for him. His pitch was all over the place and he sang way too sharp. For Paich and James, it was gruelling. I just left to drown my sorrows with whomever I could get to come along.

They managed to piece together good takes in the end, but during the two weeks that we were at Bearsville, the obvious differences between Byron and the rest of us got to be more pronounced.

That wasn't just his fault. He would go on about the trials and tribulations of the South African black man and we were from North Hollywood, so what the fuck did we know? For his part, he would be baffled by the fact that we liked to kick back and party at the end of a day, and he often as not retired to bed early. He was younger than us and didn't know anything about Zeppelin, Hendrix or any of the other stuff that we had grown up listening to. All of which made him even more of an outsider in the ranks and very sensitive about it, but since we had committed to this project, we decided to see what happened with him on tour.

In advance of that, the *Past to Present* record leapt up the charts all over Europe and in Japan. It was the number-one album all year in Holland and went multi-platinum or gold all across Europe and in Japan. Ienner seemed happy for it to be buried in the States, but eventually even in America it went platinum. To this day, we don't know why this asshole hated us. We never even got a chance to say 'Fuck you' to him – he came in hating us. It must have been some past–life shit.

Our first gig with Byron was at Forest National arena in Brussels, Belgium. Once again, we went into it being somewhat blind since we had still not got to see Byron perform. He had sat in a chair the whole time at tour rehearsals. Right before the show, we were in our dressing room backstage and he pulled on a golf glove. I asked him, 'What's with the Michael Jackson shit, man?' He told me that it was his thing, which of course was not what anybody was going to think. Next, he had pinned a sheriff's badge to his shirt, so I had advance warning that this was going to be an especially interesting and revealing evening for the band.

For that tour, we had Jeff's drums set up stage left and I was stationed to the right. We got up there and got into our opening song, which was 'Love Has the Power'. I still thank God that no one had a camera phone back in those days, because Byron came out and immediately started to dance about the stage like a fucking idiot, like fire ants were writhing in his anus. He was doing all of these extremely bizarre movements and the entire front row was stood open-mouthed with shock. Jeff and I made eye contact, and we were stunned too.

It was fucked-up-horrifying!

As the show went on and Bryon kept up his eccentric act, the crowd turned on him. There were people flipping Byron off but giving the thumbs-up to us. He didn't appear to notice, or if he did to care, because in his own mind he was a star.

The first-night reviews were scathing. Right then, we knew it was over between us and Byron, but we had to figure out how to get through the tour without having to cancel and lose a bunch of money as the tour was pretty much sold out. We had at least taken out three backing singers (Jenny Douglas, Jacci McGhee and John James) to cover for Byron, and slowly but surely as the tour progressed, we started to take his songs out of the show and push him in the background. Even still, he made things extremely uncomfortable for us and himself. Before one gig, I found him sewing pink handkerchiefs onto the side of his pants. I told him I wouldn't go onstage with him dressed like that. At another, I got so pissed at him that I actually pushed him up against a wall. I am not a fighter, but snapped after a month on the road and with him becoming increasingly conceited. There is so much more to tell but I would like to forget the whole experience. It was a blink in our history.

Martin Cole: One night in Paris, Jeff Porcaro had a riser set up stage left and behind the curtain. Without telling any of the other members, he had hired a stripper to perform during the show and so that only the band would be able to see her act. Well, when she started to dance one of our backing singers, Jacci McGhee, mistook her for a fan that had jumped up and so pulled her into the middle of the stage. The stripper proceeded to take off all of her clothes in front of the entire crowd. The only person in the building that didn't notice was Byron, because he was singing a ballad at the time and had his eyes shut tight. He thought the wild response was for him. Luke fell to his knees and backwards laughing, but didn't miss a note.

Our managers sat Byron down and tried to talk sense into him, but the cat was delusional. It was as if he genuinely thought that we were his backing band and he wouldn't listen to reason. Byron and I eventually stopped speaking to each other and things in general got to be so strained that we had no option but to pull the final leg of the tour. We got home and had Larry and Mark call up Byron to tell him that it was over with him and the band. The entire experience had lasted seven months, but between ourselves, we never spoke about it again.

Byron stayed on in LA and got a club gig. Every once in a while, I would go into a bar and he would be there. I tried to be nice, but he blamed me for what had happened because I was the most vocal about the situation. Now he likes to pretend Jeff and him were great friends. That's not true. Believe me, I was there. It was over after the first song in Belgium. It was only Byron who didn't know it yet.

I heard that he became a raving egomaniac and obsessed with hating on me. That's the way it goes sometimes. According to Byron, he was destined to be a big star. To which all that I can say is: so what's happened over the last thirty-five years, dude?

CHAPTER TWENTY

In the immediate aftermath of the Byron mistake, we took a little time off and I went and saw my best friend, actor Miguel Ferrer, who was shooting a film called *Scam* in Jamaica, and had the time of my life. I never go anywhere alone so this was a first for me. Miggy and his then girlfriend, soon to be wife, Leilani Sarelle of *Basic Instinct* fame, met me at the airport. I spent two weeks in the sun hanging out with the actor and director Edward James Olmos and his extended family. At the time, Eddie was living with Lorraine Bracco, who was in the film with Miggy; she was great.

Miggy insisted I come down. I had a blast. I even had a cameo in the film . . . blink and you'll miss me. We hung out on the beach all day with the Olmos gang, partied, swam and scuba-dived, and some of us would meet up for dinner at night.

I even got to meet and hang a little with Christopher Walken. It was a brief encounter, and I was trying to be cool. I reminded him that he worked with my dad on *The Deer Hunter* and he perked up a bit, but after I went to the bathroom he was gone. To me Christopher Walken is the same onstage as offstage – a very interesting character.

With Gregg Rolie on stage on
the Ringo tour, having a blast …
(author's collection)

Ringo Starr and His All-Starr Band outside
the green room of the Fallsview Casino
Hotel in Niagara, Canada, June 5th 2014.
left to right) Todd Rundgren, Warren Ham,
Gregg Rolie, Mark Rivera, me, Ringo,
Gregg Bissonette and Richard Page.
(© Scott Ritchie)

With Ringo Starr, working on the tracks we
wrote together. *(author's collection)*

Selfie with Eddie Van Halen, backstage at the Greek Theatre, 2017. *(author's collection)*

With Larry Carlton, Matt Resnicoff and Steve Vai after No Substitutions tour, 2001. *(author's collection)*

Steve Morse, me, John Petrucci, Sterling Ball at NAMM, 2009. *(author's collection)*

With the great Les Paul, 2008. *(author's collection)*

(left) My man Jeff Healey. *(author's collection)*

(right) High School band reunion at the Greek Theatre with Steve Porcaro and Mike Landau. *(author's collection)*

With Billy Mumy at the Greek Theatre. *(author's collection)*

Edgar Winter on An Odd Couple tour. *(© Robert M. Knight)*

With John McLaughlin at the Montreux Jazz Festival. *(author's collection)*

Lenny Castro: godfather and giant musician. The shirt says it all. *(author's collection)*

With Jimmy Page. *(author's collection)*

G3, 2012. *(author's collection)*

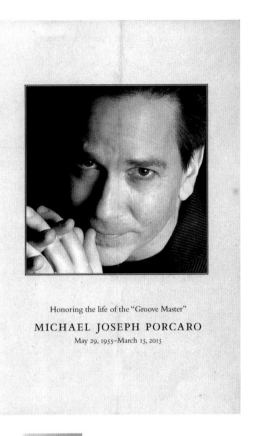

Honoring the life of the "Groove Master"

MICHAEL JOSEPH PORCARO

May 29, 1955–March 15, 2015

One of the saddest days of my life. *(author's collection)*

Notodden Blues Festival 2016: Robben Ford, me, Billy Gibbons and Steve Cropper. *(author's collection)*

With Robert Plant. I may have been over-served at this point. *(author's collection)*

(above) My best friends Miguel Ferrer and Trev at my wedding to Shawn. *(author's collection)*

(right) My *Santamental* album shoot ... *(© Robert M. Knight)*

'Big' Tony, 'Little' Tony (my son-in-law) and Trev, hanging out on my birthday in Vegas. *(author's collection)*

Simon Phillips, Joe Porcaro, Bobby Kimball, Mike Porcaro, my mom, David Paich, Steve Porcaro – Rock Walk of Fame, 1999. *(© Robert M. Knight)*

My other band, Nerve Bundle: Jorgen Carlsson, me, Jeff Babko and Toss Panos. *(author's collection)*

Alex Van Halen, me, Eddie Van Halen and David Paich, backstage at the Greek Theatre. *(author's collection)*

(left to right): Shannon Forrest, Joe Williams, Shem von Schroeck, Roger Hodgson (from Supertramp), Steve Porcaro and David Paich. *(author's collection)*

With Joe Williams and our new bass player Shem von Schroeck in 2018. *(author's collection)*

Working on *40 Trips Around the Sun*, *(left to right)*: Steve Porcaro, Joe Williams, Vinnie Colaiuta, me, Niko Bolas and David Paich. *(author's collection)*

I was talking to Jeff Porcaro on the phone a lot, plotting what I thought we should do next, which was to just be a four-piece and make a rock record, which we did. It turned out to be *Kingdom of Desire*.

While doing the overdubs for that album, we gathered at Devonshire Sound Studios in Burbank one day and I happened to bump into James Guthrie in the corridor. It turned out he was in the next room to us and engineering Roger Waters's *Amused to Death* album. Jeff Beck did most of the guitars on that record but, just as I had with Clapton, I told James, 'Man, I would do anything to play with Roger – and for free.' The producer Pat Leonard was someone I knew but had not really worked with. I offered my services if they needed anything and they called me in.

Roger, Pat and James subsequently invited me to play on three tracks and that was an absolute thrill. Roger was the complete gentleman. He is very gracious and serious-minded, too, and got straight down to business. At that point, there was a really bad vibe between Roger and David Gilmour. That was so obviously the case that I wasn't about to mention to Roger that I had got to be pals with David. James was the only guy who was able to jump between both of those camps. He was their Switzerland, if you will.

By the start of the nineties, I was entering the twilight years of my career as a regular session player. However, I would still get booked for big sessions and one of those was on Bob Seger's *The Fire Inside* record that I got through Jimmy Iovine's recommendation. I was flown out to Nashville for that session and didn't know any of the other cats on the date, but Bob was very welcoming and also something of a meticulous perfectionist. You might think that Bob's songs are simple and kind of play themselves, but there is way more to it. He's a taskmaster when it comes to cutting them and it proved a tedious process. He wanted to try many different tempos and keys and so on, so we did a lot of takes.

Barry Beckett, the famous keyboard player from all of those fabled Muscle Shoals sessions, was Bob's producer on that record.

We played the same song for two whole days, with just a tenth up or down in tempo or a change of key maybe . . . I guess Bob wanted a lot of options that he could edit together for whatever reason. He would also sing in the room, and I have to say that he brought it on every one of those takes. What he was doing mattered so much to him that every single performance counted. I would have been much less willing to do a thousand takes with someone who didn't sing so great. After the date, Bob also asked me to go out on the road with his band, but I was committed to Toto and we never saw each other again.

Experience had taught me to branch out and I was looking to make a move to the other side of the desk. Entirely fittingly when you consider what my life was like, one of the first producing gigs I got was for Spinal Tap. I had gone along with Eddie Van Halen to a private party that Marshall threw at the Guitar Center in Hollywood honouring Jimmy Page and Christopher Guest was among the other guests, but in character as Nigel Tufnel. I went up to him and whispered, 'I don't know if you're aware of this, but Jeff Beck loved the movie and thought what you did was hilarious.' Jeff had indeed told me that he found the Tufnel character very funny, though I wasn't sure he understood that it was at least in part based on him. That was the only time that evening that Chris broke character, and as much as anything with relief. He had thought Jeff might have more likely taken offence. The two of us talked some more, exchanged numbers and I said that if he ever happened to need a producer to give me a call.

Not long afterwards, Chris phoned and invited me out to meet his two fellow Tap actors, Michael McKean and Harry Shearer. We did a deal for me to produce four tracks for their *Break Like the Wind* record, which came out in 1992. I even said to them, 'All I can tell you is that you've got the right guy for the job.'

The next occasion that I got together with the guys was to work through the arrangements. They knew precisely what they wanted to do and that was the thing about them: they are three excellent musicians and were deadly serious about the music. Each of them would get everything down in one or two takes. If anything, their parts were so good on that record that it was stopped from being funny for the most part (subtle humour).

There were a couple of real high points for me making *Break Like the Wind*. For one, I got Cher to come down and sing a duet with the guys on a track called 'Just Begin Again', which she loved doing and just killed. Then there was the title track ('Break Like the Wind'), the concept for which was to have six different guitar solos in the middle of the tune. Each one was four bars and they were meant to build towards a crescendo, up a half step every time. For that we had Jeff, Brian May, Joe Satriani, Slash, Chris as Nigel Tufnel and me doing a sort of funny solo.

Both Jeff's and Brian's contributions were exquisite. Brian did his beautiful Queen thing with the harmonies. Joe Satriani's playing was so bad-ass and brilliant that I almost hated him for it but Joe is one of a kind and always brings it. They flew him down to LA to do it. As for Chris, I had to tell him that he was playing too good. In total, that was one of the most fun times that I ever had in a recording studio.

Toto spent a good chunk of 1991 working as a four-piece and on material for *Kingdom of Desire*. That also proved a thoroughly enjoyable experience. We were determined to go back to being a straight rock-and-roll band again, and in the first instance that meant getting together in a room and writing almost the whole album as a band. It felt great to be free again! The bulk of the album was made up of songs that Paich, Mike, Jeff and I jammed into being. We had also been burned so much by our experiences with lead singers that we decided to do the job ourselves. I had intended to defer to Paich in that regard, and expected him to sing on his own plus a few things with me, but instead he kept throwing the lead vocals to me. By the end of the *Past to Present* tour, I suppose that I had been singing the bulk of the leads and also started assuming a more of a frontman role, because Byron hadn't had a clue how to talk to an audience either.

Outside of the band, Danny Kortchmar wrote and produced what became the title track, which I loved for being so heavy. Kootch also brought along another song, 'Kick Down the Walls', that he had written with Stan Lynch. Stan and I had become the best of pals during my solo record so seeing him was always a groove. He's one of the funniest human beings I've had the privilege to know and an incredibly gifted lyricist and writer (as well as being a great drummer). He went on to write and produce songs for Don Henley and also the Eagles, and he had a big part in the lyric-writing process for our later album, *Tambu*, as well. We'll get to that later . . .

To cut *Kingdom of Desire*, we moved out lock, stock and barrel to George Lucas's ranch in rural California. George had bought a huge, sprawling complex, just one part of which was Skywalker Studios. We took Greg Ladanyi with us and finished up the basic tracks and a lot of overdubs in just two weeks. That period was nothing but good times. We would work hard all day long and then have a great hang over dinner each night. As we had at Bearsville, the four of us got to bunk up in log cabins, which were set around a small lake. It was truly idyllic, except for the fact that my room had to it the distinct smell of death.

This stench was utterly horrendous and I was tortured by it. Now, George Massenburg had been up at the ranch right before us working with Linda Ronstadt, and I knew from our time together on *The Seventh One* that he had a depraved sense of humour. I convinced myself that George had hidden something dead in the walls and he was fucking with me. I even called him up at home and railed at him: 'Motherfucker, for God's sake tell me what you've stashed in my room.' George couldn't answer for laughing so hard, swearing he had done nothing, and I had to endure this dreadful stink right up until the end of our stay. It was only then that I discovered the body of the rat that had died in the room.

In the middle of the recording, we went over to Europe to do a summer tour, ostensibly to have fun, make some dough, play live and try the new stuff out as the 'new' four-piece Toto band. We had got some great offers to do well-regarded festivals such as Rock am Ring in Germany, and the Montreux Jazz Festival, which we were particularly excited about playing. Looking back, and because of the dreadful event that would follow, my memories of that tour are all bittersweet. The band was roasting on those dates, and Jeff especially played his ass off. At Rock am Ring, we finished our set with Sly and the Family Stone's 'I Want to Take You Higher' and had 50,000 people sing along with us. We were one of the first rock bands to be asked to do Montreux. Quincy curated his own night there, so he came out and introduced us, and that was quite an evening, which can been seen on the 1991 DVD.

The weather throughout the tour was beautiful and we got to spend some down time in Nice in the south of France. One afternoon, we were sat out in the square restaurant drinking wine and with me holding court, when this absolute goddess walked towards us down the street. She looked like a well-known supermodel. She was named Heather and I was knocked out. When I was married, I had never before been able to partake of the fruits of the road, for lack of a better term, but now I was free to partake, and I did. Having a couple of adult beverages inside me, I was fearless. She was with a friend, also beautiful, and I hailed the two of them to come on over and have some wine with us as we had a huge table party already going.

It was a crazy enough offer for her to be interested and within fifteen minutes of her sitting down, I had won a bet with her and her friend that meant they had to show us their tits. They did. They were awesome. The two of us hit it off after that, but girls beautiful as that are always trouble. I knew that if I fell in love with her it was going to hurt, bad! I knew she would never stay with me but I dove in anyway. She came along to our next show and we went on and spent some time together in NYC, and she came to LA briefly. I was head over heels and right up until the point that I found out I was not the only one . . . I knew really, but still . . . I thought to myself that I could win her over. It was a brief affair and lots of fun.

Tina Lukather: Dad was gone on the road a lot when we were growing up, but he was nevertheless a constant presence in my life. He would make sure to call every day, even if it was just for a minute or two, and to tell my brother and me that he loved us. Christmas was the best time, because Dad would spoil both of us rotten. He would buy up almost all of Toys 'R' Us and Mom would get so mad at him. Animals were another of his favourite presents to us. We had dogs, hamsters and one time he bought me a pair of rats, which soon enough vanished into the house never to be found again.

Trev Lukather: The earliest memories that I have of my dad are of him with his early-nineties big hair. He would show up to my Catholic school in a Chucky the Doll T-shirt – and with Chucky brandishing a big knife – and a model girlfriend of that time period. The other parents would be terrified of him, which I always thought was classic.

When we got back home from the Lucas ranch and had finished all the overdubs, we started mixing the album with Bob Clearmountain at A&M Studios Hollywood. That's when the LA riots broke out, which was really scary, and we were glad it didn't burn all of LA down. We were like high-school kids all over again, which is to say filled with boundless joy and optimism for the future. That lasted for as long as it took for Jeff and me to have to fly out to New York and play our new record for our old friend Donny Ienner and his A & R goon David Kahne. Arriving at the Columbia building, we accidentally got into the same elevator as Ienner. He looked uncomfortable and began doling out insincere compliments, such as asking me if I had lost weight. The guy barely knew me.

True to form, when we got to Ienner's floor, he made us sit and wait outside his office. Yet when he did at last allow us over the threshold, he claimed to like the record. As we got up to go, he even chimed, 'That was great, guys, just great.' It was all for pretence. Literally the next day, he had someone call our managers and tell them that the label didn't dig the record and weren't going to release it. That was the last straw for us and we wanted off Columbia, but they wouldn't let us go. The fact is that we sold too many records around the world. Our managers were also looking out for their percentage. They forcefully reminded us how we had a multi-million-dollar contract with two records left to go on it, and stressed that we weren't going to be getting a better deal anywhere else.

I was told by an insider who was a friend that Ienner was going to hate the record no matter what, but what he really hated was us. We were always in the black with Columbia and Sony, and if you added up how much money they made off us playing for and writing for other Sony artists, it would amount to multi-millions of dollars. Yet we never got any love or respect.

Kingdom of Desire came out around the rest of the world in September 1992 and did really well. We had booked a tour and were selling out big arenas, including multiple nights in some. Ienner was eventually compelled by his superior, who by then was Tommy Mottola, to put it out in the States, but not for another eight months. Even then, it appeared to me to be only the most token gesture.

When Jeff and I got back to LA from that New York meeting, we were feeling utterly dejected and discouraged. However, we quickly picked each other up and began to conspire and strategise about what our next move should be.

The last time that I spoke with Jeff was on 5 August 1992, the day that he died. He called and invited me over to his place for a barbecue that same night. We were going to carry on discussing where the band should go from this point on and also knock around the likely set-list for our next tour, which was selling like crazy. Jeff told me that he was off to do some stuff around the garden and get the barbecue ready. The last words that I ever said to him were, 'Love you, bro.'

It was about 6.30 that evening when I got a call from bass player Abe Laboriel Sr. Abe had been on a session with Joe Porcaro that same evening. He asked me if Jeff was OK. I had no idea what he was talking about, but Abe explained that Joe had got a call on the date to tell him that Jeff had suffered a seizure and Joe had dashed off to Westlake Hospital. I went into full panic mode. I called around everyone else in the band, but the only person I could get hold of was Mike's wife, Cheryl, who I have always loved. She told me that they had all gone to the hospital and that I should get there fast. That turned my guts inside out.

I took a huge slug of tequila before getting in my car, which was pretty fucking stupid of me, but I was in shock and my heart was palpitating. Jeff had never been sick a day in his life. Westlake Hospital was thirty minutes on the freeway from where I lived. Traffic was jammed, and I got off the freeway and got lost. When I finally made it to the hospital, I tore right up to the emergency-room entrance. Jeff's neighbour, Jack, happened to be a doctor at Westlake Hospital and he was walking right out of the doors. He saw me and started shaking his head. I jumped out the car and implored him: 'Jack, where the fuck is Jeff? Is he OK?' Jack just went right on shaking his head and said, 'Jeff's gone. He died.'

I lost it. Everything went black at that moment in my life. I couldn't breathe.

Jack asked me if I wanted to go inside and see Jeff. I'm not sure that I knew what he meant, but I said of course. He led me into the hospital and there wasn't another soul there. The family had all gone back to Jeff's house. I walked into Jeff's room alone and there was Jeff. He was laid out on a table with all kinds of tubes shoved down his throat and still had his glasses on. The medics had obviously tried desperately to revive him. I just screamed like I had seen the devil himself. I grabbed hold of Jeff's face, which was cold as ice, and that freaked me out all the more. Next thing I remember, I was on the floor on my knees in hysterics and a nurse was holding smelling salts under my nose.

Jeff had been in his back yard spraying a pesticide. Knowing him, he wouldn't have bothered to wear a face mask or even gloves for the task, and was probably smoking a cigarette. At any event, somehow this toxic shit had got into his system. He had gone inside to take a hot shower. Coming out of it, he dropped, right there in front of his wife and three young kids. They'd had three sons by then, Christopher, Miles and Nico, who was only a three-month-old baby. I didn't find out until later that Jeff was supposedly dead before he even hit the floor. They had been hoping for some kind of miracle at the hospital.

I drove to Jeff's house on autopilot, tears streaming down my face and in total disbelief. Who dies at thirty-eight years old with no illness?

Of course, when I got there everyone else was in shock and tears. His parents and family were wrecked. His two elder kids were also still little enough that they didn't really know what was going on, but that's the kind of tragedy that you just don't get over. Later on, those boys were deeply affected by Jeff's passing because he had doted on them.

It was me that called our manager Mark Hartley to break the news. I had to tell him to sit down first, and I went on and made a bunch of those calls. However, I had no real words for anyone. None of us did. I just didn't know what to say to any of them, the kids, Susan, his parents Eileen and Joe, or my brothers in the band. This event pulled the rug out from under all of us. It was something unfathomable.

It would be unfair of me to even try to describe the family's feelings, but if they were anything like mine, they were destroyed. Even after twenty-five years, I'm still not the same guy. In many ways, all of our lives ended that day, too. I lost the big brother that I had never had and the world is a worse place without him.

Ever since then, a mean, spiteful story has done the rounds that cocaine was partly a cause of Jeff's death. It's even found its way onto Wikipedia, but it is simply not true. Jeff was the least abusive guy out of all of us. He would always be the one going, 'Are you knuckleheads going to stay up all night again?' while we would be trying to chew our own foreheads off. What none of us knew was that Jeff had a bad heart and hardening of the arteries. It was the combination of those two things, triggered by the pesticide, that caused him to have a seizure and die.

As I said, Jeff had complained of pains in his arms for years. Even on our earliest tours, after a show he would have his arms submerged in buckets of ice and need a few drinks to help to take away his aches. We all thought it was a muscular thing, Jeff included, but he worried about having carpal tunnel surgery because, if it didn't go right, he would have never been able to play again. If he had just gone to the doctor to get himself checked out, it might have saved his life. Like all of us, he thought he was bulletproof. He was very alive that morning and very dead that night. That's how fast it happens and the older I get, the scarier that becomes.

For days afterwards, I was useless. I went home, buried myself in bottles of whatever I could find and cried my eyes out. Paich holds his hand close with his emotions, but the both of us got together and wept buckets. All of us guys did.

Thousands of people turned out for Jeff's funeral, and every artist and musician he had ever worked with was there. Jeff was not just some drummer guy. He was a legendary cat and magical man who jump-started hundreds of careers! All this time later, he is still the litmus test by which other drummers measure their groove and finesse.

The band had an album about to be released and a three-month tour booked. Jeff had picked out the cover art for *Kingdom of Desire*. It was a painting of a skeleton body that had been buried alive and tried to dig itself out. Unusually for him, he had also written a line of lyrics for one song, 'Wings of Time':

> *Our love doesn't end here*
> *It lives forever*
> *On the wings of time*

Among the rest of us, we didn't even mention what we ought to do for another week or so. We all went back to our quiet corners and grieved. Jeff was the heart and soul of our band, and I presumed that we all thought that Toto was done, finished.

Gradually, though, we had to face up to our collective commitments and responsibilities. Aside from us, we had thirty-five people on our payroll. Everybody had families. We consulted with the Porcaro family. The overwhelming consensus was that us stopping playing music was never going to bring Jeff back, so we decided to do the tour as a tribute to him. Also, we hoped that with money from the tour Jeff's family might be able to start to move on with their lives.

The next question was the obvious one: who on earth could we get to sit in that chair? Nobody would ever be able to fill it, but my immediate thought, and I spoke with Paich about this, was that we shouldn't go to one of the guys we knew, or the studio cats who were friends of Jeff's. We needed to get somebody who wasn't emotionally involved because they were going to have to drive this bus. I thought also that we should go for someone who would be respectful of Jeff's playing, but from more left field. Both Paich and I hit upon Simon Phillips at almost the exact same moment. Back in 1986, I had played with Simon in Jeff Beck's band in Japan and Paich had not long been to see him do *Tommy* with the Who. Simon was a brilliant musician. He played in a totally different way to Jeff, but just like him had a great pocket in the groove.

When I phoned Simon, it was the middle of the night in the UK. Within days, he had flown over to LA to join us. Opening day of rehearsals, we walked in and Simon had a massive kit set up with double kick-drums and all kinds of other shit. Jeff was more of a minimalist, so it was a jarring sight for the rest of us and most of all for Mikey. Mike hardly knew Simon, and Mikey and Jeff had been as close as could be. The first song that we played with Simon was 'Hydra'. We went into a long jam and Simon unloaded with his double kick-drum. It sounded so extreme compared to what we were used to, but great too. It was such a relief that, at the end it, Paich and I burst out laughing and even Mike had a big smile on his face.

Right after Simon joined the band, I had a lucid dream in which Jeff came to me. In the dream, I was in an otherwise deserted theatre, stood at a sound-desk at the back of the hall, and watching Simon check his drums up on the stage. From the shadows out came Jeff. He was glowing and young and in his prime, like he was when I first met him. He was smiling at me, so that I could see that he still had the chipped tooth that Susan had made him fix. He looked over at Simon, back again at me and nodded, as if to say that we had made a good choice. I started to run to give him a hug, but he just vanished into air.

Swear to God, right there in that dream I felt as alive as I have ever done. Whenever I hear Jeff's playing now, I know that he lives on. I still feel him close and I've had other dreams in which he has come to me, though not for a while now. Jeff's death didn't make any sense to me at the time, but I have grown to believe that he must have been such an evolved soul that he didn't need to live a long life.

CHAPTER TWENTY-ONE

When I got home after being with the family on the day that Jeff died, the first person I called up was my brother Miguel Ferrer. He came right on over and sat with me while I cried my eyes out. All night long, I told him stories while we drank everything in my house. I was legless for a few days. People were worried. I could not come to grips with it. It seemed impossible. I had just heard his voice earlier that day . . .

Miggy's was one of the best and most beautiful friendships that I have had in my life. We had originally met very briefly when I was recording with Jay Gruska over at Todd Fisher's mobile studio, but it was years later at a lunch with mutual friend Billy Mumy that we really hooked up, and that was it.

Miggy was part of that young Hollywood scene and tight with a bunch of the guys that I got to know, including the Cassidy brothers, Todd Fisher, Dave Jolliffe and Billy Mumy. Our other brother Ben Weiss was very close to Miggy in school and lived near him when they were growing up. Ben was first assistant director on *Friends* (and later directed the show), doing my dad's job, and that sort of bonded us and I dug him right away. At the time, he looked like early Michael Bolton with the long hair, and would get stopped on the street to sign autographs.

Miggy was a great actor. Not good, great! Acting was in his blood as his dad was José Ferrer and his mother was the singer and actress Rosemary Clooney. Miggy wanted to be close to his dad but José refused to see Miggy perform or see him in a TV show or a movie. It crushed Miggy. He cried on my shoulder the night his father died, let it all out. José had been the first Hispanic actor to win an Oscar in 1950.

I hadn't seen Billy Mumy for a while when he invited me for that very first lunch with Miggy. Miggy had just then had his breakthrough role in *RoboCop*. Matter of fact, when I first saw that movie I spent most of it trying to figure out where I knew that guy from. There was a scene in which Miggy's character had snorted lines of coke off two girls' tits. I told him over lunch that this had prompted my buddies and me to stand up in the theatre and applaud and scream. No one else did. He loved that.

That tale might have helped us become such instant friends. We exchanged numbers that afternoon, called each other that same night and were inseparable from that moment on. I had met somebody who was just as crazy as me and it was as if I had known him for a hundred lifetimes.

Miggy introduced me to his mom Rosie and his four siblings, Gabri, Rafael, Monsita and Maria. I adore the entire Clooney/ Ferrer family. All the kids and cousins . . . they are wonderful people. They always treated me like one of their own, especially after my own parents had died, and I can't tell you how much that meant to me. I just immediately fell in love with Rosie and she also took a shine to me. She would throw the most amazing parties. For the next twenty-odd years, I spent every Christmas Eve up at her house, and Tina and Trev grew up playing with Rosie's grandkids on those occasions. My daughter Tina had her first taste of high-end caviar at Rosie's. She snuck inside to get more, not knowing it was a 1,000 a tin. My then live-in girlfriend Beth-Ami and I busted her through the window and we made piggy faces at her. It was a hilarious moment.

Rosie was always great with all of the kids and loved the hustle and bustle. Each Christmas Eve, she would sit up at the piano and sing 'White Christmas' just as she had done in the movie with Bing Crosby, and famed musician Michael Feinstein would play piano. It was always a highlight for me.

I have a picture of Rosie and me together that I keep in my office at home. In many ways, she was like a second mother to me. I would sit on the floor next to her while she sat in her favourite chair, and tell her the filthiest of jokes and my tales from the road. Her kids would say that I was the only one who could get away with doing such a thing. We would drink together and she would tell me stories about old Hollywood and Sammy Davis Jr, as he is a fave of mine. I once hired a Sammy imper-sonator for one of Miggy's birthdays, ironically at her house. I flew him in from Vegas but Eddie Van Halen spoiled the surprise. To be fair, he didn't know. He just said, 'Hey, Luke, where's the Sammy guy . . . I gotta get home.' Miggy pretended not to hear but he did.

At that time Rosie was with a guy named Dante DiPaolo who also served for her as a kind of tour manager. Dante, who was an old 'hoofer' from Hollywood, was also a fave of mine. He was one of the sweetest cats ever and was so cool to me and the kids. Sadly, he passed away a few years ago.

Rosie was singing right up until the day that she died in 2002, which is how to have a career. I even played on one of her records for fun. I was with Miguel when Rosie passed. He was there for me too when each of my folks went. That's how close the two of us were.

If I wasn't on the road with the band, then I would be hanging out with Miggy, and particularly after my divorce. Marie never really liked Miggy too much because he really came back into my life right around the time that our marriage was ending. I was living at the Oakwood Apartments and, grim as it was, that place became a magnet for our 24/7 debauchery. We would go out on the prowl most nights of the week and were a force to be reckoned with – ask anyone that knew us.

Later, when I moved back into my house, we had the keys to each other's homes and also our respective liquor cabinets. We had some heady, fun and insane times together and through Miggy I was brought into a whole other circle of people that included Lou Diamond Phillips, Brandon Lee and Sherman and Bill (Slim) Allen.

Lou happened to live just down the hill from me and his pad soon became another place to hang. Lou is a straight-ahead guy and never did drugs. He was always very gracious about inviting people round for weekends. He liked to drink a little rum and we would all hang out and play poker. Melissa Etheridge lived next door and would be round at his place all the time. This was before she'd had any kind of real success, but she would pick up a guitar and just start singing, and there was no question that she had talent. I knew she would be a star.

Lou had a band called the Pipefitters with the Allen brothers, and I'd sit in with them sometimes on the weekends. Miggy had a band called the Generators, in which he played the drums and sang, with Billy Mumy on guitar, Dave Jolliffe on guitar and vocals, Gary Stockdale on bass and vocals as well as a bunch of great cats. Miggy used to get out from behind his kit and sing Dylan's 'Knockin' on Heaven's Door' and a song of his own that he wrote with Billy called 'Pussy Whipped'. It was hilarious.

Around this time, I took up golf. I was horrible, and never got any better than horrible. I would play with another of my close friends, Sterling 'Biff' Ball, who would teach me, but I still sucked. I used to spend a lot of time with his family in San Luis Obispo and got into all sorts of trouble. But we had an incredible time. (Biff is one of the most important friendships in my life – there are so many stories with him, it could be a book on its own. He is my go-to guy for any advice on life, and he is one of the wisest and most generous people I know. He owns Ernie Ball Music Man, which has been making me the finest guitars for over twenty-five years! (I've also been using his strings since I was a kid.) He and his family are like blood to me. When I'm home I speak to him every morning.

Eddie Van Halen and Tommy Lee and I would get invited to these 'celeb-rock' golf events. One of them was an early morning celebrity golf tournament that Eddie's then manager, Ed Leffler, had organised. Eddie, Tommy Lee and I went along together and the carnage started just as soon as we had arrived at the country club. Out on the course, they had a group of girls follow us around on a golf cart dispensing shots of Jägermeister. I hit the alcoholic shots hard even though they tasted like Satan's piss and liquorice mixed together. You didn't care after the first four shots, and I chased the girls around. I believe I even caught one of them, but let's leave it at that.

I knew it would be that kind of a day when we started the morning with cocktails and bumper-car competitions. Eddie, Tommy and I got engaged in a game of bumper cars with three golf carts. We were going head to head, tearing down a hill outside of the clubhouse and smashing into each other. Finally, Ed Leffler came running out, his face blistering-red, and screamed at us: 'Stop! This is my club, you assholes!' It was my dad's old club too. (It was one of the wildest days of my life.)

Rather than go home, we rented a limo and went with Eddie back to Tommy's house and got even more shit-faced.

Ed was smashed and I was gone. I knew that I should go home but when I eventually called for a cab, I could barely speak and neither could Ed. Eddie's place is hidden away off a beaten path in the hills, and I couldn't make my directions understood. My solution was to call up Miggy, because he knew where Eddie lived.

Miggy rolled up soon after with another of our buddies, Carlos Yeaggy, who was a well-known make-up artist. Carlos was driving and I tumbled into the back seat. I said, 'Thanks, thanks, man. What a day,' but no one said anything, which I thought was weird. As we were making our way onto Ventura Boulevard, Miggy turned around from the passenger seat and waved a big bag of magic mushrooms in front of my face with a shit-eating grin. All he said was, 'Shroomies!' Like an idiot, I grabbed a fistful of mushrooms from him and shoved them in my mouth.

It was only a mile or so from there to Miggy's house, which was also up in the Hollywood Hills. We got there and Miggy had a house full of people, one of whom was Brandon Lee, who I had met about a year before when he handed me a cup of mushroom tea. We bonded that night overlooking Hollywood. Over time, I got to know that Brandon didn't do blow or anything else, but was interested in exploring psychedelics from a mind-expanding, spiritualist perspective. That night, he was on acid. He told me that it was pure LSD, the best that he had ever had, and convinced me to try it.

Ever since my teens I had been scared shitless of acid. I also hadn't eaten all day, but sucked down a quarter of a tab with a beer with God knows what else. Almost at once, I started to come on real hard and everything in the room got really weird. I had to step outside and get some air, which carried an element of risk to it at. Miggy's. He lived next door to a fellow actor, Erik Estrada, who had become famous playing a motorcycle cop in the TV series *CHiPs*. I'm not sure that old Erik had been able to leave that role behind, because he was forever sneaking up and bagging on us. 'Hey!' he would shout, emerging from the shadows. 'Are you guys high?'

Fortunately, Erik wasn't on patrol that night and I managed to make it out and sit against Miggy's flagstone house. I sat there, looking down on the twinkling lights of LA and way too high, when another guy sat down and joined me. I shit you not, his name was Stony. He was a great guy but his name and the acid made me hysterical. I tried to hold a conversation with Stony, but I was tripping so much that his face appeared to me to be made out of fine sand. In the breeze, it was blowing away. The last thing I recalled was Stony's eyes, his nose and mouth being blown off into the wind and then everything went to black.

I woke up the next morning at home, and there was a trail of food leading to the kitchen, where the refrigerator door was wide open. I had emptied the fridge. I must have walked through the house indiscriminately gorging myself with food and then passed out. Other than that, I had no idea what the fuck had happened to me. That was a little too much fun. I never did that again!

Brandon and I went on and became great friends. He was one of the sweetest people I knew and it just crushed me when he died so tragically at just twenty-seven on the set of his breakthrough film, *The Crow*. I can clearly remember him getting that part. He was so excited, yet also said to me that he'd had a premonition that something was going to happen to him. He was convinced that he was going to die young like his father, Bruce. And I told him, 'Come on, man, that shit ain't real.'

It was the late eighties when Miggy brought George Clooney over to my house for the first time. George was Miggy's maternal cousin and Miggy had persuaded him to move out to LA to take a shot at an acting career. Miggy even introduced him to me as 'Cousin George'. That was precisely how I and also my kids addressed George for the next several years. Even before George got his big break on *ER*, he would always be working. He would get a part in a pilot every season. These shows wouldn't get picked up, but George would get paid for them and so he was never short of dough. George bought a house within walking distance of me and the three of us started to hang. At the time, George lived with a great big pot-bellied pig that he had named Max.

I adored George from day one and still do. I watched his meteoric rise from up close and I've never seen anyone better handle that kind of huge success. When he was a struggling actor, George would crash on a lot of floors and couches around town. He is such a class act that he has never forgotten those acts of kindness and has retained the same group of old friends.

Mostly, we would see each other at weekends. By then, I had custody of the kids during the week. Mondays through Fridays I would be a model dad, and then Tina and Trev would go stay with Marie at the weekends, and I would turn into my monster. Most often, George would do the driving because Miggy and I were the wilder pair. We would go out to clubs and, if there was a band onstage, Miggy and George's tactic for getting girls over to our table was to have me jump up and jam with whatever local band was on. Hendrix's 'Red House' was a favourite of mine, and afterwards we would be a little more popular.

One night, Miggy called and asked me to hurry down to a Mexican restaurant in the Valley called Casa Vega. It was a little hole-in-the-wall joint and one of our favourite haunts. Tuesday nights, we would meet up there with Slash and a bunch of great people, musicians of all sorts. This was when Guns N' Roses had blown up and it had gotten too crazy for those guys to hang in Hollywood. We used to call Casa Vega the 'darkest place in the world' as it was so dark 24/7.

Turned out Miggy was on a first date and wanted for me to meet this new girl. I cruised right on down to Casa Vega and there he was sat at a table with this gorgeous blonde. Her name was Leilani Sarelle. The three of us did a few shots together. Not too long after that, Leilani caused something of a stir playing Sharon Stone's lover in the movie *Basic Instinct*, by which time she and Miggy were making plans to be married. Leilani was a fun and beautiful girl. I thought Miggy might have found a great one, and I was very happy for him.

They ended up getting married at the Little Brown Church in North Hollywood, the same place where my parents married. They had their wedding reception at Rosie's house in Beverly Hills. It was a huge event with booze in abundance and also a lot of Leilani's hot girlfriends. One girl in particular struck me in the crowd. She said she was one of the girls in Van Halen's 'Hot for Teacher' video and we got to talking.

Somehow, I managed to convince her that she needed to come home with me, but by that stage in proceedings I was considerably worse for wear. It was George who came to my rescue. 'Look,' he said, 'I live down the street from Luke and I'll drive you guys home.' That was sweet music to my ears. I grabbed this girl and pulled her with me into the back seat of George's Saab convertible, which had the top down.

By the time we hit Coldwater Canyon, I was all over this girl and to the point where my pants were around my knees. One thing led to another, and to try to drown out the noise that we were making, chauffeur George was forced to put on a cassette of his Aunt Rosie's music. Eventually, though, our act got to be all too much for him. George pulled the car over and snapped, 'Let me know when you're done.' Then he got out and walked off down Mulholland Drive. Meanwhile, Rosie's song was still playing and I was laughing my ass off. That there was a truly monumental one-night stand. The sexiest man in the world was driving me home while I was playing 'Swallow the leader' in the back seat of his car.

Leilani was mortified when she learned the gory details from me the very next day, but Miggy called Rosie up and had me tell her the full story. Rosie did say that she was glad her music had been able to help me out, but otherwise had her usual reaction to the things that I would do, which was to say: 'Oh Lukather, for fuck's sake.'

Miggy and I used to drink too much and the plain fact is that booze ruined each of our marriages. People used to make jokes about the fact that we would get so messed up that only the two of us could understand what we were saying to each other. We didn't get sloppy when we first started to hang, but as you get older your body doesn't metabolise the shit in the same way. Leilani and Miggy ended up getting divorced in 2003. I loved him no matter what state he was in, but I guess that behind closed doors and in his relationship, he would get a little darker. I wasn't privy to that and I'm sad for it, because he wasn't a dark man. What emanated from him was love and humour. He had the most infectious laugh. I always really liked Leilani and her whole family.

In 2005, he met his second wife, Lori, on a flight to Fiji and they were married in a heartbeat. I was at the wedding, but the next thing I knew was that Miggy had moved with his new wife to the outer reaches of Calabasas and wasn't five minutes away any more. I would meet him in the middle for lunch and it was always me and him, so I never got to know Lori very well. As long as he was happy, it was cool.

I was gone, too. The last eight years of my life, I have been on the road 200-plus days a year. Miggy and I would still text and talk on the phone, but I hardly ever saw him any more. Then Miggy got throat cancer.

The two of us were at Clooney's wedding in Venice in 2014. After the ceremony, we found a moment to sit down and talk. Miggy always kept his hand close to his body. He never complained and told me not to worry, that he was going to beat this thing. He had just one more cancer treatment to go, he said. Six months went by, and Miggy went back to work on *CSI* and a new version of *Twin Peaks*, and I assumed that he was on the mend. By then, I had begun playing in Ringo Starr's band, and Miggy texted me the day before we were due to do a show in nearby Thousand Oaks. It was just thirty-five minutes from where he lived and he asked for tickets. I was elated to see him, as it had been a while due to work.

On the night of the show, I was having a pre-gig dinner with Ringo and his wife Barbara, and Joe Walsh and his wife Marjorie. Marjorie is also Barbara's sister, so Ringo and Joe are brothers-in-law. Ringo asked me who I had coming along to the show and I mentioned my buddy Miggy. Walsh and Marjorie also knew Miggy through a shared passion for horses. They would go riding together, and Walsh and Miggy had become friends. I think he had helped somewhat to counsel Miggy during tough times and his stopping drinking. At the mention of Miggy's name, Walsh looked up at me and said: 'Miggy's coming out? Man, he must love you. I heard that he's been given three to six months.' The colour drained from my face. Nobody had called to let me know that Miggy had taken a turn for the worse. I was crushed.

I had to excuse myself and went back to my dressing room. Ringo came by a few minutes later to see that I was OK, but I really was not. I just sat there and wept, but I didn't want Miggy to have to see me in that state. It wasn't ten minutes before show-time when I got the word that he had arrived. I ran up a flight of stairs to the backstage door and there he was with his son Raffi and stood talking to Walsh and my son, Trev. Miggy didn't weigh eighty-five pounds. The sight of him broke my heart, but I managed to keep it together in front of him. I grabbed his face, gave him a big hug and kiss and said to him, 'Jesus, Miggy, why didn't you tell me?' He could hardly talk, but he managed to say, 'Please, don't worry about it. I wouldn't miss this night for anything.'

That night, I played for Miggy. He was sitting so I could see him from the stage. I could tell that he was digging on the music, but also that he was spaced out from being in so much pain and on so much medication. All sorts of crazy thoughts went through my head during the show. Only when I dug in for solos did I let myself just play the music, otherwise I was so worried about him. At that point, he had been given a gallon of liquid hydrocodone, which is what's prescribed for people when there's nothing more that can be done.

Miggy was in excruciating pain and for him to have come out must have taken every ounce of strength that he had left, but he did that for me.

After that, I made sure to see Miggy as much as I possibly could. I would go over to the new house in Santa Monica, where they had moved at his wife's request – I had never been there before, which was strange after being so close that we had the keys to each other's houses. He never quit and didn't ever use the word 'terminal'. There was always the hope with him that a miracle might happen. A week before he passed, I went out to lunch with Miggy and his eldest son, Lukas. It was a hysterical scene. Miggy was struggling to enunciate and my hearing is all beat down from tinnitus. Lukas had to translate for us, which gave us a few good laughs. I held him a little longer than usual at the end of that day, looked into his eyes and said, 'Man, I love you. Please stay close and call me every day.'

The next Thursday morning, 19 January 2017, I got a call from Lukas. He told me straight out, 'Daddio's gone.'

I was broken. I can't even explain. It was different than Jeff or the many other friends I have lost.

George took care of everything for Miggy's memorial service. He was a saint on that one. He got Paramount to give up their sound stage for the service and had his team edit together clips of Miggy's film and TV work. It was a beautiful get-together of old friends. I was able to bring along Tina and Trev and they got to see all of the various Ferrer kids who they had been raised along-side. Gabri Ferrer, Miggy's brother, is a priest and was a great comfort, and his wife Debby Boone has always been great and I love their kids . . . It seemed that it was all gone.

I was sad so many old friends were not there. I was getting calls like it was a gig – 'Can you get me in?' It was an excruciating scene. Joe Walsh called and asked me if I wanted to play. I just couldn't. I knew I would fall apart and I did.

There were so many kind words. Gabri related a funny story about how Miggy taught him to masturbate and told him not to worry when the end product would go flying across the room. Those of us who really knew and loved Miggy cried hard together that day. Watching the clips of his work, I was reminded of how great he was, and how much fun and trouble we had in life. God, I miss him.

Since then, I have re-connected with Leilani, who I hadn't spoken with in thirteen years. I am happy that we're friends again

I still hang with Miggy's boys, Lukas and Raffi, and we grab meals together with my kids all the time. I intend to honour my promise to him that I will be there for them and be a reminder to them of their dad. Miggy and I had a very, very special relationship. He was a true brother to me. Like when Jeff and Mike died, I don't believe I've been the same person since, or ever will be again.

After Jeff's death in 1992, we had to put on our game faces to go back out on the road and perform *Kingdom of Desire*. If we had taken even a little more time to consider the gravity of our situation, I don't believe that we would ever have played together again. As it was, none of us was able to grieve properly for Jeff, and the run we did for the album ended up being a mammoth undertaking. We went all over Europe, Australia and Japan. Altogether, we were out for three months straight. The shows were sold out and as a band we were surrounded by a lot of love from our fans, but there was a negative emotional charge to that tour. We developed this kind of psychological muscle that we would flex in order to keep ourselves going. Ultimately, that turned all of us into different, not necessarily better, people.

Personally, I was on a mission not to be alone on any single night. Outside of the shows, I was also drinking heavily. I had stopped doing 'sleep repellent'. Booze was enough for me to anaesthetise myself, but it would have an even more ruinous effect on my personal life. Of course, Mikey wasn't himself and was hanging by a thread. For just one thing, it took him time to get used to our new drummer Simon's presence on the road. Musically, Simon's a big personality and very different from Jeff. Mikey also had to deal with an emotional roller coaster and he missed his family at home.

Towards the end of the tour, emotions were at an all-time high. Mikey would lash out because he was angry about losing his brother and take it out on the rest of us. I would then bark right back at him. One time, I even threw him into an airplane seat. We had to be dragged apart. This was someone I loved. We were ragged and running on fumes, and that led to even more in-fighting. We all started to grow apart and get into our own hangs with different people post show.

In the midst of all this, the record came out everywhere but in America. However, Donny Ienner had the audacity to take out an ad in the US trade press as a memorial to Jeff. It was a picture of a snare drum and two drumsticks, and alongside was written: 'Jeff Porcaro – Rest in Peace.' I went fucking psycho when I saw it. I called up Mark Hartley and literally raged at him, for the lack of being able to do anything else. It was like being a kid and having the guy who raped your dead grandmother come on over to the house and give you a kiss on the forehead. This after he had just disrespected us so badly and dumped us seemingly for no real good reason.

The only way that we could think of to end the tour was do our own tribute show to Jeff and in the band's hometown, LA. We had our managers book the Universal Amphitheatre for the evening of 14 December 1992. One hundred per cent of the money from the gig was to go to Jeff's family and we made plans to invite some of his favourite ever musicians to join us on the night. One of the first people Paich called up was Donald Fagen. Steely was on an indefinite hiatus and Donald was back east doing shows with Boz Scaggs and Michael McDonald as the New York Rock and

Soul Revue. Donald's hatred of LA was legendary, but he and Jeff had been close and he agreed to fly out and do a couple of tunes with us.

Boz and Michael wanted to be involved as well. So did Don Henley, and to our great surprise David Crosby also offered up his services. James Newton Howard and Lenny Castro were both givens, and I secured Eddie Van Halen, who hadn't before played a major show outside of Van Halen. It quickly shaped up to be a full-blown event, and one that in all honesty I fully anticipated would be Toto's swansong.

The week of the tribute gig – after we'd come off our three-month extravaganza – I went out to a club called the Gate in LA and George Harrison happened to be there. He was sat at a private table with friends. I had a bouncer go over and ask if it would be possible for me to say a quick hello. George's guitar is the reason that I breathe and I wanted to thank him for inspiring me to play. George sent word back for me to come on over. He stood and shook my hand, and was so gracious and welcoming. I told him that he was the reason that I played music, but also that my band had recently suffered a tremendous loss and that I understood that he of all people would know what that felt like.

I ended up spending the rest of the evening at that table with George. All that he drank in that time was hot water. He told me that he had quit boozing and said that by the looks of my red face, I should too. He also informed me that I clearly had a high-acid diet, but I still had the time of my life. I asked him a plethora of geeky guitar questions and about his songs, and in turn he appeared to find the stories of my own on-the-road escapades highly amusing. At the end of the night and as he was about to split, I mentioned in passing our upcoming show for Jeff and that the last song of our set was going to be 'A Little Help from My Friends'. 'I know this is a long shot and no pressure,' I told him, 'but I'll have a couple of tickets left for you on the back door.'

A day later, we went into rehearsals, which were very emotional. We had a couple of extra keyboards set up for Steve Porcaro and James Newton Howard. Fagen turned up with Denny Dias, the original Steely guitar player. Denny's clean, perfectly played notes are all over Steely's early records. He was very close to Jeff and all of us. Henley was there too; Eddie dropped by and worked up with us a killer version of Van Halen's 'Ain't Talkin' 'Bout Love' and also 'Hold the Line'. We would be elated one second and the next realise what we were all there for and have tears in our eyes. The plan for the gig itself was that we would do a couple of our own songs, then invite one of our special guests out and repeat throughout the show. The tickets had sold out in a heartbeat and all of the Porcaro family was going to be there.

On the night, we all gathered in the main dressing room back-stage. All our kids were running around the place together. We'd had a grand piano and some guitars brought into the room so that we could work out the massed arrangement for 'A Little Help from My Friends'. As we were getting down to it, one of the crew guys tapped me on the shoulder and said, 'There's somebody here to see you.' I said not now and that I was busy, but he emphasised: 'No, someone from Liverpool is here.' My heart stopped. The door opened and there was George Harrison. Everybody just kind of flipped out. George beamed over at me and said, 'You didn't think I was going to turn up, did you?' I asked him if he would like to play on the last song and sent someone to fetch my '59 Les Paul. We were doing the Joe Cocker version of the tune, because that was the one that Jeff had used to do in his high-school band. We started to play and George shouted over to me, 'Well, me and the lads didn't do it like this!'

That might have been the best show this band has ever done. There was so much love and soul in the room and everyone's performance was just spectacular. Everybody brought their A-game and also came out and told their own personal stories about Jeff. Fagen hadn't played in LA in years. The band started to vamp on the opening groove to Steely's 'Chain Lightning' and he got rolled out from the shadows on a riser, playing his Fender Rhodes and wearing dark glasses. He was the epitome of cool and the place went ape-shit. Denny Dias took the first solo and then Donald threw the next one to me. I took an extra round as I was on such a musical high because, fuck, I wanted to jam with Donald Fagen. I am sorry, Donald . . . I had to.

Donald did a second Steely song with us, 'Josie', and brought the house down.

We got the same euphoric reaction when Boz came out and we started up 'Lowdown'. Michael McDonald got up and together with him we did the Doobies' 'Takin' It to the Streets'. Henley did an old ballad from the forties, 'Come Rain or Come Shine'. Henley's was an unusual choice, but his reading of that tune was sublime and he ended up recording it for a soundtrack. We did 'Dirty Laundry' and 'You Better Hang Up', which was the first song we ever recorded together.

Crosby came out with Mike McDonald, which was a surprise to the audience. Then I called out my brother Eddie Van Halen to close the show and we did 'Ain't Talkin' 'Bout Love', which I sang, and we ended with 'Hold the Line', which we stretched out, and we were throwing solos at each other. The place went nuts . . .

I had asked George to wait in the wings so that I could bring him on in my own words. I went out and announced, 'As if this wasn't the most amazing night ever, we have one last surprise for you. This guy doesn't need an introduction, but, ladies and gentlemen . . . George Harrison!' George came out to the most thunderous ovation and it kept on rolling and resounding around the arena. He did 'With a Little Help from My Friends'; everyone sang and it was very emotional.

I went home and doubtless would have had a bottle in my hand, but instead I looked up to the ceiling and talked to Jeff. 'I really hope you were there tonight, man,' I told him, 'because that was all for you.' There would have been no one more excited than Jeff when George walked into that room.

George had hung out at the after-show party, too, and we exchanged numbers. Thereafter, George Harrison would call and leave these great messages – which I wish I still had – on my answering machine.

One day I came home to: 'Hey, it's your new good buddy George. I'm having dinner tonight. Meet me at the Italian down on Melrose. I'm inviting a few people. Let me know . . .'

So, of course, I went.

There I was waiting, and the first cat who walks in the door – Bob Dylan.

I thought: oh fuck, George Harrison has invited me to dinner with Bob Dylan.

Thank God my buddy Jim Keltner shows up and introduces me to Bob. A whole bunch of other people turn up and then George shows up. I'm now sitting in between George and Bob, but I don't know what the fuck to say to Bob Dylan. What do you say to Bob Dylan? Of course, I'm a massive fan but I'm not going to go all fanboy on him. Fortunately, we have a mutual friend in common in Stan Lynch from the Heartbreakers. Stan told me a long time ago that Bob was into Sammy Davis Jr and Frank Sinatra. I've got myself a martini and realise I've got to say something to the cat.

'Hey Bob, Stan Lynch is a dear friend of mine and he told me that when he was out on the road with you guys you went to see Sammy. I'm a big Sammy fan and collect all his stuff.'

Bob, all of a sudden, lights up.

'I love Sammy man. I really love that kind of music.'

Then all of a sudden he stops and stares at his drink.

I now think: oh fuck, I blew it. So I lean over to George.

'Did I say something to piss off Bob, man?'

He looks at me, smiles and says, 'I haven't seen him this animated in years.'

It was a great dinner. Afterwards George said we should all go to Jeff Lynne's house and have a jam.

Holy fuck, yeah . . .

So Jeff welcomes us – he really is one of the nicest cats ever and now a friend – into his studio. Bob picks up a bass; I grab an acoustic guitar; George grabs a Rickenbacker twelve-string (Beatles style); and there's Keltner on electric drums and Lynne on keyboards.

I start playing George's song 'I Want to Tell You' off *Revolver*. I'm playing the piano part of the B section – a flat-9 – on the guitar while holding the low E open.

George says, 'Stop. How are you doing that?'

'It's a flat-9,' I say.

'I didn't know you could do that on the guitar as it's the piano on the record.'

I was in heaven; no one was going to believe that this had actually happened to me.

Another time, he called and said that he had got something with him that I might want to hear. I went over to the Bel-Air Hotel and Olivia, his wife, answered the door to me. It was the first time that the two of us had met. The poor woman looked at me and then at George as if to say, 'Are you serious?' Olivia and I did get to be friends later and she is very nice . . . but I guess that I was the unexpected friend.

George had a cassette that he wanted to play me. It was the final mix of 'Free as a Bird' that Paul, Ringo and he had just then done with Jeff Lynne. I was honoured that he shared it with me. It blew my mind right away. Here I was sitting with George Harrison listening to what would be the new Beatles single. First one out since 1970 and I got to hear it with George. Beyond cool. And I loved it. Jeff Lynne and Paul did a killer job putting that together.

George also got me into transcendental meditation. For an uptight person such as me, this sounded particularly appealing. He gave me the number of a girl named Penny Bell and said to tell her that he had suggested I call. Penny worked at a Buddhist centre on Sunset Boulevard. She came round to my house and taught me how to go into trance. It was a really wonderful experience and something that I try to use to this day. It's not a religious thing, so much as a way to centre one's own spirit. That being said, it has never been easy for me to silence the screaming in my own head. Also, I have tinnitus, so it's doubly difficult for me to go to a place of quiet.

There was another time that George called up out of the blue and asked if I knew Slash. I told him that Slash was a good friend of mine. It turned out that George's son, Dhani, was a huge Guns N' Roses fan and George wanted to see if I could fix it for him to meet Slash. I hung up, called Slash and arranged the meeting.

George rolled around to my place with Dhani in this crappy, beat-up old car. I had to ask him what's up with the fucked-up wheels. He smiled in that beatific way of his and said, 'Well, when I'm driving around town people only think that I look like George Harrison.' Dhani was just thirteen at the time and the sweetest kid. I took the two of them over to Slash's pad, which proved an eye-opening experience for both of the Harrisons.

Slash had built into the walls of his home a multitude of Plexiglas terrariums that housed his collection of pythons. He also had an alligator, named Wally, in his garage. It was a crazy scene, but Slash legitimately loved all of these animals. We had a fun day. Not normal at all!

CHAPTER TWENTY-TWO

The period following Jeff's tribute concert was tough for all of us. That night had been so much of an emotional release that it had felt like a high point for the band, but afterwards we sank back down into a deep depression. After drawing such big crowds on the *Kingdom of Desire* tour overseas, we made the mistake of going straight out again to have another crack at recovering lost ground in the States. We did two weeks of club dates. Sure, they were packed houses, but the clubs would only hold 1,000 so we weren't making any money and it couldn't be anything but anti-climactic and dispiriting. We came home to figure out what to do. The one definite was that we again needed to take time off from each other. Being stuck together for months on end and in such circumstances had put a strain on all of our relationships in the band. It was the same old story: how can I miss you if you never leave?

As a result, there was no 1993 for Toto. I had a contract with Columbia to do a second solo record so it was the perfect time for me to pick that up.

I wanted it to be a sort of live-in-the-studio record, but with songs and vocals instead of straight-up jams. We would be able to go off on musical tangents, and I had in mind moving across a landscape that was somewhere between pop, rock, Latin and fusion. Right at hand, I had the ideal group of musicians to help me do just that – the cats from my regular Baked Potato jam band, who I had been playing with a lot. Los Lobotomys was then made up of David Garfield on keyboards, John Peña on bass and Simon Phillips, who was by now established as Toto's drummer. Simon had moved into an apartment block where my dad was also shacked up. Dad and Mom had come apart, though they never stopped loving each other. The apartment was just blocks away from the family home anyway.

Simon and I, meanwhile, had gotten into a musical thing of our own and had not long since written a song together that wound up being on my record. Indicative of the carefree sense that we felt at having been released to do as we pleased, we were having a bit of a party while writing this piece, our first ever, and we had called it 'Party in Simon's Pants'.

I wrote a bunch of other cool stuff with Garfield and also Fee Waybill from the Tubes, and we went in and made the record at Capitol Studios, Hollywood. As I wanted a more live feel for this one, the idea was to cut it all live except for vocals. As well as the cats from Los Lobotomys, I had Lenny Castro on percussion, and Paich as well as Chris Trujillo from the *Kingdom of Desire* tour came in too. Tom Fletcher engineered and co-produced and his pal Kevin Curry was there to lend a third ear and be helpful any way he could. We were getting two tunes a day and it was going great. We started cutting and in just two weeks had it all down, and started vocals.

The album's title, *Candyman*, was a nod to one of Sammy Davis Jr's best-loved songs, and I had Capitol 'A' studio set up to be like a cross between a black-light room from my adolescence and a shrine to Sammy. Above my head was a real black-and-white painting of Sammy, which thrilled me no end. The painting was given to me when the record was done. We had a blast making this record because it really did turn out to be more of a live thing, with live solos, and more free form than Toto. I even did a reading of Jimi Hendrix's 'Freedom', which is not often covered.

Stan Lynch and I had both got into this Sammy adoration thing. Not only was he one of the greatest entertainers who ever lived, but also the hippest cat in the room. Over time, I had acquired quite a collection of his memorabilia, including his Candyman golf bag. I was delighted to discover that Sammy had his own face embossed on his wedge.

When we moved into the smaller 'C' room at Capitol to mix and overdub, we also adorned that with our own Sammy paraphernalia and posters. Funnily enough, Sammy's Rat Pack running mate, Sinatra himself, took over from us in the big room. I loved Frank, Dean Martin and the whole Rat Pack thing, too. Those guys were the original rock stars. I never did get to meet Sinatra, but we had a quite an eclectic, random mix of people show up at our sessions.

Miggy and Clooney would often drop by, and George Harrison came down one afternoon with Jim Keltner. At that time the Beatles red and blue best-of records were out on CD and number one in the charts. There were mega-sized cut-outs of all four Beatles on the lot, and when I took George there in the car, he was embarrassed and cracked up, saying, 'Oh my God . . .'

As good as it was to see all of them, it was more of a surprise when Claudia Schiffer dropped by. A record producer friend of mine, George Acogny, brought her down. The door opened and there was the most stunning girl. She was wearing just jeans and a T-shirt, but was so beautiful that she stopped you from breathing. I wasn't backwards in offering her a tour of the studio, that's for sure. I even tried to ask her out, figuring all she could do was say no . . . but no surprise, she had a boyfriend.

In a professional sense, it was great to have Richard Page and the great Paul Rodgers, the former vocalist with Free and Bad Company, come in and sing overdubs. Paul sang, amazingly, on

'Freedom' and his vocals were absolutely flawless. As soon as you put him in front of a microphone – pure magic.

At the beginning of the next year, 1994, I got to go over to the UK and play with Paul Rodgers' own band on what was meant to be a month-long tour. Neal Schon was supposed to have done the gig, but pulled out at the last minute. Jason Bonham, who I had gotten to know well, was drumming with Paul and his band, and he called and invited me to step in. Jason promised me it would be a lot of fun and I certainly didn't do it for the bread. It was actually more like a form of therapy, because by then I had found out that my father was dying of bone-marrow cancer. I had to take him for chemotherapy treatments every week. That beat both of us down and was one of the hardest things I have had to go through. In the same room, there would be six or seven other desperately ill people all hooked up to tubes and you could smell death in there. I was trying to keep Dad's spirits up, but he said to me, 'For fuck's sake, go on the road with your friends.' Dad passed not long after, which is an event that is engraved on my heart. It broke me down again.

I did have a blast with Paul's band and it was therapeutic for me, but I also drank too much. Indeed, my opening act was to get the whole touring party thrown out of our London hotel. First night, I went down to the bar with Jason and just got trashed, because I was so bummed about Dad. At a certain point, the barman refused to serve us any more and I threw a glass of vodka against a wall. We were all told to pack our bags, which didn't go down well with some of the touring party. Inadvertently I got us to a better hotel.

It was big fun from then onwards, though, and it was a killer band. It was a thrill to be able to play all of those classic songs by Free and Bad Company and with the guy who sang them. That stuff was in my DNA and Paul was just awesome every night. He would also fuck with the band. Each day, he would ask that we learn a new song for the next show and it would be something like the most obscure Free B-side. We got to be very determined not to let him stump us. We would learn all of these songs on the tour bus and then play each one flawlessly that same night.

I was due to continue with Paul's band on the European leg of the tour, but then LA got hit by the major earthquake. It freaked out my ex-wife Marie and scared the kids half to death, so I had to leave the tour and go home to them. Fortunately, to replace me Paul was able to bring in Reeves Gabrels at short notice. Reeves was Bowie's regular guy but had also played with Paul before. Plus, he was a lot less trouble than me, so it worked out for everybody. Thanks, Reeves!

When *Candyman* was released soon after, I went out yet again on what was my first proper solo tour. I took Simon, Garfield and Peña with me and we played all over Europe and Japan. Touring is so expensive that I could not afford to pay for a bigger band. As it was, I lost 200,000 dollars on the project because I wanted a real tour bus and even selling out rock clubs in Europe and Japan did not cover all the expenses.

That band was super-tight and so accomplished that we were able to be entirely spontaneous. Our sets would extend up to three hours and we could do everything from a forty-five-minute reggae jam that would morph into songs by Hendrix, Mahavishnu and the Police to all sorts of other mad choices.

There was a lot of partying that went on. As a whole, it was perhaps the most unhinged that I ever got and nowhere more so than when we were in Japan. I was still able to bounce back like nothing happened, which used to piss off Simon Phillips. He would see me the next day and say, 'I carried you to your room last night – there is no way you can feel good!' I was fine. I was bulletproof for many years, and then it started to hurt.

By that point on the tour, I never really got hangovers and could function after a rough night, fairly unscathed. My reckless behaviour freaked out no one so much as the girl I was dating at the time. I had met Jessica at the start of the run in Sweden and flew her out to Tokyo to be with me. On arrival, we got taken out to dinner by Sony Japan. In lieu of any food, I got into a drinking contest with the head of the label. The two of us were filling beer mugs with sake and downing them in one. I, in particular, was being an idiot and raced ahead of this guy. The vice-president of Sony ended up falling backwards off his chair, putting a paper bag on his head and throwing our presents at us before passing out. Jessica, Martin Cole and I went on to a club called Pips, where it was possible to get pure absinthe. I was already blazing, but that was no impediment to me pounding six or seven more shots of absinthe in half an hour.

Subsequent to that, I was just about able to drool to Martin that I needed to eat something, and saw a McDonald's right across the street. I hate McDonald's but I was smashed and needed food, so Martin and Jessica walked me over there. To get in and out of this place, you had to negotiate a spiral staircase. I managed going up, but when I came back down, filled with Satan's food, I slipped and hit my head on a protruding piece of sheet metal to stop rats crawling up the wall. It ripped across my forehead, peeling the skin off in a flap. Blood immediately gushed down my face and in a matter of seconds it looked like a crime scene. Martin called for an ambulance. When it came, they put me in back and, in agony, I was screaming all sorts of obscenities at everyone.

At the hospital, I was bleeding so much that they whisked me off to the emergency room, where a doctor came at me with an eight-inch needle. In broken English, this poor guy tried to tell me it that it was for my own pain relief, but I just went on ranting that he should go fuck himself. Jessica was freaking out. Over and again she kept repeating, 'You are a crazy man.' I was like an insane person. Martin eventually had to lie on top of me and the doctor got his revenge by performing a hatchet job. He gave me seven big, ugly stitches on my forehead, carelessly wrapped a bandage over the wound and discharged me. The fact I was in a band called Los Lobotomys was not lost on me. I was told not to drink any more booze that night, because it might stop the blood from coagulating. I proceeded to pop a beer when I got back to the hotel. At that moment, I think Jessica was finished with me. We lost touch but I wish her well.

Next morning, I woke up feeling as if someone had hit me over the head with a sledgehammer, but I didn't miss a show. I never have, not with illness, injuries, food poisoning or through my own stupidity. In fact, I went all around the rest of the tour chanting, 'I cannot be killed!'

Martin Cole: After Japan and for the rest of that tour, it was a rider requirement of Luke's that we be provided with a bottle of absinthe backstage at every date. Since absinthe was illegal in most countries, I would also request a local brew that would be even stronger. My cocktail cabinet at home is still filled with the remnants of the disgusting concoctions that we were given. I can remember us rolling into our hotel in Milan at seven one morning and still flying from a show we had done the night before in Montreux. A group of suited Italian businessmen was trying to check out at the same time and one or two of them started to bark complaints at the bunch of dishevelled reprobates slumped against the front desk. They were quickly silenced by Luke. He shouted back at them: 'Fuck off or I will buy you all and keep you as pets in my back yard!'

As I did not have a record deal in the US for *Candyman*, one of my best childhood friends, Scott Carlson (aka 'Serge'), introduced me to the head of A&R at RCA, a girl named Leslie Lewis. I fell for her and she moved in with me for a year or so. But, in the end, I could not take the relationship any farther and it all fell apart. But, thankfully, we're still friends now.

Finally, the band's managers called Paich and me. Once more, they pointed out the financial benefit to us of making another Toto record for Columbia. A million a record is nothing to sneeze at. I was never going to be able to go out and make a million dollars under my own name and I had a responsibility to provide for my children and family if no one else. I suppose that I had also come to accept that Jeff's life had ended, but that didn't mean that all of our lives had to stop too. Again, Paich and I went and asked the Porcaro family for their blessing. And again their feeling was that the band not playing music wouldn't bring Jeff back, so why wouldn't we do it in the spirit of him?

With that in mind, we called up one of Jeff's very favourite engineers, our friend Elliot Scheiner, who had recorded and mixed Steely Dan, and we went with him into Capitol Studios. Paich and I wrote songs together on piano and using an acoustic guitar I borrowed from Billy Mumy. Mikey and Simon came up with stuff too, and we also wrote together as a band. Elliot pushed us to go back to the earlier, more organic, acoustic Toto sound. The synthesisers took a back seat as Steve Porcaro was not very involved. What ended up being the *Tambu* record showed very much a different side of us. Also, the sound of a record is always somewhat dependent on your mood.

Together with Stan Lynch, I wrote one of my favourite songs for *Tambu*, which was 'I Will Remember'. I came up with the music on the fly one day over at Mikey's house and then Stan came up with the lyrics. It was a song about relationships and at that very same time, the pair of us shared something of a complex one. One day at the start of one of the sessions, Stan had brought his then girlfriend, Beth-Ami, along with him to the studio. She was funny, engaging and gorgeous with long black hair, and I was bowled over. We all went out to dinner that evening and when I came to kiss everyone goodnight, and having had five martinis, I very obviously lingered on Beth-Ami for a moment longer than anyone else.

Stan had cracked up at that, but also the two of them were on the verge of breaking up anyway. Once they did, and after I had first squared it with Stan, I called Beth-Ami up and asked her out on a date. Her initial reaction was to protest that she was not the type of girl that would be passed around, but I was persistent and she finally said yes. She ended up moving in with me and we lived together for the next two years. Ours would be a fiery, tumultuous and passionate relationship. It was a lot of fun but we fought a lot too because I was still a crazy party man. We hit the rocks only because ultimately she wanted to get married and have kids, while I was still smarting from my divorce. That's why it fell apart. But we're still great friends to this day.

Tambu, released in Europe in May 1995, went on to be a pretty successful record for us outside of America, enough anyway for Columbia to pick up their option on the band. More importantly and after all that we had been through together, it gave us renewed purpose and a reason to go on being. After we came off the road from touring it, I felt as if I had been righted and more positive than I had been in a long time. (We had an amazing tour in Europe, and those were the best of times for Beth-Ami and myself.)

They were still crazy times. One night, Simon and his then girlfriend Charlotte and I went up to Slash's house to shoot the shit and have a few laughs. However, I neglected to share with either of them the news that Slash had added to his eclectic menagerie of pets a cougar named Curtis. I had been up to Slash's many times and encountered Curtis as a cub, and even then he had scared the crap out of me. In big-cat terms, he was now entering his teenage years and this filled me with some considerable trepidation. Soon as we got there, Curtis stalked up to check us out. He had very much grown, but he knew me by smell at least, so that I was able to pet him somewhat. Charlotte was much less enamoured, but Slash assured her not to worry, and that if you were firm with Curtis then he would be no trouble.

Curtis sloped off and we settled into the living room. After a bit, Slash, Simon and I went off into the kitchen to fix some drinks and hang, leaving Simon's girlfriend alone on the couch. We were gone for just a few minutes, laughing away, when we heard this muted, strangled voice drifting in from the other room: 'Help . . .

me. Help . . . me.' I was going, 'What the fuck?' Then a horrible realisation dawned on Slash and he burst out, 'Holy shit – Curtis!' The three of us raced out the door to find that Curtis had got Simon's girlfriend pinned to the couch.

In reality, Curtis could have hurt her but he was just playing. Not surprisingly, the poor girl was terror-struck and had tears rolling down her face. In one quick movement, Slash scooped Curtis off her and threw him across the room. At which point, Charlotte snapped. 'Get . . . me . . . the . . . fuck . . . out . . . of . . . this . . . madhouse!' she shrieked. I looked over at Slash, shrugged, made a WTF face and said: 'I'll see ya later, man.'

CHAPTER TWENTY-THREE

As I look back now, the ensuing ten years of my life appear to me as one long crazy, jumbled blur. Certainly, that span was an emotional rollercoaster ride and ultimately drained me to the point that I was running on empty and sought to drown myself in booze. The hole in my heart just kept on getting bigger and I felt increasingly empty inside. I started to pull away from the people closest to me, including my own family. Drink had got the better of me, but I didn't want to admit that and so remained defiant and self-destructive. I also remained single for a while.

I worked incessantly with or without the band. If Toto wasn't active, I found other stuff to do to keep busy and somewhat sane. In 1997, I wrote, recorded and released my third solo record, *Luke*. I co-wrote half of the songs with Phil Soussan. He and I were close friends and neighbours at the time and I thought we wrote some interesting, cool things that were darker and dirtier than anything I had done prior. Tom Fletcher co-produced again but he was putting distortion on everything and it took time for me to get used to it. I ended up having Elliot Scheiner remix the album.

Where its predecessor was made with an altogether positive vibe running through it, the backdrop to the *Luke* record was my breaking up with Beth-Ami. She had given me an ultimatum that I didn't feel able to meet. I had lost a lot of weight from being so stressed out and some of the lyrics were darker, more autobiographical. I wrote one great song, 'Hate Everything about U', with the legendary country singer Rodney Crowell. That had nothing to do with Beth-Ami specifically, but was more of a general take on break-ups and divorce. I hadn't been so lucky in that regard. Not that I helped the situation with Beth-Ami by drinking so much and being such a madman. She had to put up with a lot from me and I'm not particularly proud of how I behaved some of the time.

Several years of working, raising my kids and insanity passed, then my guitar tech Jerry Sabatino and Elliot Scheiner invited me out to Burbank Studios to see John Fogerty film a live show for MTV. John had sung on a track on our *Kingdom of Desire* record, 'She Knows the Devil', for which he had asked to be uncredited. I went by myself – I don't know what made me do that as I hardly ever went anywhere alone. John was great, as always, but my lasting impression of the evening was not anything that he did. At a certain point in the show, this stunning woman all of a sudden appeared, looking for someone. Shawn Batten was beautiful, very self-confident and wearing a 'Star 80' T-shirt. She marched right up to me and said, 'Are you wearing patchouli oil? It smells good on you.' Instantly, I was taken. Really taken.

After the show, a bunch of us were going across the road to a bar called the Smoke House. It's an old-school place with red leather seats and I invited Shawn to join us. I found out that she was an aspiring actress. She had moved to LA from the East Coast, trying to get a break, and had been at the Fogerty bash working as a PA for a friend for the dough. We were sitting with Kenny Aronoff, who was playing drums in Fogerty's band, and began ordering cocktails. Kenny ordered a cosmopolitan, so I said, 'Sure, why not?' and Shawn asked for a double Jack Daniel's, straight up, which made think to myself, *I really dig this girl.* She had balls. She was very chatty and funny, and when she got up to leave at the end of the night, I wrote my number down for her on a napkin and asked her to call me as we'd had such a great hang, and I was not sure she knew I was interested. She told me that she was going back east to spend Christmas with her folks, so I assumed that would be the last I would hear from her.

A couple of weeks later, Shawn surprised me by calling and we ended up going out to dinner. That was the start of my next major relationship. Shawn didn't make it easy for me – you know what I mean – and there were fourteen years between us in age, but we took it slow. We partied and hung and got along like a house on fire. I fell in love. She and I seemed to fit perfectly. Shawn got a regular acting gig on a soap called *Sunset Beach* and I fell utterly in love all over again: a woman with a great-paying gig . . . it just kept getting better. She had a nice family, too.

At the very same time, Toto had a twentieth anniversary coming up. I hadn't even thought of it, but Mark Hartley made the suggestion that we dig around the vault and see what leftover songs we had lying around for a commemorative release of B-sides, stuff we left off due to time constraints or because we just didn't think the tune fit a record, and unreleased live recordings. As it happened, there was an abundance of stuff from our original demos and tracks dating back to the days before CD that we hadn't been able to fit onto our vinyl records. We picked out the best of this bunch and released them as the *Toto XX: 1977–1997* record in 1998.

Since that record encompassed all eras of the band and we were in a state of flux anyway, Dave Paich and I had the idea of bringing Bobby Kimball, Joe Williams and Steve Porcaro back for a short promotional tour. We had lined up a few shows in key European cities and I thought it might be fun for the fans and also give us fresh impetus. Joe, Steve P. and I had remained good friends, but as a band we hadn't had any contact with Bobby in more than eight years. We got in touch and had him come by Paich's house. The two of them sat around the piano playing different things and Bobby's voice was sounding great, as good as ever. Steve Porcaro agreed to come back too, which thrilled me as he was always my friend and I had missed his 'thing' that no one else can do. So we all got together and rehearsed and then went off to Europe and had a really good time. The slate had been wiped clean and if we were going to press on as a band, it seemed to make sense for us to go back to the egg.

Back home in LA, Paich and I began to meet up at his beach house to write songs on piano and acoustic guitar. It was just the same way that we had kick-started the *Tambu* record and I was in a really good head space. We had a clear plan for the band. We were going to make a new album with Bobby and then do a full reunion tour with him. As well, I was forty years old, had met this great girl and wanted to settle down. It wasn't long, though, before the same old frustrations came rushing back into play.

As was ever the case, Bobby had a tough time in front of a microphone in the studio. Paich was a patient man and he and Elliot excelled at getting vocals out of Bobby so it was sort of left in their laps, and perhaps it was easier for Bobby without everyone else in the room. Dave and Elliot, who was co-producing, did manage to get great vocals out of him, but with a lot of time being used up and infinite patience. In retrospect, we also cut too many tracks for what became the *Mindfields* record. It ended up running to fourteen songs and would have benefitted from us trimming the fat. I always felt that, but in that era Dave kept saying, 'Let's use up all the CD time.'

Next, we ran into the same hurdle that we had for the previous ten years,d which was that Columbia initially refused to release the record in the States. My old friend John Kalodner was working at Sony and, because of our friendship, had said he wanted to work with us on the record, which would have really helped us, except he never helped at all. He showed up at the end of the record and called me to say he hated it. I said he was wrong. He said he knew I would say that, and that was the last time I spoke to John Kalodner. I used to work on all his records and I thought we were friends. It was as if Ienner had called him and said, 'Bury these assholes.' And he did.

Joe and Steve didn't join us for the subsequent tour, which took in Europe and Japan. However, Bobby's return proved a big draw and we were again filling arenas. In Paris, we played to 17,000 people at the Bercy Arena. Ironically, right before the show that night, Columbia presented us with plaques for selling twelve million records across Europe and getting all sorts of awards. Overall, it was a good run. Everyone got on and audiences seemed to dig having that voice back in the band, but towards the end of it we could hear that Bobby was once again labouring. He would have a good night, then a bad one. As he had gotten older, it was even harder for him to reach his top range. We were forced to lower the keys of some songs and also throw the ball around a bit with the lead vocals. There was nothing wrong with lowering the key as no one thought we would still be doing some of these songs all years later, but the situation was getting bad again.

Right in the middle of us making *Mindfields*, I got a call from Larry Carlton's then manager Susan to invite me to do a series of shows in Japan with Larry. I couldn't resist being able to play with Carlton and also it was a good payday, so I begged a couple of weeks off from the studio. We showed up with no rehearsals and figured out some jams at soundcheck. We played to packed houses all over Japan, doing two sets a night, and got an overwhelming response. Each show that we did was basically an extended jam. We had a designated start and end to our set, but whatever happened in between was always open to change. Larry and I would spend an hour or two together before each show, which also meant that I was able to pick his brain and learn a lot.

Things were going so well that we decided to record the remaining shows. The band were killer: Gregg Bissonette, the late great Chris Kent on bass and Rick Jackson on keys and we tore it up. Steve Vai and Ray Scherr had just then started up their own label, Favored Nations, and after I got done with the Toto tour, I brokered a deal to release Larry's and my record. It eventually came out as *No Substitutions* in 2001. Steve Vai, our pal Matt Resnicoff and I went through all the takes, picked the best ones and did some editing and mixing, and the following February won a Grammy for Best Pop Instrumental Album. That's the category where they dump everybody that they don't know what to do with, and it was hardly a pop record. Yet it was an unexpected thrill.

Not long after we won that Grammy, I was once more a married man. Shawn and I were wed in Malibu on 11 May 2002. Trev was my best man and afterwards Shawn and I enjoyed a blissful honeymoon in Hawaii. I thought the two of us were the perfect match and for a good while we were. It was hands-down one of the best times of my life, and I flew home to yet another irresistible surprise. Elliot Scheiner and Al Schmitt were also in the process of launching a record label and asked me to be their first artist on Bop City Records. More specifically, they wanted me to make them a Christmas record. I cracked up and said, 'OK, guys, what the fuck about me says Santa Claus to you?'

Elliot and Al put a small budget at my disposal and I had a week to do the record from top to bottom. As the title suggests, *Santamental* turned out to be one of the most fun records I have done. I went into it with the notion of cutting high-energy, fucked-up versions of traditional Christmas tunes and put together a core band of John Pierce, Jeff Babko on keys and, on drums, Gregg Bissonette. There was no time for us to be able to rehearse and we had to do the tracks live in one or two takes. It was the middle of June and Bissonette, God bless him, showed up with Christmas lights and decorated the whole studio.

I've got to hand it to Jeff Babko, who arranged most of the

songs with me, because some of the re-voicings are just crazy and not what you expect at all . . . The guy's a genius. Thanks, man!

We did 'Silent Night' and 'Greensleeves', as well as 'Winter Wonderland' with Edgar Winter.

For a big-band version of 'Jingle Bells', I got permission from Sammy Davis Jr's widow, Altovise, to sample his voice and have him do a posthumous duet with me. That was meant as a tongue-in-cheek kind of thing – I even made the guitar solo a little out of tune just to tweak people – but in reality came out too good to be funny. I also had Eddie Van Halen, Steve Vai, Slash, Mike Landau and a host of other friends come down and trade solos with me for the record.

Belatedly, Elliot and Al presented me with the greatest challenge of *Santamental* and that was to add a couple of original Christmas songs of my own. How do you even begin to go about writing such a thing, right? In the first instance, I had Babko help me with a tune we called 'Look Out for Angels'. Then Stan Lynch weighed in with a great lyric for the other track that Jeff and I worked up, 'Broken Heart for Christmas'. I think it would be fair for me to claim that this latter song is still unique in the annals of Christmas records. After all, it was about Santa Claus wanting to get laid and not being able to.

This record led, years later, to the yearly thing of performing Christmas songs with my new band Nerve Bundle, featuring Babko, Toss Panos on drums and Jorgen Carlsson from Gov't Mule on bass. It was Jorgen's idea to put the band together. I'm glad he did as we have done sell-out December shows at the Baked Potato for the last seven years.

Toto's twenty-fifth anniversary in 2002 seemed to have rolled around in the blink of an eye. Our deal with Columbia was done and we had a new offer from EMI, but hadn't got any new material together whatsoever. At a band meeting, we had the idea of instead marking this latest milestone with a covers album and to do our own versions of songs that had influenced each of us as kids. Simon had got a home studio by then and we moved into his place for the month and a half that it took us to make *Through the Looking Glass*.

All told, that record was made up of a very weird and eclectic bunch of songs. Of the more obvious stuff, we did an inevitable Beatles tune, 'While My Guitar Gently Weeps', which I wanted to dedicate to George after his passing in 2001, and Elton John's 'Burn Down the Mission' because we knew very well that Bobby would be able to nail it and we all love Elton, but also a left-field take on Bob Marley's 'Could You Be Loved'. We called in an English cat, name of DJ Tippa Irie, to rap on the Marley track, and by way of just throwing stuff against the wall. That was Paich's doing. David's very open-minded musically, and I think he wanted to be black at some point in his life.

My wife Shawn lobbied for us to do the Elvis Costello tune, 'Watching the Detectives', which groove-wise was a bookend to 'Could You Be Loved'.

Costello had always hated our band. He had said so many shitty things about us in the press that it seemed a good way of goading him back. For the vocal, I did a sort of obnoxious, cartooning take on his distinctive singing style. I happen to think that he's a really good songwriter and I don't carry around grudges about other artists. As for Costello, I'm not sure that he even bothered to hear what we had done to his song, but he made some money off us. Maybe money helped to chill him out in his old age.

For the longest time, I had been driven to distraction fretting about what people thought of us, but we had at last reached the point of not caring about it any more. And just as well. *Through the Looking Glass* came out to very mixed reviews. Even our fans were like, 'What the fuck?' Some people dug it and most people thought it the worst, most offensive shit that we had ever done. The critics already hated us. This was like sending them some lube and a photo of me smiling.

Hardly anyone 'got it'. These were songs from our childhood we did for fun in Simon's living room as we had not played together in quite some time, and it meant that we could tour for our twenty-fifth anniversary. The guys at EMI liked it, and then everyone turned on us. At least we got a DVD out of it and the record sold OK, surprisingly enough, but our time at EMI was already over.

We did a lot of touring through the next couple of years and a good deal of it was fun. In 2003, we did the 'Night of the Proms tour' with some great people including our pals INXS, John Miles, Huey Lewis and En Vogue with a full orchestra and choir, which was a lot of fun. Too much fun sometimes.

As time passed I began to look around and started to think to myself that this wasn't truly the band we started in 1977. In 2003, after the second show, Simon got sick and had to go home to get well. In the interim my dear friend Jon Farriss from INXS stepped in. He did a brilliant job of learning our set in one night. But the promoters wanted us to have our own band. We then brought in studio man and ex-Steely Dan drummer Ricky Lawson (RIP) to fill in. Ricky had played with Stevie Wonder and Clapton, but his vibe was the complete opposite of Simon's. He would only play in a certain way and not want to meet us in the middle. Next thing, Paich's sister fell seriously ill and he also went home. We got in Greg Phillinganes, who we all loved, for Paich but I couldn't help but think that we were turning into the best Toto tribute band ever.

For me, there could not have been a worse period for us to start our Italian misadventure, which would come back to haunt us a few years down the line.

In 2005, we were approached by a guy named Serafino Perugino with an offer that sounded too good to be true. Perugino was from Naples and, apparently, stinking rich. He had founded his own record label, Frontiers Records, and wanted to pay us a shitload of money to make a classic-sounding Toto record. Perugino had basically been collecting up his favourite rock bands from the 1980s. Nevertheless, we met with Perugino and he was so accommodating to us that we couldn't refuse him.

We pulled out all of the stops on a new record. Just as *Kingdom of Desire* had been, *Falling in Between* turned out to be a band album in the truest sense. Everybody co-wrote songs and it was a very big-sounding record. Paich and Simon were back with us in the studio. Paich wanted Phillinganes to remain with the band because he was going to have to be back and forth with his sister. Steve still didn't want to tour – he was happy staying at home, being a dad and doing music for TV and film – but he worked on that record too. Joe even dropped by and sang on some stuff alongside Bobby. We had Lenny Castro do percussion, as we did on all our records. Jimmy Pankow from Chicago did horn parts, and one of our childhood heroes, Ian Anderson of Jethro Tull, came and played flute on a song called 'Hooked'.

When we put that record out in February 2006, we got some of the best reviews that we had ever had. It was universally well received, which was virgin territory for us. Back out on the road we went, but even before the first night the wind had dropped from our sails. Paich had intended to join us, but his sister took a turn for the worse and was dying. He had to go be big brother and hold the family together. The opening show was in London and that night Bobby's voice went south. The band was on fire and we had a great production to back us up, but his lead vocals were screaming way out of tune. Of course, Bobby blamed it on the monitors, which he always did. He may even have had a case on this occasion. I think one of his monitors did give out, but to compensate he over-sang and was way too sharp. He wasn't even in the ballpark of the tune. After the show, people were coming up to me with appalled or horrified looks on their faces, asking me: 'What the fuck?'

Surprise: I went to the bar.

As the tour wound on, Mikey also began to experience problems.

He'd had trouble with his left thumb while we were making the album and had gone for tests, which were inconclusive. We had put it down to something like a slipped disc or trapped nerve, but his condition worsened. On stage, you could see the stress written all over his face. His brain would send the signal, but his hands wouldn't move quite as instantly as they should. We couldn't help but see how much he was struggling. It got to where he would feel so weak that he would have to sit down to play.

We did a year on the road and had some further festival shows lined up, but it became apparent that Mikey simply couldn't go on. He picked Lee Sklar to come out to join us and Mikey went back to LA for more tests. We thought of everything that might be wrong with him, except, that is, for the worst possible diagnosis. None of us even considered the concept of amyotrophic lateral sclerosis (ALS), or motor neurone disease as that dreadful affliction is also known. As far as we were concerned, Mikey would get over whatever it turned out to be.

The rest of us hung in there and did the best that we could, but there was a lot of denial going on in general. There would be good nights, but others when Bobby just wasn't able to deliver. Towards the end of the run, there were times that he was even forced into lip-syncing. At the same time, I was thinking of Mike's whole family, his wife Cheri and their kids. I got to be so miserable that I drank all the more. The routine I had of guzzling to sleep at night got to start a little earlier each day and then the guys would bitch at me about my boozing. From my perspective, the situation became them against me and got to be ugly. Bobby in particular would bust my balls. I would be like, 'Really? This is coming from the guy that can't sing.' Lee was one of my oldest friends and has never boozed or done drugs, but he would hang all night with me because of his insomnia. Otherwise, I was something of a pariah among guys who hadn't even had anything to do with any of our hit records.

Leland Sklar: I loved doing that tour with the guys, but at the same time there was a certain amount of tension in the air and Luke had a hard time dealing with a lot of the things that went down. My friendship with him goes way beyond music and I became his go-to guy whenever things got difficult. I was glad that he would come and confide in me. Those were tough times for him, but he's very strong-willed and that also helped him to prevail.

In the end, I gave the band and the management an ultimatum, which was to pay me twice as much as anyone else or I would walk. After all, I was the only original member who never missed anything Toto. Really, I was just looking for a way out and they were never going to cough up. They said no to me. I announced my decision to quit the band in the summer of 2007. I called up Paich first and told him of my intention to leave. He said, 'What took you so long?' Latterly, I had just been doing it for the money, going through the motions, and I couldn't live like that any longer. None of the other guys owned the Toto name either, so the band was over.

CHAPTER TWENTY-FOUR

I had imagined that leaving the band would make me a better, happier person. In fact, all too soon the reality ended up being quite the opposite and I got to find my rock bottom. It is true that much of that was self-inflicted and, to this day, it's hard for me to have to rake back over that ruined ground. I was touring a lot with my solo band, with keyboard giant Steve Weingart, his wife Renee on bass and vocals and drummer Eric 'Biggie' Valentine; we had a lot of fun. However, I take some comfort from the knowledge that I was eventually able to get back up on my feet. That was an achievement in itself, I think. In those next two years I took a series of hits, any one of which would have knocked me out had I not been gifted with a strong and stubborn instinct for survival.

To begin with, I threw myself full-force into my solo career. I quickly made another record, aptly titled *Ever Changing Times*, which was released in 2008. One of the best bits about it was that I was able to have my son Trev involved. He had gotten to be a very talented musician and all through his own hard work and dedication, which made me enormously proud. The two of us wrote a couple of songs together, 'New World' and 'Tell Me

What You Want from Me', and I had him come down to the studio and cut both of them with the band and me. I have an indelible memory of sitting back at the desk and producing Trev alongside Lee Sklar, Abe Laboriel Jr and Jeff Babko. He played great, too. This record came to pass because of my dear friend Randy Goodrum, who wanted me to be the first artist on their new label.

> **Trev Lukather:** *I used to jam on drums with my dad. Those are some of the fondest memories I have of being a kid. I played drums from four till twelve and then I got to see Toto play. First song, Dad went and ripped into a solo. It was so sick and all of the fans were reaching out to touch him. Right then, I thought, 'Man, I want to do that!' I went to Dad and pleaded with him to teach me guitar, said I wanted to be just like him. He got me a guitar, tuned my E string to a D, so that it would sound like a power chord, said, 'Have fun, man,' and left the room. He had no patience for tutoring.*
>
> *The advice that Dad did give me was not to sit learning scales all day long, but to practise how to write songs. Dad said that being a flash player would only get you so far, but the business was all about songwriting. Or as he would put it, 'It's all about the mailbox money, man!' Dad was my mentor. He produced my first demos, which led to me getting my first professional gig. At seventeen, I was made Lindsay Lohan's musical director. Dad gave me a lot of freedom, too. He would say, 'Go out and do your thing, but if you mess it up . . .' and give me the evil eye. That's a Lukather trait – the hairy eyeball and a stare that can paralyse you on the spot.*
>
> (Note from Dad: Trev came on tour in Europe with me at thirteen and was caught backstage with a photographer's four-teen-year-old daughter in a state of partial undress. I knew then my dream of him becoming a doctor would never happen.)

Sklar looked up to me at one point that day and gasped, 'I can't believe this, man. I'm out here playing with the kids of people that

I've known and worked with all my musical life.' Time surely had sped by. I was closing in on fifty and Shawn had been after me for long enough for us to have our own child. We had been trying by then for a couple of years but nothing had happened, and probably because I was poisoning myself most every day. Eventually, I stopped drinking for a while and Shawn fell pregnant. We had ourselves a beautiful baby girl, Lily Rose, our little angel, and it was a trip for me to be a father again at that age. I fell in love so hard with that baby and was very happy. My older kids, Tina and Trev, all of a sudden had a baby sister, which must have been a little weird at first, but now everyone is really tight. Shawn and I had a second child, Bodhi, and it makes me feel great that my little ones have two big siblings to keep my vibe around them when I go to the great gig in the sky.

I jumped right back into work and made another record of my own, *All's Well That Ends Well*, which was co-produced, co-written, engineered and mixed by C. J. Vanston, one of the most brilliant musicians I've ever worked with (I brought him along to work with us on *Toto XIV*). The album came out in 2010, and then we put a band together and went out on the road again. Toto had lain dormant ever since I had walked out, but the core of us remained like family and when one hurt, we all did. Mike finally got his ALS diagnosis, which was shattering. I felt for his wife Cheri and their kids Brianne, Sam and Jeffrey, and for Mike too, of course – one of the best people ever, who had been given this fucked-up disease. It was so cruel.

Then Steve went to his doctor complaining of headaches. He had an MRI scan and they found he had a huge brain tumour. Fortunately, it was benign, but they still had to go in and take it out, and one of the risks of doing that was that they might damage crucial ear nerves.

Steve was scared by the odds, but went in and had the operation. They managed to remove the tumour, but at the cost of him losing his hearing in one ear. This was the guy who was king of stereo imaging and so he was beyond devastated. He got really depressed for a time and had to completely relearn his craft, but I've never seen anyone be given lemons and turn them into lemonade faster. My admiration for him grew to be even greater through that very emotional period but, goddammit, it seemed as if we were beset with disaster and illness at every corner.

True to form, my own lowest point arrived directly after we had gotten a tremendous boost. Towards the end of 2009, Toto was inducted into the Musicians' Hall of Fame in Nashville. That was a big deal for us because only fellow musicians can vote you the honour. It's not bestowed by twelve angry music journalists in Ramones T-shirts that are way too small for their beer bellies, jumping off Champ amps at the Christmas party while they scream, 'Rock is dead,' or whatever arrogant rock journos do. There wasn't even a band as such at that point, but Paich, Steve, Hungate and I went along to represent Toto at the induction ceremony.

I got back to LA for my fiftieth birthday and played with my solo band at the Roxy. We had a party, at which I pummelled myself real hard. In any event, by then I looked like shit and felt like it all of the time. Bobby got all pissed off with me as if I had kept him out of the Hall of Fame thing, but the honour was given to the musicians. I had nothing to do with it.

I was not doing well. Emotionally I was empty. Looking around me, I knew this feeling was wrong, but I was trying to work and money was tight at that time, and I was sad inside. But my baby Lily made me happy and I just hung in boozing my way through it.

The day after my fiftieth birthday gig I was sitting in the garage, first thing in the morning. Shamefully, I needed a hair of the dog, just a beer or something. That's a bad sign right there when you start boozing before breakfast to make the pain go away. Plus, I had a hacking cough from way too much smoking. I opened up the freezer and saw that I had left in it an ice-cold bottle of Absolut vodka. I did one of those look left, look right moves, but in my demented, still half-drunk mind, I thought that it was my pain medicine. I took the bottle out, tipped it up and glugged on it. I lit a cigarette, took a second gulp and that was when I noticed Shawn standing in the garage doorway and staring at me.

She just shook her head and said, 'So it's come to this now, huh?'

I was busted, having turned into something I swore I never would be, which was a hopeless fucking drunk.

I had tears in my eyes and was so ashamed. I looked back at Shawn and said to her, 'I know, but that's it, I quit.' She didn't even begin to believe me. She said that she knew how it was with me, that I would stop for a couple of weeks, maybe even a month, but then slip right back into a bottle again. I told her not this time, and ever since that morning I've not touched another drop of drink or had even a puff of a smoke. I never went to rehab or an AA meeting either, I was just done. That isn't to say that AA hasn't been incredibly beneficial for others. I had many friends who were then going through the twelve-step programme and I did reach out to them but, ultimately, I did this on my own.

It was ironic that a whole bunch of my guitar-playing, drinking buddies also stopped around that very same time – Eddie, Slash, Neal Schon, Zakk Wylde etc.. We were all well-known lunatics, but all of us got ourselves back together. For each of us, it was also a very private thing. Shawn was the only person who I even told about my new-found sobriety. I didn't want to make a grandiose announcement, because if you fuck up everyone is liable to go, 'Ah, told you so.' When he eventually found out about it, even my own doctor was stunned. He told me, 'Dude, you're a medical anomaly. I wouldn't have bet a dime on you being able to pull sobriety off, and I like you.'

For all of that, 2010 was still the toughest, weirdest fucking year of my whole life. Sobering up brought me the clarity of mind to take a long, hard look at myself and the way that I had been living. My most uncomfortable realisation was about the state of my marriage. Shawn and I had grown so far apart that we were more like reluctant room-mates than husband and wife. It was as if all the love between us had left the house and, try as we did, it couldn't be brought back. No one was to blame really. We were great party buddies, but we were both on a different page at that time. I think she wanted out but didn't want to make the first move.

It was an awful time for both of us and made much harder by the fact that Shawn got pregnant again even as we were coming apart. Well, kids, it is true you can have sex once and get pregnant. I had cleaned up for about six months by then and I was leaving to do a tour in France and . . . well, you know what happened. It was kind of weird. There was no love in it at all, and I was immediately off to the airport in a car that had been sent for me. In April, we found out that we were having a baby and Shawn moved out soon after. It was a really bad time for us.

For a time, things were just as difficult between us as could be imagined and all that we did was argue and butt heads, but very gradually the situation got to be easier. We went through a mediation process and I wanted for us to have as fair and amicable a divorce as possible, which ultimately we were able to do. She bought a house and lives eight minutes from me, and after almost nine years clean we're now best friends.

Our son Bodhi was born on 12 December 2010. I was out watching Lee Ritenour play with my pal and bassist Tal Wilkenfeld, and Shawn called to tell me that her water had broken (two weeks too early), and asked me to take her to the hospital. I said of course. We went through the whole birthing process as if we were still man and wife. It was a very unique and bizarre situation, of course, but it didn't mean that I adored our son any the less. If anything, the whole sorry episode brought me closer to both of our children and eventually to Shawn, too. I look back on a lot of that period with such sadness and regret. Although it took a lot of work for us to get there, Shawn and I are now the best of friends. I have the utmost respect for her and, when I'm not on the road, we share the parenting of the kids fifty-fifty. We speak every day. I see the kids on FaceTime or Shawn will say, 'Come by and see the kids.' We spend family birthdays and, every other year, Christmas together. For alternate Christmases, she goes back east to her family, and the kids have a great time with their grandparents, aunt, uncle and cousins on the Jersey shore. I used to go when we were married and really enjoyed it.

That's the way that both Bodhi and Lily have been brought up and they don't know any different, but they do know that their mom and dad are utterly devoted to them.

Around the time that Shawn and I were splitting up, my mom was drinking herself to death. God rest her soul, she got so miserable once Dad had died that she crawled deep inside a bottle and never came out. I saw her wither away before me and it was horrible to have to watch. Having been sober for six months and quit smoking after thirty-five years, I tried to be an example to her, saying, 'Mom, if I can do it . . .'

At the end, she was not more than eighty pounds wet. On Father's Day 2010,* Trev, who was living with his girlfriend at the time, wanted to take me out for breakfast. While we were on our way out, I got a call from my mom, desperate and wheezing. She sounded very weak and just about managed to say, 'Steven, help me.' Mom was the only person to ever address me as Steven.

Trev and I found her dead on the couch. She had a look of horror frozen on her face, cigarette still burning and a tumbler of shitty vodka on the table. I was crushed, and my oldest son had to see this?

---

* I lost my father to bone marrow cancer in 1993. The memories are still so painful that I can't begin to write about them.

Poor Trev was stood there in complete shock, while I was crying and going, 'Holy-fuck-holy-fuck-holy-fuck!' I didn't know what to do. I called my sister. Lora was living in Kansas at the time and was obviously freaked out. As the two of us were talking, I couldn't help but stare at Ma and she looked like something out of a bad horror film. It was so wrong and fucked up that I just started to laugh nervously. When Lora heard me, she did too. The two of us laughed and then cried, or else did both at the same time. Eventually, I asked Trev to get me a sheet to put over my mother until Lora and I could figure out who was going to come and take care of her body. My mom had wanted to be cremated and made all necessary arrangements. My sister and her then husband really bailed me out with the selling of Mom's house and going through things because I was working on the road.

That was the day that I became an orphan. Another thing hit me, too. If you look at these things in a chronological order, then I am the next in line to go in our family. That's a very strange place to be, and especially when you have young children. I was also breaking up with my pregnant wife, so it would be true to say that my emotional state was somewhat fragile. It was an all-too-intense time and, by that same summer, Mike had also got to be really sick. This was truly the lowest I had ever been.

After Lee Sklar had taken over from him in the band, Mike had really begun his descent into health hell. He started to lose muscle control. At first, he was able to still get around with the aid of a cane, then slowly but surely ended up being confined to bed. That's the creeping nightmare of ALS. When we were kids, we had never heard of it. Maybe one in a million people would contract it, but like a lot of neurological diseases, it's more prevalent now. I'm convinced that's down to the chemicals that they put in our food or nasty shit in the air and water that no one tells us about. I don't know whether that's true, but when you are losing a best friend, you try to make sense of it. My heart was broken for his wonderful wife and my friend Cheri and their kids, who I adore.

As Mike deteriorated, his medical bills ratcheted up. Paich called me one day and said that we had to do something for Mike and his family, since he was unable to work. Mark Hartley had been pushing for us to get the band back together anyway, but, when I look back on it, he was probably just missing his stipend. The only way that I would ever have done it was for the right cause. Also, Paich and Steve Porcaro had to come back and a final stipulation of mine was that Joe Williams be our singer. With Bobby, it was never a personal vendetta for me – singing those songs is a hard gig – but people had heard just how much Bobby was grasping on the last tour we had done and we had got some wretched press.

Rather begrudgingly, Simon Phillips came back on board too. Lee couldn't because he was committed to doing the James Taylor and Carole King reunion, so Paich suggested we get Nathan East instead. Nathan was into it and later that year, in the summer of 2010, we did a tour of Europe. The response was amazing and we had the best time ever. We made a chunk of change for Mike and put some dough in our own pockets as well. I'm not going to lie: without Toto, money had gotten to be tight. For me also, it was a joy to look around the room and see my old high-school buddies again.

At the end of the run, we had all had such a blast that we agreed to do it all over again the next year. As that tour loomed the good vibes spread once more. We were intending to film a gig in Italy to mark our thirty-fifth anniversary in 2012, but Perugino had other ideas. He countered that we owed Frontiers Records another studio album. None of us was aware of this, but when we looked into it, there it was in the fine print of our contract. Somehow, it had been missed.

We had filmed a big show in Italy at a castle but, for reasons that remain unknown to me, our main lighting director Astro was demoted and our old guy, Andy Doig, came in and took over without me being told. Now, Andy is great and did a lot of tours with us, but he came in that day with no rehearsal. He was to do the outside lighting of the castle and check out the overall look, while Astro, who was killing it, was to do the rest. Things were really intense and weird, and the vibe was thick. Andy had to do the show blind, there were technical mishaps and it was not a great gig. It was a night I would like to forget. I barked at my dear pal, director Nigel Dick, for no reason other than I was pissed off at the world. Sorry, Nige. Dave and I bought and shelved the film, never to be seen, so that we didn't burn my friend Ed van Zijl at Mascot Records, a man I still work with on my solo stuff.

CHAPTER TWENTY-FIVE

The end of 2011 was a trip. I was booked to host an event at the Grammy Museum in LA. That night I was sitting with Scott Goldman, vice-president of the Grammy Foundation, before an audience of around 250 people over-stuffed into a room, answering questions about my career. People were laughing their asses off at my insane life. Scott had a bunch of questions to ask me about my whole life and career and had obviously done his homework. I had not been briefed on the questions as I wanted my answers and reactions to be fresh and real. It was fun, and that led to the idea that I should write a book. And here we are . . .

Around the same time, I was asked to join Ringo Starr & His All-Starr Band for a 2012 tour, which opened up a new and entirely wonderful chapter in my life. I could not tell anyone yet as he was finishing a tour with his old band in 2011 and I was asked to keep quiet. I had always wanted to be in Ringo's band. Earlier that year, Toto and the All-Starr Band had been touring Europe at the same time and Gregg Bissonette, my long-time brother and monster bad-ass drummer, came out to the Toto show in Paris. Gregg had already been in a couple of incarnations of the All-Starr Band and I had told him many times, 'If you ever need a guitar player, singer, etc . . .' So Gregg brought with him Dave Hart, who was Ringo's agent and producer, whose job it was to corral together various musicians and book the tours. Gregg thought that, if Dave saw me and liked me, he would tell Ringo and maybe I would get the call.

Ringo had launched his band back in 1989. The first line-up was a stellar one and featured Joe Walsh, Dr John, Clarence Clemons of the E Street Band, Nils Lofgren, Billy Preston, both Rick Danko and Levon Helm of the Band fame, and our mutual friend Jim Keltner. Since then, there had been eleven successive variations of the All-Starr Band, and Ringo would go out and tour with them a couple of times a year. They would all perform his own solo and Beatles songs, and each of the various band members would also get to front two or three of the hits that they were associated with. When we met that night, Dave Hart was in the process of assembling a twelfth version of the band for Ringo when he saw me play and I told him how much I wanted to be in the band. I wanted very much to work with another of my musical heroes, but also believed that I could really bring something to Ringo's band as a team player.

Gregg and Dave sold Ringo on the idea of me. My brother Jim Keltner put a good word in, too, because he and Ringo are close, and I was invited on board. The rest of the band was going to be Gregg, Todd Rundgren, whose music I loved, Gregg Rolie, who had been keyboard player with both of Santana and Journey, Richard Page, on bass and killer vocals and old friend, and saxophonist Mark Rivera. Mark was also Ringo's musical director and the sweetest of cats. We have become very close friends. He has done so many things, including playing with Billy Joel for decades and putting down *the* sax lick on Peter Gabriel's 'Sledgehammer'. The plan was to go out in the early part of summer 2012, so again I had to get time off from Toto. I was really nervous beforehand, simply because I wanted Ringo to like me.

That June, we were flown up to Canada to start All-Starr Band rehearsals. Ringo had taken over a place called Casino Rama, which is a luxury resort complex on Native American reservation land in Ontario, where we were to rehearse for a week. I got given a beautiful room that overlooked the Niagara Falls.

It wasn't until the first night there that I actually met Ringo in person. As I stepped out of the elevator on our floor, he opened up the door to his room to me. He gave me a big-ass hug, wished me well and said, 'OK, I'm off to bed now.' Clearly, the Boss meant for me to get an early night too. He didn't know me yet. By then, I was going to bed at around 9 p.m. and up around 6 or 7 a.m. every day no matter what. A far cry from the 'They tell me I had a great time' years.

Rehearsals started first thing the next morning. The initial day for a new band like that is always difficult because everybody is feeling how it all fits together, how we groove together and how we get along. I don't get nervous often but I was that morning. Todd was the only one of the guys who I didn't really know, in spite of the fact that we had just recently worked together. He had produced a track for the amazing Australian bass player Tal Wilkenfeld. The day itself was fun, but Todd was very reserved. It turned out that he did warm up, but it took a little time. Todd's also super-smart. If you ask him a question, for sure he will know the answer. I learned never to bet against him on things like that.

All of the guys were seasoned pros, worked hard and we clicked together right away, both musically and personally. After the first day, I knew we were going to be OK. It was going to be a great tour.

After a couple of days, Ringo asked me, 'Do you know Bill and Bob?' I hadn't a clue who or what the fuck Bill and Bob were, but he was being very serious about it. My confusion must have been obvious, because he fired straight back, 'Are you sober?' I wasn't aware that it was a Bill and Bob that had written the original AA handbook. Their names are used as a code among recovering alcoholics. I told Ringo that I had stopped drinking, smoking cigarettes and doing any illegal drugs many years prior but wasn't in AA and had personal counselling. Ours has developed into a great friendship and that's something that I really cherish.

Our version of the All-Starr Band has been the longest running and became a great family. I went into it with no expectations, because Ringo seemed to have wanted to change things up every year or so, but we have just kept on rolling together these last five years plus. It felt like a real band.

Ever since that summer 2012 tour, we have gone out together at least twice a year. It's been nothing but great fun and has blessed me with a great second act. I get to play not only the parts that George Harrison did on all of Ringo's Beatles and solo songs, but also Carlos Santana's with the legendary Gregg Rolie, plus all the cool Mr. Mister stuff that Richard Page brought and, in fact, all the music is fun to play. I know Todd hates playing 'Bang the Drum All Day' – it's a running joke – but I am also familiar with his deep cuts. He's a very musical guy.

Ringo also treats us like kings. We only stay at the best hotels and travel everywhere in a private G4 jet. It is a paid vacation for me. I get up early and do all the management stuff for Toto and practise, just like when I am at home. The only bummer is that I miss my kids so much. I must admit FaceTime is a life-saver in so many ways.

Ignorant critics have over the years ragged on Ringo's playing, but I will come to blows with anyone who doesn't recognise that he is *the* rock-drumming great of all time. He brought drums to the forefront of rock-and-roll. You have to first understand that the man never played to a click track. He created all of those parts himself and by never playing what was obvious. 'Tomorrow Never Knows', 'Ticket to Ride', 'A Day in the Life' . . . the list goes on and on. Every one of those amazing songs was made even more special by what Ringo did. He brought a unique swing to each of the Beatles' records. He's not a basher, but a very musical player. He swings hard and has a mean pocket, but it's as if he is caressing the backbeat. If you would have put any other drummer in there, then the Beatles would have been a completely different-sounding band and that can't be underlined hard enough.

In rock drumming terms, Ringo is the chicken that laid the egg. Drummer guys will understand what I mean: without Ringo, there wouldn't even have been any of the later drumming legends. Jeff Porcaro, for just one, gave him all the love. Ringo's very humble about all of that, but he explained to me once that the way that he plays is out of necessity. He's left-handed, whereas most other drummers lead with their right. He leads with his left, so he had to be more creative about how he got from one side of the kit and back to the other. He is also unschooled in the sense that he isn't able to read music. What Ringo does is 100 per cent heart, soul and instinct. Does anything else matter?

He can be quite funny about the Beatles. He doesn't want to sit around and talk about them all day long. In the All-Starr Band, we have asked him to do a Lennon–McCartney song, but he has been adamant that he won't, but there was one time that we were doing a soundcheck with no one else around, and I started to play 'I Should Have Known Better'. Everyone else in the band joined in and then Ringo jumped in. He gave it the full Ringo, too, hitting really hard, old-school, and doing that side-to-side thing with his head. The building was deserted, but there is a sound-desk recording of that jam that exists somewhere. I know that to be a fact because at the end of the song Ringo leaned down into his snare mic and said, 'Did you get that for Mr Lukather?', in his unmistakable Liverpudlian accent.

The fiftieth anniversary of the Beatles' first appearance on *The Ed Sullivan Show* came around in February 2014. Ringo asked me to be part of the TV special that CBS conceived to mark the event, *The Night that Changed America*, in LA, where it was being filmed before an invited audience. Don Was, who was musical director of the show, and I had worked on an Elton John record many years before. The concept was for artists such as Stevie Wonder, Alicia Keys, Brad Paisley, Pharrell Williams and Katy Perry to each sing a Beatles song, and be backed by an all-star band that Don put together. That band included my pals Peter Frampton, Greg Phillinganes, Kenny Aronoff, Lenny Castro, Don himself on bass, Rami the keyboard player from Foo Fighters and me. Ringo was also going to perform the tune 'Photograph' from his 1973 *Ringo* album at that 2014 Grammys, so I rehearsed for two things at once.

Katy Perry was going to do 'Yesterday', which I thought was an interesting call. Not being a teenager, I didn't personally know Katy, but she was dating John Mayer at the time, who's a great guitar player/songwriter I really dig, and the two of us had met. In advance of the filming, Don asked me to come down to Capitol Studios and sit with Katy to help her to figure out a key. She had no idea who I was. We were sitting in Don's office at Capitol Records and I was just being myself – I don't edit my act for anybody – and Katy was looking at me kind of funny, as if to say, 'Why are you even talking?'

The next time I saw her was at the gig and she was completely different towards me, super-nice. Maybe John had said something to her.

There were sensational moments as well. For a start, the hang was incredible and the band killer. Don invited us all over to Capitol to talk things through and he had with him the original sixteen-track masters of *Abbey Road*. Don was able to push up the faders and there was George singing 'Here Comes the Sun'. It was the lead vocal and you could hear the bleed through George's headphones. Man, I had chicken-skin arms. In my world, it doesn't get any better than the Beatles. All these years later, those recordings are pristine hi-fi, each of them beautifully played, recorded and sung. That's the gold standard of music.

On the night itself, there was a cool version of 'While My Guitar Gently Weeps' fronted by Joe Walsh and Gary Clark Jr, with Dave Grohl joining us on drums. Paul McCartney showed up with his amazing band, and watching him and Ringo sing 'Sgt. Pepper' into 'With a Little Help from My Friends' was a mind-fuck. There I was with Lenny Castro and Al Schmitt and Don Was watching the rehearsal (the only three people in the room beside the techs) when they did the 'Sgt. Pepper' transition into 'Little Help' for the first time. We were jumping out of our seats, freaking out. It was like a personal concert of the first time they had ever done this. It was unreal.

A few days later, right before we were due to go on to do the real show, I looked up and saw clips from *A Hard Day's Night* were being shown on the stage screens. Up until then, I had been consumed with remembering all of the parts and keys, since they were often going to be different from the originals. I didn't want to be the guy who fucked up on the gig. That moment hit me like a ton of bricks. I had made my paternal grandmother take me to see that film a hundred times and now I was among those chosen to honour the very same band that had changed all of our lives.

CHAPTER TWENTY-SIX

The realities of my own day-to-day life and also of being in Toto were sometimes hard for me to bear. When my youngest son Bodhi got to be three years old, he was physically fine but Shawn and I were concerned that he didn't talk a whole lot. We took him to the doctor for his regular check-up and he had Bodhi do a series of aptitude tests. Afterwards, he said that he wanted to refer Bodhi to a specialist to establish if he was 'on the spectrum', a code phrase for autism.

It was much the same routine with the specialist. He ran all the tests, but Bodhi didn't pay them a great deal of attention. Afterwards, the specialist looked Shawn and me right in the eye and told us, 'Your son is definitely autistic.' He informed us that we had caught this early and that there were treatments and therapies that could work for Bodhi, and that if we did this and that, by a certain age he might well have caught up with other children. I was hardly able to take in his words, because Shawn and I were crying in each other's arms.

However, once we got over the initial shock, for both of us it was a case of doing whatever we had to do, and we were going to love our boy twice as much. It was just a hurdle that was thrown into our lives to make things a little bit harder. As a spiritual person, I also happen to think that Bodhi was sent into this world to teach me what patience is all about and perhaps to heal the pain of our divorce as well. All of a sudden, something much bigger and more intense hit us both. We needed each other to get through it all.

I come from a long line of impatient, quick-tempered Lukather menfolk, including my own father. Bodhi has given me more than I could ever possibly give him in return, because he is the most pure-hearted spirit. He loves to be hugged and kissed, and to laugh. He is incredibly smart and a problem solver. See, so many people think autism is retardation: it is not! He is also a really good-looking kid, thanks to his mom, but one who just happens to be wired differently. Not a problem. His old man's a little different, too.

Somebody I know who also has an autistic son explained to me that Bodhi understands everything that's going on around him, but that his condition means that he sees things totally differently than we do. He has made great progress. By the time he's twelve, or thirteen, if not before, hopefully he's going to be in a regular class at school. The only thing that I live in fear of is that some wise-ass bully will make fun of him, because that would break my heart. Like any parent, I am hyper-protective of all of my kids. And I was bullied as a kid too.

In 2012, I returned to the studio to make a further solo album, *Transition*, with my pal, keyboard master and co-producer C. J. Vanston. That was a really good, positive experience, but I was in deep pain inside myself. I had failed as a husband again and I felt like shit about myself, because, after I sobered up, I saw things different. Bodhi was a huge wake-up call about how fragile life is.

Making this record was like coming out of darkness and back into the light. I had finally calmed down and got myself in order, and Shawn and I were establishing a friendship from out of the dust of our marriage. Returning to Toto, though, I was plunged yet again into rougher, more turbulent seas. The saddest part of our contractual dispute with the Italian record company on what we thought was a one-time-only record deal was that it tore us apart from our long-time managers, Mark and Larry. It was heartbreaking for me especially, because Mark, I thought, was a dear friend. Yet there was a lot of grumbling going on behind the scenes and the fact was that neither Mark nor Larry was stepping up on our account. The vibe was so thick you could not cut it with a chainsaw.

By then, the pair of them were all about Nashville. Larry had lived there for years so we had hardly even seen or heard from him for a long time. We had drifted and had nothing in common any more. The only thing that they seemed to care about was their country acts. In our case, they didn't seem to be driven to do more than pick up the phone, book a tour and ask for their percentage.

Paich and I went back and forth on what I thought was a personal email, and then we would forward our concerns to Mark.

Mark sent out a group letter by return and I was really disappointed with what he had to say. Meaning to forward it on to Paich, I wrote, 'We've got to bale,' and made a derogatory remark about our soon to be ex-managers as fake hillbillies. It was a fucked-up, sarcastic thing to say but I thought I was just writing to Paich. I hit 'Send'. Even as the little ball was spinning around on my screen as the email was sending, I realised that I had replied to everyone. I felt terrible about it and hadn't meant to hurt anyone, but at the same time it was almost like divine intervention. We had a lot of great years with those guys, but it had got to be like being in another broken marriage.

However, any relief that we felt at the divorce from Mark and Larry was short-lived. It seems impossible to me now, but we spent the next three years going from one set of managers to the next, mired in legal battles and being drained of money by lawyers and pay-offs. Doc McGhee's was the first organisation that we went with. I had met with someone from his office; he was slick and said all the right things but little did I know he wasn't senior management. We thought Doc was going to be more hands on. Doc was a big-hitter and had made a formidable reputation for himself managing both Bon Jovi and Mötley Crüe to huge success. He appeared to be just what we needed, and most especially as we were about to go to war once more with Columbia Records and the whole of the Sony organisation.

In turn, Columbia/Sony made a settlement offer, which was less than we were hoping for. We didn't want to go to court, because in that scenario it's only the lawyers that win. Each time that we even picked up the phone to our lawyers, five guys would be on the end of the line and all of them charging us hundreds of dollars every fifteen minutes.

To add to our woes, Simon had also gotten to be pissed off and not really interested in Toto any more, or so it seemed. In his mind, Toto was no longer the band that he had joined twenty years previous. Things were way different. We had Paich, Steve Porcaro and Joseph Williams back on board and that had changed the business structure. Simon wanted more of a say in our business decisions, but at the time Paich was fixed upon having me and him run things. I think Simon had also grown tired of filling in for deceased guys – Keith Moon in the Who and Jeff with us – and had decided to do his own thing. We had felt him drifting away from us and he was booking gigs with Hiromi, one of his side projects. It wasn't such a shock when he upped and left at the start of 2014. There were no hard feelings. I wished Simon well and we have remained friends. I love the guy for what he brought to us over those twenty years, not to mention the friendship. I learned a lot working with him and we had some amazing times.

The band was still in a precarious position because of the Frontiers Records contract and with lawsuits from that flying all over the place. The next manager we went with was Ken Levitan. Ken had worked with Frampton, Meat Loaf, Lyle Lovett and Emmylou Harris, and pitched us all the right things. My close friend and business manager for thirty years, Gary Haber, had suggested Levitan and thought he would be great for us. He said, 'Ken is my best friend. He will never fuck you.'

Ken brought along Ross Schilling to be our day-to-day guy. I like Ross but I thought Ken was our manager. The thing with many of these manager guys is that they have twenty or thirty acts. I manage Toto now, and just one act is an insane amount of work if you want it done right, so I don't know if it is possible to be great for all those acts.

Ken and Ross got off to a good start by booking us onto a co-headline tour of the States with Michael McDonald, which ran through that summer. The United States was always our Achilles heel and we are still determined to break that wall down. It is start-ing to happen as things are now going great in the USA and the song 'Africa' has become something of a phenomenon with the kids today. All of a sudden, we have a ton of young people at our shows and pieces from our whole *Toto IV* album have been sampled at one point or the other, including by Jay-Z, as well as the EDM DJs ending their sets with 'Africa'. Slowly but surely our hard work and persistence is paying off. This was the first proper tour around America that we'd had in many years and took in prestigious venues like the Greek Theatre in LA. We had Keith Carlock from Steely join us on drums and the whole vibe of the tour was positive.

Until, that is, we got home and realised that we had lost money on the venture. Nobody had been looking too closely at the budget. For just one example, we had been billed thirty-thousand dollars for after-show food. For fucking burgers. It was a disaster financially and it was time for another change. We were then told that Levitan was suing us for $100,000, money that we had intended for Mike's family. He won. How we will never know.

In the midst of all this, we had been working on the record that we owed to Frontiers. That could easily have been thrown together ad hoc, but we went in with the mindset to do something really good and dug deep. As a whole, *Toto XIV* ended up being a record that we were all proud of and one that proved the point that we could still write valid new material. It came out in March 2015 and instantly wailed up the charts all over Europe and in Japan. At that point, though, we were hurting too much to celebrate. Just before it was released, Mike died.

Here we were, devastated by Mike's death and the record company was pissed off about a video we did for our single, which Steve Porcaro's oldest daughter Heather directed as she had done a spectacular job of the *Toto XIV* album cover. Frontiers gave us 500 bucks and expected a video like 'Sledgehammer' or something. Once again, we were faced with the sort of temper tantrums you might expect from a five-year-old who'd forgotten to take his mood-elevator medicine.

The ALS had left Mike paralysed and barely able to talk when the end was near. His mind was every bit as sharp as it had ever been, but he couldn't move his pinkie finger. It got to be really hard to see him deteriorate like that, and most especially for his poor family

I would come by for visits when I was in town or when Mike felt like seeing someone, but he saw very few people during the last year. Mike had a temper – like we all do, and who would not be pissed off at the world in his shoes? – but his wife Cheri and kids truly were saints and looked after him 24/7. She had hardly been out of their house in seven years and they had tried everything under the sun, every legitimate treatment, every snake-oil salesman, just in hope.

I went to visit Mike the night before he passed. I leaned over his bed, gave him a kiss and told him that I loved him. He managed to gasp out that he loved me back, which took everything that he had. There were tears in his eyes and mine. I had this very strong feeling that I wouldn't see him again.

The next morning, I got the call from Steve P that Mike had gone. On the one hand, I was relieved because I had seen first-hand his suffering. On the other, I was devastated to lose yet another of my best friends and also for his wife and kids, his sister Joleen and her husband Steve, and for Eileen and Joe, Mike's parents. They had already lost one son. How are you meant to bury two of your own kids? It's just not supposed to go down that way. Mike's was a beautiful service, but another of those tough days. Cheri asked me to get up and say something. I hadn't spoken at Jeff's funeral, because I couldn't: it was too intense and shocking. I didn't write anything down, but stood and spoke from the heart. I still keep pictures of Mike around me, alongside ones of Jeff, my parents and other dear friends who have passed.

I know that Mikey and Jeff aren't far away. I can sense each of them, but miss being able to physically touch them and hear them play live and laugh.

Maybe it was Mike's passing that encouraged me to be more in control of Toto's future and money. Paich and I had met briefly with our dear old friend Craig Fruin, who went back with us to the Boz days and was now managing Jeff Lynne and Lenny Kravitz. Craig told us that we wouldn't want to pay him his percentage because he only handled solo artists, and that anyway we were smart enough not to have to. That gave me the impetus. I said to the rest of the band, 'Give me six months and, if I fuck this up, I'll pay back any money that I lose.'

We took on a couple of great guys to help, Keith Hagan and Steve Karas, who I had worked with on my solo stuff. I love those guys and we all get on great. Keith hooked us back up with Sony again and I brokered a new record deal. Karas is a beast with details, and along with Jack Albeck, Rob Markus and Brian Ahern at WME, Kirsten Baumeister and Eric Wagner, our European and US tour manager, and Trish Field and the guys at Gelfand, we now have a winning team. (I've also got to give a shout-out to Ron Remis – he looked after my money for twenty-five years and I adore the cat. He's now retired. Party on, Ron!)

A whole lot of positive things started to unfold for us. We got out from under the legal mess we were in, made a deal for a loan to consolidate all debt until we're paid off. The *XIV* album put us back in the game and we got booked onto a second major tour of the US with Yes, one of our favourite bands.

Keith Carlock had commitments to Steely Dan that overlapped timewise and he had to make a choice, but David Hungate recommended to me this cat named Shannon Forrest. I knew Shannon from meeting and hanging with him many years before, and he was playing on all of the hit records coming out of Nashville. He was very influenced by Jeff and Hungate told me, 'Shannon's the closest guy to Jeff that I have ever played with.' That's a pretty big statement, but it held a lot of water for me because Hungate knew Jeff from when he was seventeen years old, but that is not to say that Shannon is a copycat. Shannon joined up, and what's more I also persuaded Hungate out of retirement and Lenny Castro came back too. Shannon just has the groove, as does Hungate, and with Lenny, who has always been a huge part of our sound, we were more and more like the original band again in terms of where we felt things groove-wise.

Hungate never meant to do more than that one tour but we held on to him a bit longer. He finally said that he'd had enough touring and wanted to chill on the farm with his wife April. I love him and learned a lot playing with him. Lee Sklar then briefly returned to our ranks. It was great to have him along for the ride again and we parted on the best of terms. He's back with Phil Collins now.

The fans loved the tour. With Hungate, Lenny and Shannon, we sounded closer than ever to the old band and went down a storm. We also got to have an empathetic relationship with the Yes camp. I had been in regular contact with Chris Squire about all of the arrangements for the tour. I was an early Yes fan, and we had got to know each other over the years. I had found out that he had cancer, but not that it was terminal, and he died almost just before the tour began. After that, each band was really sensitive to the fact that the other had just lost a key member and brother.

I was genuinely excited to meet Steve Howe of Yes for the first time, since he was another of my teenage idols. It turned out to be an unusual introduction. Opening night, I made a point of seeking out Steve backstage. He seemed very nice and approachable, but when I put out my hand to shake his, he said, 'Oh no, I don't do that.' Somewhat reluctantly, he did shake my hand after all and I went on and told him how much I admired his work. He was very thankful. Toto had opened the show and in return he said that he had heard me play that night and thought it was great, which meant a lot to me.

The whole tour that we did for the *XIV* record was a raging success. It sold out across Europe and wound up in front of a packed house at the Budokan in Tokyo. We were back on an upward trajectory in the US and also able to really raise our guarantees overseas and now we're making European money in the US. Against all the odds, we were going to make it through to our fortieth anniversary and in better shape than we had been for many decades. And from that point on, I decided that the word 'no' was going to be erased from our band's vocabulary. For example, we were told we could not get on TV with our new 35th anniversary DVD by all three management companies. Paich and I made that happen, so WTF . . .?

CHAPTER TWENTY-SEVEN

All along I have been mindful that any success that Toto had was our best form of revenge and right now is payback time. When we got back together to help Mikey in 2010, it was meant to be for just one run but it was so successful and we had so much fun. Well, there's a lot of life left in this old band.

One of our team, Keith Hagan, arranged for Sony to 'reintroduce' themselves to us. The new people at Sony Legacy, including the president of that department, John Jackson, came to see us at the Barclays Center in New York when we were playing there with Yes and brought along plaques to commemorate us having sold forty million records. The guys at Spotify told me recently that we have had over half a billion streams since 2010, making us still a very viable touring act. Around the world we are doing arenas, as well as sheds and theatres in the United States, and it's all going better than we had hoped.

The band these days has four main guys: Paich, Steve P, Joe and me. Other cats come and go. Lenny and Shannon are still with us and have become a steaming force of groove, but Lee Sklar is one of the busiest guys in the business. Steve found us a new bass player/

singer, a guy by the name of Shem von Schroeck who had previously been out with Kenny Loggins and Don Felder. This cat plays his ass off and also has a high, perfect-pitch voice. We brought back Warren Ham from the eighties to play horns and sing. He has a huge, strong voice as well, and he plays in Ringo's band with me too.

For those of us who have been there from the very start of this long and winding story, our fortieth anniversary is a big deal. We never thought that we would get ten years, let alone forty, but my ambition is for us to have one more grab at the brass ring. Things have not been this good since 1983 in terms of live work and interest in the band and we are even starting to get a little respect. Even if you hate our music, you have to give it to us for hanging in for forty years against all odds and all the horrible things that have happened to us. Something keeps dragging us back to Toto.

We have two to three years of touring commitments already lined up and that, God willing, will see us into summer 2020. The anniversary has also brought our brothers back to life. While working on the boxset that we put together to mark it, we found in the archives five unfinished tracks that we had cut with Jeff and either Hungate or Mike. With Joe Williams jumping in on vocals and pretty much leading the Toto production team, Paich, Steve and I were finally able to complete those and at the same time get to play with Jeff and Mike once again. That was a great thing for us to be able to do, of course, but also very moving emotionally. It was as if both of them were there in the room with us and you could hear Jeff doing the count-offs. There isn't a day goes by that I don't think of those guys and miss them.

The other thing that I recalled from those old basic tracks was just how distinctive the groove was that we had with Jeff and Mike or Hungate. Lenny coming back was the cherry on top. It was a trip for us to not only play with Jeff and Mike, but to play with our twenty-something selves as well. It was all so natural. The songs were recorded by Al Schmitt and/or Greg Ladanyi too, so they sound alive and of the moment, not like they were recorded over thirty-five years ago. To me, it's that honesty that is the essence of classic rock. Everybody these days is so used to hearing records that are absolutely lined up time-wise, auto-tuned and tweaked to death. They are beyond polished, but the greatest music was never so perfect. Human beings are not perfect. We used to be called 'slick', meaning we played in tune, in time and well, like that was bad. Our records were polished – they still are, we like it to be right – but they were not over-polished. The people who like our music like it like that. They expect it from us.

These days, we play for our audience and can get direct to them. They are the people who spend their hard-earned money on us. We listen to constructive critique and that's what counts.

We want to give them a great time and we have fun doing it. We don't get paid for the two hours on stage: we get paid for the other twenty-two hours of isolation, being away from family and the travel that can sometimes be brutal. Try flying to South Africa from LA, thirty hours door to door. By the time I got to Cape Town my underwear probably looked like a used coffee filter.

I have made my peace with Bobby Kimball, too. I hadn't seen him in eight years when he surprised me at the NAMM trade show in LA in January 2017. As I was walking through the back-stage door at the Anaheim Convention Center, I got stopped by this guy. He told me that he was producing a record with Bobby and not to hate him. I didn't even know the cat and I've never hated Bobby. Next thing, I was standing at the Music Man booth for a couple of minutes talking with my friends, the Ball family, when someone poked me in the back. I turned around and Bobby's face was literally two inches from mine.

He grabbed hold of me, hugged me and said, 'Hey man, I love you.' It was only then that I realised that gathered around us there were all of these other guys with cameras. They were shooting pictures and people started to applaud. He was being a bit erratic and everybody was staring at the two of us. I don't believe that I've ever felt so uncomfortable in my life, but then again, it seemed to me as good a time as any to bury the hatchet. I told Bobby that it was good to see him. From my end, I think we're cool. We're all going to die, but when my time comes at least I won't have any bad blood left over with him and I feel better for knowing that.

During my most recent major recording sessions, I wrote a couple of songs with Ringo for his most recent album, *Give More Love*.

The first one was a straight-out rock-and-roll tune called 'We're on the Road Again'. I played all of the instruments on that (bar drums) and Ringo and I worked on the lyrics together. Ringo was also looking to do a ballad, so I said that I would get started on something and bring it to him for us to finish off. I sat down at the piano at home and soon enough found that my hands were doing an impression of what in my mind was a Paul McCartney-ish song. The reference was going to be so obvious that I decided to write a 'Maybe I'm Amazed'-style guitar solo too, something very melodic, and then an equally signature bass part. I left the track with Ringo and he wrote the subsequent song, 'Show Me the Way', for his wife Barbara, who is a most awesome woman.

In the studio, Ringo likes to work on his vocals with just his engineer, Bruce Sugar, a talented and mellow guy, in the room with him. After he was done with his vocal and the song was about to be mixed, he called me to come over and played me the track. The lead vocal that he had cut really brought the song to life. I think it's one of his finest ever (although I am partial) but Ringo said that he still wasn't satisfied. 'It's the bass,' he told me. I said to him not to worry, that mine was just a guide part, a place-holder, and that he should call up Nathan East or someone he felt was right for the tune.

'No, I have something else in mind,' he replied. 'Paul's coming over this weekend and he's going to do something on our tracks.'

I think I stopped breathing.

I had worked with Paul before, but a track I co-wrote that has Ringo and Paul on it? If you would have told me at age twelve that when I was sixty years old this would happen, I would have said, 'Yeah, and I'll be the first man on Venus too!'

Paul subsequently played on both 'Show Me the Way' and 'We're on the Road Again'. He pulled out every classic McCartney trick in the book, alongside Ringo doing all of these classic Ringo drum fills.

I couldn't believe what I was actually hearing when Ringo played me the mixes at his house. I was speechless, which doesn't happen very often, and had tears in my eyes. I told him, 'You have just presented me with the greatest gift I've ever been given except for my kids!'

Ringo ended up giving me a big hug and telling me that he loved me. For me, it was the highest of highs.

I felt so euphoric right then . . . A bucket-list moment.

Perhaps that's what I should have called this book. There have been so many bucket-list moments. I have had a chance to work with most of my heroes, I've seen the world several times over, I have four wonderful kids and even my exes are cool with me and I them. I just turned sixty years old. It's been one hell of an interesting, crazy, wonderful, WTF-you-have-to-be-kidding-me kind of a life. I can only hope for a little more before the final 'dirt nap' occurs, and I certainly hope God has a great sense of humour during my life review!

One of the most exciting and also harrowing things I did in 2012 before Ringo was G3. This is Joe Satriani's baby with Steve Vai in second position most of the time. Joe called and asked me and my band to be on it for the Australia and New Zealand leg. Now I know these guys! They are musicians' musicians – take one look at Mike Keneally, he's fucking genius and eats Zappa music for breakfast, as does Vai. They are also dear friends of mine. I think they asked me along for the humour part of my personality and certainly not because of my playing. I was to open but was hesitant at first when Joe asked me. I said, 'I'm not sure your audience will like me'. Joe laughed and assured me he thought I would be perfect. Now, I LOVE these guys, so I said yes and thought, I'm just gonna be me and not even try to compete. How could I?

First day of rehearsal in New Zealand my gear wouldn't turn on. I was freaked and everyone was waiting for me to rehearse the jam songs for the encore. We had a blast, though, and all the bands and musicians travelled together, making this one of my fave tours ever.

Humour was everywhere and, man, I was so honoured to have been asked to be a G. That is like winning a Super Bowl ring as a guitar player. I know those guys wipe the floor with me, but they asked me to do Mexico as well with John Petrucci stepping in for Brother Vai! He is also an alien with his unreal playing and again one of the nicest men ever. Mick Brigden is Joe's manager and a prince of a man who helped me a lot. It was a great time and to have been a G at all is a big deal to me. Thanks again, Joe, Steve, John and all the fantastic musicians for treating us so well and to the fans who accepted me as I was hardly what they expected.

CODA

I feel truly blessed. I wake up every day and thank the good Lord for my good fortune. I was this punk-ass kid from North Hollywood who saw the Beatles on *The Ed Sullivan Show*. Fifty years later, I got to walk out onstage with Paul and Ringo for their fiftieth anniversary show.

I had the old 'billion-to-one chance' speech from my dad and school teachers tell me that I was a bum and would never amount to anything ringing in my head. By the grace of God, most of the dreams that I had growing up got to become my reality.

Being in Toto and also in Ringo's band has led me to now spend 200-plus days a year on the road. No complaints: it's what I do and I thrive on it. I can't stand it when other musicians gripe about having to go out on tour, except when they talk about missing their families. We have the best job in the world and nothing to bitch about. Sure, we all have bad days, but I have done every kind of touring there is from taking a fusion band out in the back of a van to flying everywhere on private jets, and they all have an equally special place in my heart. I also have these other intermittent bands such as Nerve Bundle at the Baked Potato in December and Supersonic Blues Machine. That band only came to me in 2016. The core of it is a producer and musician, Fabrizio Grossi, a great blues player and singer named Lance Lopez and my dear friend Kenny Aronoff, who I have done countless sessions with. Kenny has almost as sick a sense of humour as me so we have got on great ever since the first time we met decades ago. They welcome aboard a roving cast of guitar players, including Billy Gibbons, and it's a joy to play music with him. He is the coolest man alive – his vibe is so intense and hip, and his sound is so unique. He's a really nice man, as is Robben Ford, who I have known and revered since I was young and his playing blew my mind. It's a lesson for me every time we jam together. Walter Trout is a new friend who squeezes out so much soul from his guitar. And another mic-drop talent Doug Rappoport. And then there's me. We head out every once in a while to play our demented version of Texan blues mixed with everyone's style, make ourselves a few bucks and then go home. A great time had by all.

I have been in some other jam bands, too, including El Grupo, which came out of a one-off project for Japan ten years or so ago with the amazing Nuno Bettencourt, Steve Weingart, Joey Heredia and Oskar Cartaya. We had an outrageous tour many years ago . . .

Then I stole some of the guys to start my own solo band with Steve Weingart, who is a genius-level player, Eric 'Biggie' Valentine and Steve's wife Renee, who is great, on bass and vocals. We toured the world and had a million laughs along the way. I owe a lot to those three, plus the other musicians who joined us for a while, the crews and the promoters, and especially Alec Leslie who booked all the shows.

Ringo is a big inspiration to me as well as becoming a great friend. I look at him and think, 'If he is what seventy-seven looks like, I'm in!' He has made getting older a lot less scary for me. If you stay moving and in the groove, if you keep working, use your mind and be creative, then age doesn't have to be a barrier or big deal. People ask me all the time now when I'm going to retire. Retire to do what? Watch television? I'm enjoying my career now more than ever. I spent my sixtieth birthday being out on the stage with Ringo. What else would I have done? Get a birthday cake with sixty candles? Jesus, I would have needed a fucking iron lung just to blow them all out.

The one negative is that I am gone from home and my kids a lot. That's the way the business is these days. Records don't bring in the money like they used to, so you have to tour to earn. The way that I reconcile it is that my father was gone all the time too, and I didn't love him any less.

I was having a conversation with my ten-year-old daughter Lily just the other day. I'm always making poop jokes with the two youngest kids and I said to Lily, 'When you talk to your friends, what do you say about your dad?' She looked on over at me and shot back, 'I tell them my dad is insane.' I laughed at that for about five minutes straight. She meant it in a good way, and I'm quite sure I'm not like other dads.

Tina, my eldest, is with her husband Tony, living in a beautiful house they bought overlooking the Strip in Las Vegas. She wants to have a kid and I'd like to be a grandpa. That's one of the things in life that I've never done and that I am looking forward to. My sister Lora and my nephew Luke live in Vegas too, along with Marie and Tina's in-laws, Anna and big Tony, so Tina has around her a great family support unit. I also get up there as much as I can, and there's always a room for me at Tina and Tony's house.

My older son is my very best friend. Trev's very much the Mini-Me with his killer sense of humour and we hang hard. He's starting to do great with his music and his band Biotin Babies got signed directly to Spotify, which is a sign of the times. They have put out a couple of singles. The first one he wrote with Trevor

Rabin's kid Ryan and the second with his cousin, Jake Hays, who's also real talented. I love Jake and his dad, Robert Hays . . . Yes, that one who starred in *Airplane!*

Trev's keeping it in the family. The face on all of his band's artwork is his little brother Bodhi. When I leave this planet, my little ones are going to have Trev and Tina as surrogate parents and represent the Lukather side, and that makes me very happy. I raised great kids and I'm super-proud of all of them.

Oddly enough, there was symmetry to the two big relationships of my life. I was together with Marie and Shawn for fourteen years each. In each case, we were married for nine of those years and had a girl and then a boy. Marie and I went years without speaking to each other, but just last Christmas I picked up the phone and called. I said to her, 'Look, this is ridiculous.' This made Trev very happy. We calmly straightened things out. We are cool with each other now. The day that Tina got married, I sat right next to Marie and held her hand, and we enjoyed the day together. Those bonds don't break.

I love Shawn, too. Lily and Bodhi were so young when we broke up that they have no memory of us being at each other's throats. We're tighter than ever these days and go out for dinner, to school events and on holidays with each other all the time. Shawn still helps me out a lot and is a great mom to our little ones.

There is only a very small handful of people that I would call enemies. None of them have ever tried to make things right with me, so that's why they remain on the 'fuck-you' list. I could have gone after other people who have wronged me but then they would just get a chance at rebuttal and the bad feelings would never die. And why give an asshole free press? They know who they are.

People are otherwise dying all around me. Since Miggy went, I have lost a couple more close friends and a few more have become sick, and that's really fucking depressing. I've sworn to myself that I'm going to make the most of whatever time I have left. The warranty is up, so I want to try to rid myself of all of the resentments and bullshit that have bothered me over the years, including some of the things I have written about here. I might finally have realised how petty they are. I get no joy from a bad vibe. I am sorry to anyone I ever hurt through the years. There's less than a handful, so that's not bad for showbiz.

I have a routine check-up every year, believe it or not. My doctor of twenty-five years, Rob Huizenga, is also my friend. I find myself naked with this guy, who knows me so well, literally inches from his face while he is kneading my ball sac for tumours and saying to me, 'So, how's the tour going?'

When a man has your balls in his hands, the rubber gloves and all, touring is the last thing on your mind. Then it gets worse. The whole room slows down as I hear the words, 'OK, turn around to the gurney and take your underwear down.'

(Rob is still my doctor . . .)

It's like forty-plus years in showbiz and two divorces. I didn't feel a thing.

Years ago, after a yearly check-up, he said that they were going to have to test me for Hodgkin's lymphoma – a type of cancer – because I had an uncontrollable itch all over (and that's one of the symptoms). For an hour, in my mind I had gotten a death sentence. I sat there on my own with all the thoughts racing through my head that anybody would have with a family, a life and a career. I got a little taste of fear. My whole life passed before me.

Turned out I didn't have anything seriously wrong with me, but thanks, Doc, for giving me an hour's worth of pure terror. He says the word 'cancer' a thousand times a day and didn't realise he scared the shit out of me.

Now, when my time's really up, I can't imagine what that's going to be like, but I'm guessing that I'm going to have that fear amplified by a billion per cent. I have somewhat of a strange obsession with death: what happens to us after we die. I have a great deal of faith in God and an afterlife, which should be a comfort, but the end is now closer than the start.

There's a lot of great stuff happening for me right now, and all told I'm in pretty good shape for sixty, with the exception of a serious shoulder injury as a result of a tour-bus accident in Europe. It has left me in constant pain, so don't come and whack me on the left shoulder!

But as my doctor once said to me: 'I've got good news and bad. The good news is that you're going to live. And the bad news is that you're going to live.'

THE GOSPEL ACCORDING TO DAVID PAICH

Question 1: Can you recall where and when you first met Luke, and what your initial impressions of him were?

DP: I remember hearing about Steve Porcaro's high school band from Andy Leeds. Andy took me to Taft High School because he wanted me to check out the two guitar players. (The other one was Mike Landau.) I'll never forget that night as we were entering the darkened auditorium; I could hear echoed guitar playing. It sounded like Hendrix so I assumed the band was on a break and they were just pumping records through the PA. When I got in there, I saw a little guy playing a Strat and he was unbelievable. It was Mike Landau.

The next thing you know a guy comes flying through the air and lands on his knees (like Pete Townshend), playing a Les Paul. He was a little odd. I thought to myself: 'Is that what he looks like?' Little did I know it was Luke with a rubber monkey mask on singing and playing 'Johnny B. Goode', and he sang like Edgar Winter.

Just then Jeff walks up beside me and says, 'There's our guy! We need him, he's a star!' Just like that!

Question 2: Luke told me that you and Jeff strung him along for the longest time over whether or not he was going to be in Toto. Is that how it went down from your perspective?

DP: Not exactly how I remember. I don't think Jeff or I ever strung it out to mess with him. It was such a major decision we had to be sure in our gut and our hearts and ears.

Luke was an incredible live player and performer, but we weren't aware of how much recording experience he'd had, so we might have deliberated on that a bit. I think we counted on the fact that he was such a fast learner.

Question 3: What did Luke bring to the band from the get-go?

DP: Fire and a youthful sense of adolescent antics. Did I mention he has GREAT time?

Question 4: How did you all deal with the enormous success you had, and in particular, around the *IV* album?

DP: It was surreal. We were always the guys behind the scenes. This was the first time we were being covered, media-wise, with TV interviews around the clock as well as being up against our good friends in some major categories. It was a trip.

Question 5: What do you think are Luke's strengths?

DP: His work ethic and his ability to wear different hats. He is a father, the band manager and a fellow band mate, with a seemingly tireless passion for all of them.

Question 6: When have you seen him at his best?

DP: When he is on stage playing 'Red House' or with his kids, who he adores.

Question 7: And his lowest ebb?

DP: Luke wears his heart on his sleeve. What you see is a true emotional barometer at all times. I think the passing of his mom had a major effect – as it did for me when my mother passed – except I spiralled downward. I think he went the opposite direction.

Question 8: Do you have a favourite story about Luke that you could share?

DP: I played a joke on him in Japan. I came out in a gaucho hat with a rose between my teeth, doing a faux Spanish dance during the flamenco-esque part of his acoustic solo. He returned the trick in Switzerland when, during my solo spot, a polka came blasting out of the speakers and searchlights followed me everywhere on stage. (I could run but not hide!)

Question 9: How would you sum him up as both a musician and a man?

DP: The kid with the harlequin face who can unleash a maelstrom of notes with a delicate touch. He also has the ability to adapt like a chameleon, musically. And, he has the biggest heart in the world . . .

His endless range of emotions can be found anywhere from bluesy, tear-rendering melodies to sudden, violent, fulminating, screaming sforzandos.

A man with a huge heart of gold, not only for his family, but also for the fellow musicians he is surrounded and admired by.

Also his compassion for those who may be challenged or less fortunate than him is immense. Rarely have I met or heard a guitarist so naturally gifted and virtuoso-like.

He is familiar with every contemporary guitar style imaginable. If Brian May, John McLaughlin and Eric Clapton had a baby, it still wouldn't live up to how awesome this guy's musical wheelhouse is. It's off the bloody Richter scale!!!

At the same time he has the finesse of a violinist, the light touch of a butterfly and the growling edge of a machine-gun/power saw.

Luke has an intelligence that seems to be driven viscerally, when he approaches solos and parts that are outside our musical solar system. Definitely an alien!

His Zen-like flow on guitar has continued to raise my level of playing and approach (as well as everyone around him).

Luke doesn't just play guitar, he disembowels it with surgical precision, while at the same time caressing notes out of it!

He's most definitely one of a kind. (As is his unique sense of humour, which is an acquired taste!)

God broke the mould when he made Luke!

Shit I Better Remember!

To my older kids, there is nothing shocking here for them. They were there and now are happy and in their thirties. They were honest with me about their experimentations and life experiences. To this day, we have an open relationship. There is nothing they could do that would shock me. My parents had *no* idea what lived in my bedroom, or how insane me and my friends were. I don't mean Hannibal Lecter insane, but that we were up to no good most of the time. They loved me in spite of it all and my silly dreams. I loved them madly and I miss them every day. It's funny how when you are a kid you think your parents are stupid or not cool . . . All the shit they said about just waiting to have kids of your own 'and then you'll see.' They were right. I understand their worry and care and love more than ever.

I got lucky. I have four great kids. And two great mothers of my children. We are all still close friends, particularly Shawn, my last ex and I, as we have the little ones together and speak every day. I still have so much love for her. Great moms make a difference. It did for me and my kids!

My first wife Marie and I are now great pals again, which means a lot to me and my older kids. I don't wanna go out with the mothers of my kids hating me! I am most grateful for peace in my world now and post the insane years.

'Mimi' – Miriam Posada-Barrientos-Posada: I could write a book just about this wonderful, kind, soulful, patient woman who has looked after me and my kids for damn near thirty-five years. She is our guardian angel. I must have been real nice to her in a past life or something. I couldn't function without her and how she is with the kids and the animals. She is truly one of God's kindest creations and I will thank Him in person for having her in our lives . . . Assuming, of course, I don't have a hot poker up my ass and with the devil laughing at me for all eternity. Mimi's in the will.

My oldest son Trev is in the family business now. Check him out, Google his stuff. It is diverse and great and I am very proud of him. Making a living as a musician in the 2000s is *way* different to the seventies and eighties, yet he is really talented and got his first gold record for co-writing the band Halestorm's first hit. That was a very proud moment for old Dad here.

I am equally proud of my oldest, now-married daughter Tina. Cristina for real but only her mom calls her that. My first baby has family around her and that is important. Maybe I will be a grandpa one day . . . one of the things I want to feel before I leave this world.

Thank you to the one and only Martin Cole. He is the man I owe my road life to from the time he joined us in Toto in 1987. Martin was with me on solo tours as well. He got me out of so much trouble, or helped me to cause it. He used to push me into my room, lean against the door so I couldn't get out again and scream in his classic British accent: "Go to BED!" Then he would catch me in a glass elevator with my bare ass cheeks pressed against the window for everyone in the bar to see.

I could write another book just about the two of us and the trouble I got him into and he got me out of . . . Bar fights, drug benders, countless drunken rages and a trillion laughs. I promised him I wouldn't say much so . . . All I can say is everything you've heard about rock-and-roll is true and I did it all. Some of it was so insanely fun and funny, and some was very dark and sad. I love the man. He is happily married now and retired. I miss him, but he deserves to enjoy the rest of his life doing nothing but what *he* wants to do. He worked incredibly hard for us and for *me*. I will never be able to repay him, but 'Tay': I love you and always will. Thank you again and again, 'cause without you, Lord knows what would have happened to me – ha-ha!

In telling the story, to Larry and Mark I say I am sorry if I have hurt your feelings. BUT I have found out *so* much since taking over the management of our band myself. It is heartbreaking and just as it was when it ended so badly between us, and in the sense that we don't now speak. I don't hate you guys. Ivy, Anita, Michelle, Kimiko, Chad, these were great, honest hard-working people and for a long time it was great between all of us . . .

It was not all bad. If that is how I have made it seem, I am sorry. But like many long-term relationships, it ended poorly. For my part, I did not end the relationship well and I am sorry also for that. There were some great times and an amazing amount of laughs, and Larry and Mark helped us a lot through the first part of Toto's career. Thank you to them for that.

Thank you to the fans for keeping us alive during the darker, less successful years. David Paich is the softest, most gentle man I have ever known. He just gave me the reins and said to take it over when his sister Lori was so sick and then sadly passed. David asked our brother Greg Phillinganes to help out and he did a great job for us. But as great as that version of the band was in terms of musicianship, it started to not be Toto any more. At least not in the classic sense and I lost myself . . . boozing out of control, filled with self-loathing and hatred and regret. I thought I was done, but I would not let this band die. We should have been toast the day Jeff died, but *something* kept us going and kept *me* going and from not giving up on the band or myself.

Thank you to 'The Thread'. The guys in it have become a nice diversion. To the uninitiated, it's a secret internet hang with famous guitar players and interesting people from other walks of life. Things are shared – amazing video stuff I have never seen and humour. There is a great camaraderie of players and from way above my pay grade, but I am a funny guy so they let me in. Nice cats and it's private, so to the ones who are *in*, I salute the kindness and friendship.

Toto is my main thing and always has been. However, over the years I have always been asked to do cool side projects and I must mention some of the really fun things I've been blessed to do outside of our band.

I have had the honour of doing many tours with so many amazing musicians and heroes of mine. I've got to thank all my solo band guys past and present. The amazing unreal talent of Steve Weingart – aka 'Keynis' for reasons only we know – and his awesome wife Renee – 'Ne Ne' – who played bass and sang with me. It was her first rock-and-roll experience and she was a trouper. She had a great vibe and always played and sang her ass off.

My man on drums – Eric 'Biggie' Valentine. He is a bad-ass and funny as hell. We spent some great years travelling together and putting up with some crazy shit: the 'murder hotel', hours and hours on buses, laughing and playing. I love these guys. There were a few people who came and went in that band and we had a great crew, too.

Speaking of which, I wanna thank *every* crew person I ever worked with and that is a novel of its own. If I name-checked everyone I knew or have worked with then this would be an encyclopaedia. You know who you are and I am so very grateful for the hard work and laughs and friendships.

I did a tour of Europe and Japan called the Odd Couple with Edgar Winter in 2000. Edgar was a childhood hero of mine (his brother Johnny, too), a giant musician and a really nice man. It was awesome to play with Edgar and an honour to do that tour.

I have missed him as we don't see each other that much anymore. He and his wife Monique are such kind people. To get to do some of Edgar's classics along with some of my stuff was great fun.

One particular festival Edgar and I did in Finland, the Pori Jazz Festival, introduced me to a giant of a guitar player and man, Jeff Healey. We immediately hit it off and spent a few days jamming and having many drinks and laughs. We remained friends and I used to go pop in and jam at his club in Canada every year after that. We had a blast and I loved the guy. I got to say goodbye to him the night before he passed. He took my call and he was suffering. I said, 'I love ya, man' one last time. I know we will meet again. When we toured the jazz circuit in Europe, I did some fucked-up things to Jeff: pounding on his door and running away in the morning after a rave-up (this was before we both stopped boozing). He ran out into the hall of the hotel in just his underwear and screamed, 'I can smell you Lukather!' He was an amazing man I miss very much.

I got a call from Bill Evans, Miles Davis's sax-playing legend and now a great friend. He put a band together with trumpet legend Randy Brecker, Robben Ford, who I think the world of as a guitar player and has been a friend for decades, bass legend Daryl Jones from Miles's band, Rolling Stones, Rodney Holmes and the drummer from Wayne Shorter's band, who was awesome. The band was called SoulBop and every person in it had played with Miles or worked with him at some level, so I was deeply honoured to get the call and do the tour we did of Japan and Asia. We had a blast too, and it was the first tour that I did sober. It was weird at first. I was *so* used to the post-gig bar hang that I became a tad reclusive. The shows were wild, though – Robben on one side of the stage and me on the other with these amazing musicians in the middle. Great fun and I'd love to do it again sometime.

I also did a permutation band with Bill called Toxic Monkey. We played a week of shows in New York City at the Blue Note.

That's where I met Keith Carlock, Steely Dan's drummer, and I tried to steal him from them for Toto. Keith is an amazing drummer – world class and a great cat. We *tried* to make it work. He did a fantastic job on *Toto XIV* and a tour with us in Japan. He was *in* and then conflicts in schedule came up with Steely and Walter, may he rest in peace. We had somewhat of a bidding war. They won and I love Keith. We will work together again.

My man and dear friend Will Lee helped put Toxic Monkey together. Will and I go way, way, way back to the seventies when we met and worked together on sessions in LA. I always love to see him and his most awesome wife, Sandrine. I brought Weingart in from LA. We had one rehearsal, everyone brought in tunes like we had with SoulBop and we threw the ball around. It was jamband stuff and packed houses.

I have a yearly jam band that only plays together in December. It's called Nerve Bundle, formerly Sphinctersayswhat? For the last seven Christmas seasons, we have played in LA at the Baked Potato for three nights and six shows, two a night. We just go and it is so much fun. We play stuff off a Christmas record I did, *SantaMental*, a one-off project Elliot Scheiner and Al Schmitt got me into and which also gets put out every year, and other stuff too, and the shows sell out months in advance.

Jeff Babko did some amazing arrangements for the tunes on *Santamental*. I would give him some ideas and he would run with them and make them brilliant. We got together and tried to fuck up standard Christmas songs in a fusion style. It was really fun and with great players.

Nerve Bundle was born from my friend Jorgen Carlsson, the bass player from Gov't Mule, bugging me about doing something on our hillside hikes many years ago. We got 'Babs' in and an amazing drummer, Toss Panos, who I knew but didn't get to play with much until this happened. He is like a rock-and-roll Elvin Jones. He swings like a bull's ball sac, but can rock too! He has wicked feel. We're all pals in the band and this year we are expanding to do a week of shows in Japan at Billboard live clubs. They are larger jazz venues and I look forward to it.

Back in the early 2000s, there was an ill-fated band, El Grupo, that I started up with my old friend, guitar legend and bad-ass Nuno Bettencourt from Extreme and with Joey Heredia on drums and Oskar Cartaya on bass. We did a tour in Europe, some LA things and a little EP that my old friend Bob Bradshaw recorded. Bob and I go way back. I love the guy and miss him as I haven't seen him in years. We were inseparable for a time. He toured with me and Toto as my tech and I used all his gear. Bob's is great stuff and I still have it all. I met him through Buzzy Feiten and Mike Landau, who showed me the amazing rigs Bob built for him in 1983. I *had* to have one and the rest is history. Bob was a huge part of the eighties guitar sounds for many greats. He still is! Over the years, he custom-made some amazing gear for me and, boy, did we get into many nights of trouble. Great fun!

The thing with El Grupo was that I was starting to drink too much, so had some off nights. That was odd for me, because it never affected me much, but I had escalated and that started a downward spiral for me. It carried on into my first solo tour for *All's Well That Ends Well.* I was nuts on that tour. Life was falling apart inside of me for lots of reasons. It was a fun tour – too much fun sometimes. I'm sorry for a few sloppy nights, but I was sick in many ways.

I want to give out HUGE thanks to the best tech I have had. I've had some of the very best through the years, but my man for the last six has been Jon Gosnell. Jon goes beyond. He is an incredible guitar player himself, a total gear-head and one of the nicest people I have ever met – his wife Kat, too. Jon has been with me with Toto, Ringo, my solo stuff and Nerve Bundle. He's built me several pedal boards and is always one step ahead of me. He has great ideas on how to make things better and cares so much. *That* is rare. Jon really is on it and I love him dearly and owe him a lot.

There is much I have left out of the book and people I forgot to mention, and I am sorry. It's hard to put sixty years into a few hundred pages. Perhaps if this book does well I can do another and expand in more detail the rest of my life, and give so many more details on the thousands of sessions I have done. And more on the insane things that have gone down in my life!

If I have missed you, it's not meant as an insult. I am getting older now and my memory is a bit foggy during 'the lost years' at the end of my drinking career. Eight-plus years free of that shit and cigs as well. I like feeling good every day. Of course, now after the tour bus accident of a couple of years ago I will be forever fucked up with my left shoulder: *no* strength. I can't even lift a coffee cup with it – can't get it past my tits. It hurts all the time. I see my doctor every month and we are dealing with it, but I can't risk an operation and lose my left hand, so Catch-22. I can't take a year off and not play in the hope I could re-teach myself to play after a one-year wait.

Believe me, I work hard for the $s. I missed so much of my kids growing up that it sometimes brings me to tears at night when I'm alone. And I am alone a LOT! There is a price for it all. I didn't sell my soul. I worked and still work fucking hard.

And also to Paul Rees (my co-writer) who made sense of my rantings and then I went over the book word by word with my publisher Andreas Campomar and my agent Matthew Hamilton, editing and rewriting to sound more like me – and not a proper Englishman – in terms of the way it read. I put the real me in here, the way I *really* talk with lots of swearing, because that's how I am. It is expressive rather than foul for the sake of it and surely no one can be shocked by the word 'fuck' any more. It's 2018 for fuck's sake. You dig?

Speaking of 'time', as I'm sixty now, that is a more important word. I better get busy . . .

PARTIAL DISCOGRAPHY

(Special thanks to Arend Slagman, who has run stevelukather.com for over twenty years, for compiling this discography. Love to him and his entire family.)

Artist	Album	Year
Boylan, Terence	*Terence Boylan*	1977
Browne, Jackson	*Running on Empty*	1977
Clarck, Michael	*Free as a Breeze*	1977
Dal Bello, Lisa	*Lisa Dal Bello*	1977
Jameson, Bobby	*Unreleased Songs*	1977
Kisugi, Takao	*Zigu Zagu*	1977
Peck, Danny	*Heart and Soul*	1977
Ross, Diana	*Baby It's Me*	1977
Scaggs, Boz	*Down Two Then Left*	1977
Thudpucker, Jimmy	*The Greatest Hits*	1977
Cadd, Brian	*Yesterday Dreams*	1978
Carter, Valerie	*Wild Child*	1978
Champlin, Bill	*Single*	1978
Cliff, Jimmy	*Give Thanks*	1978
Cooper, Alice	*From the Inside*	1978
Criss, Peter	*Peter Criss*	1978
Dal Bello, Lisa	*Pretty Girls*	1978
Donohue, Dane	*Dane Donohue*	1978
Fuller, Craig and Kaz, Eric	*Fuller/Kaz*	1978
Gärdestad, Ted	*Blue Virgin Isle*	1978
Hall & Oates	*Along the Red Ledge*	1978
Hodges, James & Smith	*What Have You Done for Love*	1978

Jabara, Paul	*Keeping Time*	1978
Jordan, Marc	*Mannequin*	1978
Kiss	*Peter Criss*	1978
Ladd, Cheryl	*Cheryl Ladd*	1978
Lynn, Cheryl	*Cheryl Lynn*	1978
Mathis, Johnny & Williams, Deniece	*That's What Friends Are For*	1978
McClusky, David	*A Long Time Coming*	1978
Newton, Juice	*Well Kept Secret*	1978
Newton-John, Olivia	*Totally Hot*	1978
Nolan, Kenny	*Song Between Us*	1978
Omura, Kenji	*Kenji Shock*	1978
Pockets	*Take It On Up*	1978
Reddy, Helen	*We'll Sing In The Sunshine*	1978
Sager, Carol Bayer	*Too*	1978
Sayer, Leo	*Leo Sayer*	1978
Sharretts, The	*You Turn Me Around*	1978
Soundtrack	*What Have You Done for Love*	1978
Steve T.	*West Coast Confidential*	1978
Streisand, Barbra	*Songbird*	1978
Tan Tan	*Trying To Get You*	1978
Toto	*Toto*	1978
Wells, Cory	*Touch Me*	1978
Wells, Cory	*Ahead Of The Storm*	1978
Baby O	*You've Got It*	1979
Bishop & Gwinn	*This Is Our Night*	1979
Brooklyn Dreams	*Joy Ride*	1979
Cerrone	*Angelina*	1979
Cheap Trick	*Dream Police*	1979
Cher	*Take Me Home*	1979
Currie, Cherie & Marie	*Messin' With The Boys*	1979
Dee, Kiki	*Stay With Me*	1979
Earth, Wind & Fire	*I Am*	1979
Eaton, Steve	*Steve Eaton*	1979
Edelman, Randy	*You're The One*	1979
England Dan & Coley, John Ford	*Dr. Heckle and Mr. Jive*	1979
Evans, Linda	*You Control Me*	1979
Gil, Gilberto	*Realce*	1979
Goffin, Louise	*Kid Blue*	1979
John, Elton	*Victim of Love*	1979
Jones, Quincy	*Superdisc*	1979
Jordan, Marc	*Blue Desert*	1979
Kipner, Steve	*Knock the Walls Down*	1979
Kunkel, Leah	*Leah Kunkel*	1979
Ladd, Cheryl	*Dance Forever*	1979
Manhattan Transfer	*The Extensions*	1979
Mason, Harvey	*Groovin' You*	1979

Mayall, John	*Bottom Line*	1979
McIan, Peter	*Playing Near The Edge*	1979
Mitchell, Adam	*Readhead in Trouble*	1979
Noguchi, Goro	*Last Joke*	1979
Patton, Robbie	*Do You Wanna Tonight*	1979
Ritenour, Lee	*Feel the Night*	1979
Sands, Evie	*Suspended Animation*	1979
Sayer, Leo	*Here*	1979
Scaggs, Boz	*Hits*	1979
Sorrenti, Alan	*L.A. & N.Y.*	1979
Soundtrack	*Fast Company*	1979
Streisand, Barbra	*Wet*	1979
Tanner, Marc	*No Escape*	1979
Toto	*Hydra*	1979
Trooper	*Flying Colors*	1979
Williams, Deniece	*When Love Comes Calling*	1979
Wilson Brothers	*Another Night*	1979
Wood, Lauren	*Lauren Wood*	1979
Wright, Gary	*Heading Home*	1979
Airplay	*Airplay*	1980
Allen, Peter	*Bi-Coastal*	1980
America	*Alibi*	1980
Austin, Patti	*Every Home Should Have One*	1980
Berger, Michael	*Beausejour*	1980
Carmen, Eric	*Tonight You're Mine*	1980
Cher	*Prisoner*	1980
Criss, Pete	*Out of Control*	1980
Desario, Teri	*Caught*	1980
Earth, Wind & Fire	*Faces*	1980
England Dan & Coley, John Ford	*Best of England Dan & John Ford Coley*	1980
Farina, Sandy	*All Alone in the Night*	1980
Franklin, Aretha	*Aretha*	1980
Grimaldi & Zeiher	*Recidive*	1980
Hamada, Shogo	*Home Bound*	1980
John, Elton	*21 at 33*	1980
Kennedy, Ray	*Ray Kennedy*	1980
Kunkel, Leah	*I Run With Trouble*	1980
MacGregor, Mary	*Mary MacGregor*	1980
Nash, Graham	*Earth and Sky*	1980
Okumoto, Ryo	*Makin' Rock*	1980
Scaggs, Boz	*Middle Man*	1980
Sciuto, Tony	*Island Nights*	1980
Seals, Dan	*Stones*	1980
Sheller, William	*Nicolas*	1980
Soundtrack	*Urban Cowboy*	1980
Soundtrack	*Cheech and Chong's Next Movie*	1980
St. Nicklaus, Dick	*Sweet and Dandy*	1980

Summer, Donna	*The Wanderer*	1980
Syreeta	*Syreeta*	1980
Takeuchi, Mariya	*Miss M*	1980
Taupin, Bernie	*He Who Rides the Tiger*	1980
Tavares	*Supercharged*	1980
Tosti, Blaise	*American Lovers*	1980
Triumvirat	*Russian Roulette*	1980
Alpert, Herb	*Magic Man*	1981
Benson, George	*The George Benson Collection*	1981
Berger, Michael	*Dreams in Stone*	1981
Bertucci, Anne	*Anne Bertucci*	1981
Brothers Johnson, The	*Winners*	1981
Byrne & Barnes	*An Eye for an Eye*	1981
Cetera, Peter	*Peter Cetera*	1981
Champlin, Bill	*Runaway*	1981
Char	*USJ*	1981
Claudia	*Claudia*	1981
Crawford, Randy	*Secret Combination*	1981
Cummings, Burton	*Sweet Sweet*	1981
Dash, Sarah	*Close Enough*	1981
Dore, Charlie	*Listen*	1981
Essex, David	*Be Bop The Future*	1981
Forsey, Keith	*Dynamite*	1981
Frampton, Peter	*Breaking All the Rules*	1981
Franklin, Aretha	*Love All the Hurt Away*	1981
Jarreau, Al	*Breakin' Away*	1981
John, Elton	*The Fox*	1981
Jones, Quincy	*The Dude*	1981
Jones, Rickie Lee	*Pirates*	1981
Jürgens, Udo	*Leave a Little Love*	1981
Kane, Madleen	*Don't Wanna Lose You*	1981
Kobayashi, Katsumi	*Guitar Technic of Steve Lukather*	1981
Lake, Greg	*Greg Lake*	1981
Leslie, Kelly &		
Coley, John Ford	*Leslie, Kelly and John Ford Coley*	1981
Manhattan Transfer	*Mecca for Moderns*	1981
Marian	*Marginal Love*	1981
Matsui, Kazu	*Time No Longer*	1981
Newton-John, Olivia	*Physical*	1981
Nitty Gritty Dirt Band	*Jealousy*	1981
Ozaki, Ami	*Hot Baby*	1981
Pages	*Pages*	1981
Preston, Billy	*The Way I Am*	1981
Russell, Brenda	*Love Life*	1981
Sager, Carol Bayer	*Sometimes Late at Night*	1981
Sciuto, Tony	*Be My Radio*	1981
Sorrenti, Alan	*Sorrenti*	1981
Soundtrack	*In Harmony*	1981

Soundtrack		
(Jerry Goldsmith)	*Omen 3: The Final Conflict*	1981
Sugano, Anri	*Show Case*	1981
Toto	*Turn Back*	1981
Alessi Brothers	*Long Time Friends*	1982
Alpert, Herb	*Greatest Hits*	1982
America	*View from the Ground*	1982
Bade, Lisa	*Suspicion*	1982
Benson, Gary	*Moonlight Walking*	1982
Branigan, Laura	*Branigan*	1982
Bugatti & Musker	*The Dukes*	1982
Caldwell, Bobby	*Carry On*	1982
Cher	*I Paralyze*	1982
Chicago	*Chicago 16*	1982
Crawford, Randy	*Windsong*	1982
Criss, Pete	*Let Me Rock You*	1982
Ford, Dwayne	*Needless Freaking*	1982
Hancock, Herbie	*Lite Me Up*	1982
Henley, Don	*I Can't Stand Still*	1982
Imperials, The	*Stand By the Power*	1982
Jackson, Michael	*Thriller*	1982
Jans, Tom	*Champion*	1982
Katsuragi, Yuki	*L.A. Spirits*	1982
Kerr, Richard	*No Looking Back*	1982
LaBounty, Bill	*Bill LaBounty*	1982
Loggins, Kenny	*High Adventure*	1982
Manchester, Melissa	*Hey Ricky*	1982
Mars, Steve	*Somebody Somewhere*	1982
Mathieson, Greg Project	*Baked Potato Super Live*	1982
McDonald, Michael	*If That's What It Takes*	1982
Mitchell, Joni	*Wild Things Run Fast*	1982
Mizukoshi, Keiko	*I'm Fine*	1982
Newton-John, Olivia	*Greatest Hits*	1982
Night Plane	*Night Plane*	1982
Roberts, David	*All Dressed Up*	1982
Sayer, Leo	*World Radio*	1982
Sedaka, Dara	*I'm Your Girlfriend*	1982
Simmons, Richard	*Reach*	1982
Soundtrack	*Zapped!*	1982
Stevens, Jon	*Jon Stevens*	1982
Summer, Donna	*Donna Summer*	1982
Toto	*IV*	1982
Tubes, The	*Completion Backward Principle*	1982
Ware, Leon	*Leon Ware*	1982
Warwick, Dionne	*Friends In Love*	1982
Watts, Ernie	*Chariots of Fire*	1982
Webb, Jimmy	*Angel Heart*	1982
Williams, Joseph	*Joseph Williams*	1982

Woods, Stevie	*Take Me to Your Heaven*	1982
Yazawa, Eikichi	*It's Just Rock 'n' Roll*	1982
Yazawa, Eikichi	*PM 9*	1982
Young, Jesse Colin	*The Perfect Stranger*	1982
Zevon, Warren	*Envoy*	1982
Alpert, Herb	*Blow Your Own Horn*	1983
Anka, Paul	*Walk a Fine Line*	1983
Bertucci, Anne	*Cool Hand*	1983
Carnes, Kim	*Cafe Racer*	1983
Cocciante, Ricardo	*Sincerita*	1983
Crawford, Randy	*Nightline*	1983
Cross, Christopher	*Another Page*	1983
Eye to Eye	*Shakespeare Stole My Baby*	1983
Henderson, Finis	*Finis*	1983
Holland, Amy	*On Your Every Word*	1983
I-Ten	*Taking a Cold Look*	1983
John, Elton	*Too Low for Zero*	1983
Jordan, Marc	*A Hole in the Wall*	1983
Karizma	*Dream Come True*	1983
Lee, Rita	*Bombom*	1983
Longfellow, Barron	*Barron Longfellow*	1983
Manchester, Melissa	*Greatest Hits*	1983
Newman, Randy	*Trouble in Paradise*	1983
Nicks, Stevie	*The Wild Heart*	1983
Nielsen/Pearson	*Blind Luck*	1983
Richie, Lionel	*Can't Slow Down*	1983
Rivera, Danny	*Danny*	1983
Rogers, Kenny	*We've Got Tonight*	1983
Ross, Diana	*Ross*	1983
Sayer, Leo	*Have You Ever Been in Love*	1983
Soundtrack	*Two of a Kind*	1983
Soundtrack (James Horner)	*Gorky Park*	1983
Soundtrack (Jerry Goldsmith)	*Psycho II*	1983
Tubes, The	*Outside Inside*	1983
Tutone, Tommy	*National Emotion*	1983
Various artists	*Winners*	1983
Walsh, Brock	*Dateline: Tokyo*	1983
Benson, George	*20/20*	1984
Blake, Karen	*Just One Heart*	1984
Champaign	*Women in Flames*	1984
Cocker, Joe	*Civilized Man*	1984
Crane, Stephen	*Kicks*	1984
Easton, Sheena	*A Private Heaven*	1984
Gruska, Jay	*Which One of Us Is Me*	1984
Iwasaki, Hiromi	*I Won't Break Your Heart*	1984

Jacksons	*Victory*	1984
Jones, Rickie Lee	*The Magazine*	1984
Kennedy, Joyce	*Looking for Trouble*	1984
Khan, Chaka	*I Feel for You*	1984
McCartney, Paul	*Give My Regards to Broad Street*	1984
Mirage	*Give Me the Night*	1984
Schmit, Timothy B.	*Playin' It Cool*	1984
Soundtrack	*Footloose*	1984
Soundtrack	*Arthur*	1984
Streisand, Barbra	*Emotion*	1984
Toto	*Isolation*	1984
Toto	*Dune*	1984
Various artists	*The Official Music of the 1984 Olympic Games*	1984
Waybill, Fee	*Read My Lips*	1984
Atkins, Chet	*Stay Tuned*	1985
Clapton, Eric	*Behind the Sun*	1985
Dees, Rick and The Cast of Idiots	*I'm Not Crazy*	1985
Far Corporation	*Division One*	1985
Kawai, Naoko	*9½*	1985
Loggins, Kenny	*Vox Humana*	1985
Lords of the New Church	*Killer Lords*	1985
Manchester, Melissa	*Mathematics*	1985
Martin, Eric	*Eric Martin*	1985
Mitchell, Joni	*Dog Eat Dog*	1985
Newton-John, Olivia	*Soul Kiss*	1985
Rogers, Kenny	*Heart of the Matter*	1985
Soundtrack	*White Nights*	1985
Soundtrack	*Wildcats*	1985
Soundtrack	*St. Elmo's Fire*	1985
Stealin Horses	*Stealin Horses*	1985
Benson, George	*The Best of George Benson*	1986
Browne, Jackson	*Lives in the Balance*	1986
Chicago	*Chicago 18*	1986
Diamond, Neil	*Headed for the Future*	1986
Jackson, Jermaine	*Precious Moments*	1986
Lover Speaks, The	*The Lover Speaks*	1986
Raymond, Brett	*Only Love*	1986
Richie, Lionel	*Dancing on the Ceiling*	1986
Rogers, Kenny	*They Don't Make Them Like They Used To*	1986
Santana, Beck & Lukather	*Lotus Gem*	1986
Soundtrack	*Back to School*	1986
Soundtrack	*Raw Deal*	1986
Toto	*Fahrenheit*	1986
Various artists	*Hands Across America*	1986
Cher	*Cher*	1987

Feehan, Tim	*Tim Feehan*	1987
Grass Roots, The	*Greatest Hits, Vol. I*	1987
Larsen, Neil	*Through Any Window*	1987
Lynn, Cheryl	*Start Over*	1987
Milsap, Ronnie	*Heart and Soul*	1987
Soundtrack	*Turning Rebellion Into Money: Conflict*	1987
Watson, Helen	*Blue Slipper*	1987
Weckl, Dave	*Contemporary Drummer + One* (lessons)	1987
Anderson, Jon	*In the City of Angels*	1988
Diamond, Neil	*Best Years of Our Lives*	1988
Garfunkel, Art	*Lefty*	1988
Imperials, The	*Legacy 1977–1988*	1988
L.A. Workshop	*Norwegian Wood I*	1988
Newman, Randy	*Land of Dreams*	1988
Pasquale, Joe	*Prey*	1988
Rankin, Kenny	*Hiding in Myself*	1988
Scaggs, Boz	*Other Roads*	1988
Think Out Loud	*Think Out Loud*	1988
Toto	*The Seventh One* (album)	1988
Various artists	*Guy Laroche Paris, Feel the Power*	1988
Beck, Robin	*Trouble or Nothing*	1989
Bishop, Stephen	*Bowling in Paris*	1989
Bolton, Michael	*Soul Provider*	1989
Bridge 2 Far	*Bridge 2 Far*	1989
Carlisle, Belinda	*Runaway Horses*	1989
Cher	*Heart of Stone*	1989
Chicago	*Greatest Hits 1982–1989*	1989
Choir, Yves	*By Prescription Only*	1989
Clemons, Clarence	*A Night with Mr. C*	1989
Cooper, Alice	*Trash*	1989
Crosby, David	*Oh Yes I Can*	1989
Falk, Dieter	*Dieter Falk*	1989
Guitar workshop	*Tribute to Otis Redding*	1989
Harnen, Jimmy	*Can't Find the Midnight*	1989
Jones, Booker T.	*The Runaway*	1989
Jones, Quincy	*Back on the Block*	1989
Karizma	*Cuba*	1989
Kawauchi, Junichi	*Sweet*	1989
Los Lobotomys	*Los Lobotomys*	1989
Lukather, Steve	*Lukather*	1989
Marx, Richard	*Repeat Offender*	1989
Megu	*Le O Deta*	1989
Rodgers, Michael	*I Got Love*	1989
Saraya	*'Timeless Love'* (single)	1989
Saunders, Fernando	*Cashmere Dreams*	1989
Sloppy Seconds	*Destroyed*	1989
Soundtrack	*Homer and Eddie*	1989

Soundtrack	*Road House*	1989
Soundtrack	*Shocker*	1989
Soundtrack (Alan Silvestri)	*Abyss*	1989
Sugiyama, Kiyotaka	*Here & There*	1989
Various artists	*A Very Special Christmas*	1989
Weisberg, Tim	*Outrageous Temptations*	1989
Werner, Pe	*Weibsbilder*	1989
Alston, Gerald	*Gerald Alston*	1990
Anderson, Michael	*Michael Anderson*	1990
Asia	*Then and Now*	1990
Cotton, Paul	*Changing Horses*	1990
Feehan, Tim	*Full Contact*	1990
Foster, David	*River of Love*	1990
Frankfurter Rock Orchestra	*Classic Toto Hits*	1990
Garfield, David and Friends	*L.A. Keyboard Project*	1990
Grimaldi, Bernard	*Toute Ressemblance Avec Des Personnes Ayant . . .*	1990
Horn, Jim	*Work It Out*	1990
Hungate, David	*Souvenir*	1990
John, Elton	*To Be Continued*	1990
Landau, Michael	*Tales from the Bulge*	1990
Schascle	*Haunted by Real Life*	1990
Toto	*Past to Present 1977–1990*	1990
Various artists	*Rock Guitar Legends*	1990
Various artists	*Legends, The Music of Desmond Child*	1990
Wilson Phillips	*Wilson Phillips*	1990
Yazawa, Eikichi	*Eikichi*	1990
3rd Nation	*One Nation*	1991
Carter, Raymone	*Raymone Carter*	1991
Cher	*Love Hurts*	1991
Child, Desmond	*Discipline*	1991
Cross, Christopher	*The Best Of Christopher Cross*	1991
Crusaders, The	*Healing the Wounds*	1991
DeFrancesco, Joey	*Part III*	1991
Gianco, Ricky E.	*È Rock 'n' Roll*	1991
Goodrum, Randy	*Caretaker of Dreams*	1991
Hamada, Mari	*Tomorrow*	1991
Ingram, James	*The Power of Great Music, Greatest Hits*	1991
Kawauchi, Junichi	*Private Heaven*	1991
Marx, Richard	*Rush Street*	1991
Midler, Bette	*For the Boys*	1991
Nicks, Stevie	*Timespace: The Best of Stevie Nicks*	1991
O'Kane, John	*Solid*	1991
Peeples, Nia	*Nia Peeples*	1991
Richman, Jeff	*The Way In*	1991

Seger, Bob	*The Fire Inside*	1991
Stewart, Rod	*Vagabond Heart*	1991
Van Halen	*For Unlawful Carnal Knowledge*	1991
Various artists	*Guitar's Practicing Musicians Vol. II*	1991
Yemoto, The	*Olympic Matsuri*	1991
Zappa, Dweezil	*Confessions*	1991
Bissonette, Gregg	*Siblings*	1992
Champlin, Bill	*Burn Down the Night*	1992
Fields, Brandon	*Other Places*	1992
Foster, David	*A Touch of David Foster*	1992
Frampton, Peter	*Shine On: A Collection*	1992
Hadley, Tony	*The State of Play*	1992
Himuro, Kyosuke	*Himuro Masterpiece*	1992
Howell, Kurt	*Kurt Howell*	1992
Hughes, Glenn	*L.A. Blues Authority Vol. II:*	
	Glenn Hughes – Blues	1992
Manhattan Transfer	*Anthology: Down in Birdland*	1992
Nakajima, Fumiaki	*Girl Like You*	1992
Parton, Dolly	*Straight Talk*	1992
Powell, Cozy	*The Drums Are Back*	1992
Richie, Lionel	*Back to Front*	1992
Schultz, Ben	*Tri Ality*	1992
Soundtrack	*Straight Talk*	1992
Soundtrack	*Olivier, Olivier*	1992
Soundtrack		
(Alan Silvestri)	*Father of the Bride*	1992
Spinal Tap	*Break Like the Wind* (incl. 'Bitch School')	1992
Toto	*Kingdom of Desire*	1992
Tubes, The	*The Best of the Tubes*	1992
Various artists	*The Guitarist*	1992
Various artists	*Global Guitar*	1992
Watanabe, Misato	*Hello Lovers*	1992
Waters, Roger	*Amused to Death*	1992
Wilson Phillips	*Shadows and Light*	1992
Cher	*Greatest Hits: 1965–1992*	1993
Cocker, Joe	*Best of Joe Cocker*	1993
Cross, Christopher	*Ride Like the Wind*	1993
dB's, The	*Ride the Wild Tomtom*	1993
Goodrum, Randy	*Caretaker of Dreams*	1993
Gorky Park	*Moscow Calling*	1993
Sayer, Leo	*All the Best*	1993
Scaggs, Boz	*Starbox*	1993
Soundtrack	*Bopha*	1993
Summer, Donna	*Donna Summer Anthology*	1993
Toto	*Absolutely Live*	1993
Webb, Jimmy	*Suspending Disbelief*	1993

Beacco, Marc	*Scampi Fritti*	1994
Champlin, Bill	*Through it All*	1994
Clooney, Rosemary	*Still on the Road*	1994
Crawford, Randy	*The Very Best of RC*	1994
Falk, Dieter	*Instrumental Collection*	1994
Far Corporation	*Solitude*	1994
Goodrum, Randy	*Words and Music*	1994
Hausmylly	*Peilipallo*	1994
Lukather, Steve	*Candyman*	1994
Pasquale, Joe	*Ricochet*	1994
Seger, Bob	*Greatest Hits*	1994
Various artists	*Night of the Proms*	1994
Various artists	*Return of West Coast Pop, Vol. I*	1994
Various artists	*18 Rock Classics*	1994
Wetton, John	*Voice Mail/Battle Lines*	1994
Coryell, Larry	*I'll Be Over You*	1995
Di Bart, Tony	*Turn Your Love Around*	1995
Goodrum, Randy	*Songbook*	1995
Henley, Don	*Actual Miles: Henley's Greatest Hits*	1995
Houston, Whitney	*'Exhale' (single)*	1995
Jackson, Michael	*HIStory*	1995
Kleptomania	*Turn Your Love Around*	1995
L.A. Workshop	*Norwegian Wood Vol. II*	1995
Randolph, Joyce	*I Send Him Roses*	1995
Sherwood Ball 'n Chain	*White Light*	1995
Soundtrack	*People*	1995
Soundtrack	*Waiting to Exhale*	1995
Tesh, John Project The	*Sax on the Beach*	1995
Toto	*Tambu*	1995
Toto	*Best Ballads*	1995
Tubes, The	*The Best of the Tubes 1981–1987*	1995
Van Halen	*Balance*	1995
Various artists	*Jeffology, A Guitar Chronology*	1995
Various artists	*In From the Storm, The Music of Jimi Hendrix*	1995
Various artists	*People: A musical Celebration of Diversity*	1995
Various artists	*Sounds of the Eighties: 1983–1984*	1995
Various artists	*Africa Fête 3*	1995
Andreas, Teddy	*Innocent Loser*	1996
Brooklyn Dreams	*Music, Harmony and Rhythm*	1996
Cher	*Best of the Casablanca Years*	1996
Crawford, Randy	*Best of Randy Crawford*	1996
Dan, England and Coley, John Ford	*The Very Best of England Dan and John Ford Coley*	1996
Dee, Kiki	*Amoureuse*	1996
Diamond, Neil	*In My Lifetime*	1996
Earth, Wind & Fire	*Elements of Love: Ballads*	1996

Jackopierce	*Finest Hour*	1996
Jarreau, Al	*Best of Al Jarreau*	1996
Lil' Kim	*Hard Core*	1996
Lynn, Cheryl	*Got to Be Real: Best of Cheryl Lynn*	1996
McDonald, Michael	*Sweet Freedom*	1996
Meat Loaf	*Live Around the World*	1996
Mitchell, Joni	*Hits*	1996
Rake and Surftones	*Surfers Drive Woodies*	1996
Richie, Lionel	*Louder than Words*	1996
Sayer, Leo	*The Show Must Go On: Anthology*	1996
Sayer, Leo	*20 Great Love Songs*	1996
Soundtrack	*For Me and My Gal*	1996
Soundtrack	*Singin' In the Rain*	1996
Tamas	*Blue Syndicate*	1996
Tavares	*Live Hits*	1996
Toto	*Greatest Hits*	1996
Toto	*Legend: The Best of Toto*	1996
Tubes, The	*Genius of America*	1996
Various artists	*Gute Zeiten Schlechte Zeiten Vol. IX*	1996
Waybill, Fee	*Don't Be Scared By These Hands*	1996
Williams, Deniece	*The Best of Deniece Williams: Gonna Take a Miracle*	1996
Zevon, Warren	*I'll Sleep When I'm Dead* (anthology)	1996
Breaux, Zachary	*Uptown Groove*	1997
Garfield, David and Friends	*Tribute to Jeff*	1997
Jackopierce	*Decade 1988–1998*	1997
Jackson, Michael	*Blood On the Dance Floor*	1997
Kassav'	*Dife*	1997
Lake, Greg	*From the Beginning: Retrospective*	1997
Lavezzi, Mario	*Voci e Chitarre*	1997
Loggins, Kenny	*Yesterday, Today, Tomorrow: The Greatest Hits of Kenny Loggins*	1997
Lukather, Steve	*Luke*	1997
Man Doki	*People In Room No. 8*	1997
Manchester, Melissa	*Essence of Melissa Manchester*	1997
Marx, Richard	*Flesh and Bone*	1997
Mathis, Johnny	*That's What Friends Are For*	1997
Scaggs, Boz	*My Time, The Anthology*	1997
Soundtrack	*Balko*	1997
Various artists	*The Carols of Christmas II*	1997
Various artists	*One Step Up/Two Steps Back: The Songs of Bruce Springsteen*	1997
Various artists	*Pop Classics, The Long Versions*	1997
Various artists	*Ohne Filter Musik Pur, Vol. IV*	1997
Various artists	*Best of Smooth Jazz I*	1997
Various artists	*Windham Wonderland*	1997
Werner, Pe	*Die Hits*	1997

Williams, Joseph	*3*	1997
Be Five, The	*Trying to Forget*	1998
Bissonette, Gregg	*Gregg Bissonette*	1998
Chicago	*25 Years of Gold*	1998
Currie, Cherie & Marie	*Young and Wild*	1998
Earth, Wind & Fire	*Greatest Hits*	1998
Garfield, David and The Cat	*I Am the Cat, Man*	1998
Gebhard, Nicky & Gee Fresh	*No Cry, Just Music*	1998
Gurtu, Trilok	*Kathak*	1998
Man Doki	*So Far*	1998
Newman, Randy	*Guilty: 30 Years of Randy Newman*	1998
Nicks, Stevie	*Enchanted*	1998
Sayer, Leo	*Best of Leo Sayer*	1998
Soundtrack	*Footloose* (expanded edition)	1998
Tamas	*Live in Budapest*	1998
Terrana, Mike	*Man in the Machine/Shadows of the Past*	1998
Torpey, Pat	*Odd Man Out*	1998
Toto	*XX*	1998
Van Halen	*Van Halen III*	1998
Various artists	*Merry Axemas, Vol. II*	1998
Various artists	*Best of Smooth Jazz Vol. III*	1998
Various artists	*Tones of Christmas*	1998
Various artists	*The Sexy '80s*	1998
Wright, Gary	*The Best of: Dream Weaver*	1998
Bolton, Michael	*Timeless/The Classics, Vol. II*	1999
Cher	*The Greatest Hits*	1999
Chicago	*The Heart of Chicago 1982–1997*	1999
Clapton, Eric	*Clapton Chronicles: The Best of EC*	1999
Cooper, Alice	*The Life and Crimes of Alice Cooper*	1999
Dante, Ron	*Favorites*	1999
Fabian, Lara	*Lara Fabian*	1999
Jones, Quincy	*From Q With Love*	1999
Klimas, Larry	*Retro-spec(t)*	1999
Sayer, Leo	*Original Gold*	1999
Torpey, Pat	*Y2K*	1999
Toto	*Mindfields*	1999
Toto	*Livefields*	1999
Toto	*A Rock and Roll Band*	1999
Turtles, The	*Back to Back*	1999
Various artists	*ELT Songs from L.A.*	1999
Various artists	*Not the Same Old Song and Dance, Tribute to Aerosmith*	1999
Various artists	*Humanary Stew, A Tribute to Alice Cooper*	1999
Various artists	*Sounds of Wood and Steel, Vol. II*	1999
Various artists	*Pop Music: The Modern Era 1976–1999*	1999
Various artists	*Instrumentally Yours: Classic Love Songs*	1999

Various artists	*Modern Rock*	1999
Walker, Gary	*Storybook*	1999
Wolf, Peter	*Progression (Linzer Klangwolke)*	1999
America	*Highway, 30 Years of America*	2000
Asia	*Very Best of Asia: Heat of the Moment*	2000
Benson, George	*Anthology*	2000
Benson, George	*Les Incontournables*	2000
Crawford, Randy	*Best of RC and Friends*	2000
I-Friends	*I Will Get There*	2000
Niacin	*Deep*	2000
Okui, Masami	*Neei*	2000
Sayer, Leo	*20 Greatest Hits*	2000
Sayer, Leo	*The Very Best Of*	2000
Soundtrack	*Pokémon 2000: Power of One*	2000
Summer, Donna	*The Collection*	2000
Tolle Project, Christian	*Better Than Dreams*	2000
Tube	*Sha La La/Remember Me*	2000
Tubes, The	*Tubes World Tour 2001*	2000
Various artists	*Bat Head Soup, Tribute to Ozzy*	2000
Various artists	*Supergroups of the '80s*	2000
Wehipeihana Project, Lynda	*Lynda Wehipeihana Project*	2000
Williams, Deniece	*Love Songs*	2000
Wilson, Nancy	*Friends in Love*	2000
America	*Definitive America*	2001
Austin, Patti	*The Very Best of Patti Austin*	2001
Cher	*Essential Collection*	2001
Cross, Christopher	*The Definitive Cristopher Cross*	2001
Crowell, Rodney	*The Houston Kid*	2001
Davis, Miles	*The Last Word*	2001
DiMaggio, Robin	*Blue Planet*	2001
Iijima, Mari	*Right Now*	2001
Jackson, Michael	*Greatest Hits HIStory, Vol. I*	2001
Jones, Quincy	*Q: The Musical Biography*	2001
Karizma	*Lost and Found*	2001
Lukather, Steve and Carlton, Larry	*No Substitutions*	2001
McDonald, Michael	*The Voice of Michael McDonald*	2001
Newman, Randy	*The Best of Randy Newman*	2001
Russell, Brenda	*Ultimate Collection*	2001
Sanchez, Roger	*First Contact*	2001
Scaggs, Boz	*Dig*	2001
Shankar & Gingger	*One In a Million*	2001
Sherinian, Derek	*Inertia*	2001
Toto	*Super Hits*	2001
Tubes, The	*Extended Versions: The Encore Collection*	2001

Various artists	*Stone Cold Queen, A Tribute to Queen*	2001
Various artists	*Essential Metal Masters*	2001
Various artists	*Favored Nations Promo*	2001
Various artists	*While My Guitar Gently Weeps*	2001
Various artists	*Tae Bo Mix*	2001
Various artists	*Light Mellow AOR Collection*	2001
Wetton, John	*Anthology*	2001
Williams, Deniece	*17 Greatest Hits: Collection*	2001
Wilson, Jim	*Cape of Good Hope*	2001
AOR	*L.A. Reflection*	2002
Asia	*Anthologia: 20th Anniversary*	
	Geffen Years Collection	2002
Chicago	*The Very Best of Chicago*	2002
Cox, Carl	*Global Carl Cox*	2002
Crawford, Randy	*Hits*	2002
Cross, Christopher	*The Very Best of Christopher Cross*	2002
Davis, Miles	*The Complete Miles Davis at Montreux*	2002
Earth, Wind & Fire	*Essential Earth, Wind & Fire*	2002
Gore, Jackie	*The Real Thing*	2002
Gregorian	*Masters of Chant, Chapter III*	2002
Jones, Quincy	*Ultimate Collection*	2002
Lee, Tommy	*Never A Dull Moment*	2002
Loggins, Kenny	*Essential Kenny Loggins*	2002
Love Solution	*I'll Be Over You*	2002
Man Doki	*Soulmates* (incl. 'I lost My Heart in China')	2002
Okumoto, Ryo	*Coming Through*	2002
Rundgren, Todd	*Todd Rundgren & His Friends*	2002
Toto	*Through the Looking Glass*	2002
Toto	*Greatest Hits . . . and More*	2002
Tubes, The	*Best of the EMI Years*	2002
Various artists	*One Way Street, A Tribute to Aerosmith*	2002
Various artists	*Pigs and Pyramids, Songs of Pink Floyd*	2002
Various artists	*Guitars for Freedom, Vol. II*	2002
Various artists	*Movie Soundtracks*	2002
Various artists	*Air Guitar Heaven*	2002
Various artists	*American Rock Legends*	2002
Various artists	*Best of Night of the Proms Vol. I*	2002
Various artists	*Capitol Records 1942–2002*	2002
Various artists	*Guitar Attitudes Heroes*	2002
Various artists	*Best Dance Album in the World . . . Ever!*	2002
Various artists	*Movie Soundtracks*	2002
Various artists	*Drew's Famous Big Country Hits*	2002
Waters, Roger	*Flickering Flame, The Solo Years, Vol. I*	2002
AOR	*Dreaming of L.A.*	2003
Asia	*20th Century Masters – The Millennium*	2003
Benson, George	*The Greatest Hits of All*	2003
Cher	*The Very Best of Cher*	2003

Chicago	*Chicago Story: The Complete Greatest Hits 1967–2002*	2003
Cocker, Joe	*The Ultimate Collection 1963–2003*	2003
Frampton, Peter	*20th Century Masters – The Millennium*	2003
Garfield, David and Friends	*Giving Back*	2003
Heimlicher, Matthias	*Running Back to You*	2003
Lake, Greg	*From the Underground Vol. II*	2003
Lukather, Steve	*Santamental*	2003
Mitchell, Joni	*Complete Geffen Recordings*	2003
Richie, Lionel	*The Definitive Collection*	2003
Rogers, Kenny	*Heart of the Matter*	2003
Rundgren, Todd	*Re-mixes*	2003
Rundgren, Todd	*Greatest Classics: With a Twist*	2003
Sayer, Leo	*Love Collection*	2003
Sayer, Leo	*You Make Me Feel Like Dancing and Other Hits*	2003
Sayer, Leo	*The Essentials*	2003
Sherinian, Derek	*Black Utopia*	2003
Sure, Al B.	*The Very Best of Al B. Sure*	2003
Toto	*25th Anniversary Live in Amsterdam*	2003
Toto	*Love Songs*	2003
Toto	*Circa 1980s*	2003
Toto	*Africa*	2003
Toto	*The Essential Toto*	2003
Tramp, Mike	*More to Life Than This*	2003
Tschuggnall, Michael	*Tears of Happiness*	2003
Tschuggnall, Michael	*Michael Tschuggnall*	2003
Various artists	*Hazy Dreams, (not just) A Jimi Hendrix Tribute*	2003
Various artists	*Voodoo Crossing, A Tribute to Jimi Hendrix*	2003
Various artists	*Influences & Connections, Mr. Big*	2003
Various artists	*Stairway to Rock, (not just) a Led Zeppelin Tribute*	2003
Various artists	*Night of the Proms 2003*	2003
Various artists	*Mariya Takeuchi Songbook 'Sincerely II'*	2003
Various artists	*A Brief Glimpse of the Relentless Pursuit*	2003
Various artists	*Breathe, Tribute to Pink Floyd*	2003
Various artistst	*Talking to Angels*	2003
Washington, Grover	*Feels So Good / A Secret Place*	2003
Yardbirds	*Birdland*	2003
AOR	*Nothing But The Best*	2004
Benson, George	*Very Best Of: The Greatest Hits of All*	2004
Budka Suflera	*Jest*	2004
Cher	*20th Century Masters: The Best of Cher, Vol. II*	2004
Cocker, Joe	*Heart and Soul*	2004
Diggs, David	*Jazzwerk*	2004

Iijima, Mari	*Gems*	2004
Jackson, Michael	*Ultimate Collection*	2004
Larson Band, Travis	*Burn Season*	2004
Los Lobotomys	*The Official Bootleg*	2004
Potato Salad	*Potato Salad*	2004
Sherinian, Derek	*Mythology*	2004
Thomas, Mickey	*Over the Edge*	2004
Tramp, Mike	*Songs I Left Behind*	2004
Tubes, The	*Then and Now*	2004
Van Halen	*The Best of Both Worlds*	2004
Various artists	*Spin the Bottle, an Allstar Tribute to Kiss*	2004
Various artists	*A Guitar Supreme, Tribute to John Coltrane*	2004
Various artists	*Bedroom Mixes, Vol. III*	2004
Various artists	*Tribute to Stratocaster*	2004
Various artists	*Fantasia*	2004
Winter, Edgar	*Jazzin' the Blues*	2004
Asia	*Gold*	2005
Cher	*Chronicles*	2005
Davis, Miles	*Munich Concert*	2005
Earth, Wind & Fire	*The Essential Earth, Wind & Fire*	2005
Jackson, Michael	*Essential Michael Jackson*	2005
Jones, Ricky Lee	*Duchess of Coolsville, An Anthology*	2005
Logan, Oni	*Stranger in a Foreign Land*	2005
Lukather, Steve & El Grupo	*El Grupo Live*	2005
Man Doki Soulmates	*Legends of Rock*	2005
McDonald, Michael	*Ultimate Collection*	2005
Miles, Jay	*9 Hours*	2005
Mitchell, Joni	*Songs of a Prairie Girl*	2005
Odd Man Out	*Greatest Hits*	2005
Osbourne, Ozzy	*Prince of Darkness*	2005
Osmond, Donny and Marie	*Together*	2005
Paul, Les and Friends	*American Made World Played*	2005
Radioactive	*Taken*	2005
Schwarz, Siggi and the Rock Legends	*Woodstock, Vol. II*	2005
Soundtrack	*Dragon Ball Z and Dragon Ball Z2*	2005
Soundtrack	*Dragon Ball Z3*	2005
Summer, Donna	*Gold*	2005
Tolle Project, Christian	*The Real Thing*	2005
Travers & Appice	*Bazooka*	2005
Various artists	*Gypsy Blood: A Tribute to Jimi Hendrix, Vol. II*	2005
Various artists	*Visions of An Inner Mounting Apocalypse: A Fusion Guitar Tribute*	2005
Various artists	*The Loner, A Tribute to Jeff Beck*	2005

Various artists	*Back Against the Wall*	2005
Various artists	*Hurricane Relief, Come Together Now*	2005
Various artists	*Welcome to the Nightmare: An All Star Tribute to Alice Cooper*	2005
Various artists	*A Special Tribute to Pink Floyd*	2005
AOR	*L.A. Attraction*	2006
AOR	*L.A. Concession*	2006
Cerrone	*Cerrone: by Bob Sinclair*	2006
Cocker, Joe	*Gold*	2006
Fowler, Bernard	*Friends With Privileges*	2006
Jones, Quincy	*Q Digs Dancers*	2006
Jones, Ronnie	*Again*	2006
Kiss	*Ace, Gene, Peter and Paul* (solos box set)	2006
Levin, Tony	*Resonator*	2006
Rodgers, Dave	*Blow Your Mind*	2006
Soussan, Phil	*Vibrate*	2006
Toto	*Falling in Between*	2006
Toto	*Bottom of Your Soul, Summer 2006 – Tour Edition*	2006
Various artists	*Guitar Gods: The Classic Rock Anthems*	2006
Various artists	*The Royal Dan, A Tribute*	2006
Various artists	*Flying High Again: The World's Greatest Tribute to Ozzy Osbourne*	2006
Various artists	*Guitarists 4 the Kids*	2006
Various artists	*Butchering the Beatles*	2006
Austin, Patti	*Intimate Patti Austin*	2007
Clapton, Eric	*Complete Clapton*	2007
Gurtu, Trilok	*Twenty Years of Talking Tabla: The Definitive*	2007
Kawai, Naoko	*Origial Album Box*	2007
Mendoza, Marco	*Live for Tomorrow*	2007
Moog-ly	*Sex & Soul: Mixed by Moog-Ly*	2007
Toto	*Falling in Between Live*	2007
U–Nam	*Back from the '80s*	2007
Various artists	*Magna Carta Guitar Greats, Vol. I*	2007
Various artists	*World's Best Dad*	2007
Various artists	*Club Pineta: 50th Anniversary Edition*	2007
Various artists	*25 Years at New Morning*	2007
Various artists	*Top Musicians Play The Wall*	2007
Vinylworxx	*Stop Lovin' You*	2007
Borghi, Simone	*Online*	2008
Champlin, Bill	*No Place Left to Fall*	2008
Cuesta Voce	*Timepieces*	2008
Culbertson, Brian	*Bringing Back the Funk*	2008
Jackson, Michael	*Thriller* (25th Anniversary Edition Deluxe)	2008
Jackson, Michael	*100 Favourite Nursery Rhymes & Songs*	2008

Jackson, Michael	*King of Pop*	2008
King of Balance	*A Rockwalk Through the Toto Years*	2008
Lukather, Steve	*Ever Changing Times*	2008
Paul, Les and Friends	*A Tribute to a Legend*	2008
Stereoboys	*I Won't Hold You Back*	2008
Various artists	*Rock the Bones, Vol. VI*	2008
Various artists	*Led Box: The Ultimate Tribute to Led Zeppelin*	2008
Various artists	*The Dream of the Electric Guitars, Vol. I*	2008
Various artists	*Jeff Porcaro Session Works*	2008
Various artists	*We Wish you a Metal Xmas . . . and a Headbanging New Year*	2008
Various artists	*Guitar Idols*	2008
Various artists	*Classic Rock Magazine Presents Buried Treasure*	2008
Various artists	*Six Strings Maestros*	2008
Various artists	*In Session*	2008
Various artists	*Guitar Heroes, Led Zeppelin Instrumental Renditions*	2008
Williams, Joseph	*This Fall*	2008
AOR	*Journey to L.A.*	2009
Benson, George	*Songs and Stories*	2009
Bolton, Micheal	*MB Collector's Tin*	2009
Henley, Don	*The Very Best of DH*	2009
Jackson, Michael	*This Is It*	2009
Man Doki Soulmates	*Aquarelle*	2009
Noy, Oz	*Schizophrenic*	2009
Stewart, Rod	*The Rod Stewart Sessions 1971–1998*	2009
Various artists	*Abbey Road: Tribute to The Beatles*	2009
Various artists	*Rock Biographics: Pink Floyd*	2009
Various artists	*Let the Madness Begin: Ozzy Osbourne – The Ultimate Tribute*	2009
Benson, George	*Classic Love Songs*	2010
Kulick, Bruce	*BK3*	2010
Lukather, Steve	*All's Well That Ends Well*	2010
Lukather, Steve and Winter, Edgar	*An Odd Couple Live*	2010
Miguel, Luis	*Luis Miguel*	2010
Nelson	*Lightning Strikes Twice*	2010
Ritenour, Lee	*6 String Theory*	2010
Various artists	*Rock Biographies: Led Zeppelin*	2010
Various artists	*Rock Biographies: The Beatles*	2010
Grand Illusion	*Prince of Paupers*	2011
Pushkin	*The World as We Love It*	2011
Schwarz, Siggi & Friends	*Still Got The Blues, A Tribute to Gary Moore*	2011
Sherinian, Derek	*Oceana*	2011

Weingart, Steve and Jones, Renée	*Dialogue*	2011
West, Leslie	*Unusual Suspects*	2011
Bolin, Tommy & Friends	*Great Gypsy Soul*	2012
Evans, Bill	*Dragonfly*	2012
Felder, Don	*Road to Forever*	2012
Shearer, Harry	*Can't Take a Hint*	2012
Condor, Thierry	*Stuff Like That*	2013
De Rosso, Alex	*Lions and Lambs*	2013
Lee, Will	*Love, Attitude and Other Distractions*	2013
Lukather, Steve	*Transition*	2013
Man Doki Soulmates	*Budapest*	2013
Pomeranz, David	*You're the Inspiration*	2013
Culbertson, Brian	*Another Long Night Out*	2014
Toto	*35th Anniversary Tour – Live in Poland*	2014
Varady, Andreas	*Andreas Varady*	2014
Starr, Ringo	*Postcards from Paradise*	2015
Toto	*Toto XIV*	2015
Various Artists	*Rock Against Trafficking*	2015
C.T.P.	*Now & Then*	2016
Chiklis, Michael	*Influence*	2016
Porcaro, Steve	*Someday/Somehow*	2016
Toto	*Live at Montreux 1991*	2016
Montrose, Ronnie	*10x10*	2017
Soundtrack	*Stranger Things: Music from the Netflix Orginal Series*	2017
Starr, Ringo	*Give More Love*	2017
Super Sonic Blues Machine	*Californisoul*	2017
Ball, Sterling; Ferraro, John; Cox, Jim	*The Mutual Admiration Society*	2018
Kratz, Michael	*Live Your Life*	2018
Smalls, Derek	*Smalls' Change (Meditations on Ageing)*	2018
Toto	*40 Trips Around the Sun*	2018